Bud Lilly's
Guide to Fly Fishing
the New West

Bud Lilly and Paul Schullery

Bud Lilly's
Guide to Fly Fishing
the New West

PAM LANZA

Bud Lilly and Paul Schullery

Frank Amato
PORTLAND

Frank Amato Publications, Inc.
P.O. Box 82112, Portland, Oregon 97282
503•653•8108
All photographs courtesy of Bud Lilly unless otherwise noted.
Title page illustration by Pam Lanza

Book and Cover Design: Kathy Johnson

Printed in Hong Kong
Softbound: ISBN: 1-57188-186-7   UPC: 0-66066-00397-3
Hardbound: ISBN: 1-57188-187-5   UPC: 0-66066-00398-0
1 3 5 7 9 10 8 6 4 2

Dedicated to the memory of my parents,
Violet and Bud Lilly

Prologue   8

Section One: **A Western Fishing Life**   10

Chapter 1. **Montana Beginnings**   11

Chapter 2. **An Angler's Apprenticeship**   14

Chapter 3. **Other Loves**   18

Chapter 4. **Five Dollars and a Clean Shirt**   22

Chapter 5. **Glory Days**   27

Chapter 6. **A Fly-fishing Family**   32

Chapter 7. **Clients and Other Challenges**   38

Chapter 8. **Celebrities and Experts**   40

Section Two: **Tackle and Techniques for Western Fly Fishing**
(with some thoughts on attitude)   52

Chapter 9. **So You Want to Fish the West?**   53

Chapter 10. **Great Expectations**   54

Chapter 11. **Tackle Basics**   56

Chapter 12. **Flies**   63

Chapter 13. **Finding the Fish**   79

Chapter 14. **Presentation**   82

Chapter 15. **Guidance and Guides**   89

Chapter 16. **Floating**   94

Chapter 17. **Fishing Manners**   99

Chapter 18. **Releasing Fish**   101

Section Three:

Western Waters, Western Seasons   **104**

Chapter 19.	**Big Rivers**	**105**
Chapter 20.	**Small Streams**	**108**
Chapter 21.	**Spring Creeks**	**110**
Chapter 22.	**Still Waters**	**114**
Chapter 23.	**The Backcountry**	**119**
Chapter 24.	**Early Spring** (the season before the season)	**121**
Chapter 25.	**Spring**	**124**
Chapter 26.	**Summer**	**126**
Chapter 27.	**Fall**	**129**
Chapter 28.	**Winter** (the season after the season)	**132**

Section Four:

A Trout's Best Friend   **134**

Chapter 29.	**Why Western Fishing Has Gotten Better**	**135**
Chapter 30.	**Winning the Trout Wars**	**138**
Chapter 31.	**Access**	**145**
Chapter 32.	**The Total Experience**	**148**
Chapter 33.	**Once a Guide**	**151**

Epilogue:	**The Best Fish**	**156**
Appendix:		**157**
Index:		**157**

Prologue

From the Authors

IT TOOK MY FRIENDS A LONG TIME TO GET ME TO agree to do a book. The first one was *Bud Lilly's Guide to Western Fly Fishing*, which Nick Lyons convinced me to take on in 1986, with Paul Schullery helping me put the thoughts together in a logical sequence. As we worked on that book, we accumulated many fishing stories that Nick didn't think were necessary in a manual on fly fishing, so we eventually decided to make them into a second book, *A Trout's Best Friend*, an "angling autobiography." The Guide was published in 1987, and Pruett Publishing brought out *A Trout's Best Friend* the following year. Both got nice reviews and many kind comments, but both are now out of print.

As the years passed, Paul and I often talked about the books and what we liked or didn't like about them. Most of all, we talked about how much we would like to take all that information, add a lot more, and produce one big book that did the whole job—telling my story, sharing all the advice on Western fishing, and preaching a few sermons on conservation and good sportsmanship. After ten years of thinking about it, taking the occasional fishing trip to do "field research," and accumulating new ideas, this book is the result. Rather than just a guidebook or an autobiography, it blends the stories with the lessons, which makes the learning a little more fun and the stories a little more meaningful.

Let me explain how it's written. Though Paul functioned as co-author, we agreed that the most sensible way to write it was in the first person; there are times when Paul just can't keep an opinion to himself and has to say something, and then he speaks for himself. Otherwise, the "I" you're hearing from is me, Bud Lilly.

We're grateful to many people for their help: Nick Lyons and Jim Pruett, who published the original books; our families for their patience and enthusiastic support; the thousands of people I've advised and guided, who were teaching me things as I was teaching them; all the people who have encouraged me to set my ideas down on paper rather than just tell them to friends and clients one at a time; and especially to Frank Amato for his enthusiasm for bringing out this new edition.

And a special thanks to my cousin, Dave Miller, author of the book *Call of the Headwaters*, which preserves and celebrates so much of the wonderful history of the country and rivers in my part of Montana; his research greatly enriched this book, too. If we tried to thank all the people who have helped us and the fishing we love, we'd need a separate volume as long as this one. This book, with the lessons it offers, the stories it shares, and the hope for the future that it represents, is our best way of saying thank you.

Bud Lilly
Bozeman, Montana

WHEN BUD SUGGESTED THAT WE CALL THIS BOOK A "guide to fly-fishing the New West," I couldn't have agreed more. Bud's career as an angler, guide, and conservationist has parallelled the development of the very idea of a "New West," and he's had a lot to do with shaping the attitudes that the New West represents. The book doesn't go into the politics and history of this idea; after all, it's a book about fly fishing. But I figure it's worth explaining that idea a little bit here at first, because Bud is so important in the story.

It turns out that people have been using the term "New West" for more than a century, but Western legal scholar Charles Wilkinson dates the current use and meaning of the word to the spectacular growth of the ski industry in Colorado in the 1960s and 1970s, which was part of a dramatic change not only in regional economies but also in who was attracted to the West from other parts of the country. Charles describes this change in terms of "an upswelling of values" that shifted America's perception of the region. The traditional heavy industries of the West—mining, logging, agriculture, energy—are still there, and are still economically important and politically powerful, but they've been counterbalanced by everything from skiing to wilderness enjoyment to high-tech industries beyond counting. The wonderful natural resources of the West, so long primarily the domain of people who wanted to extract some "commodity" for sale, are now more and more often the domain of people who think those resources have a higher value—and are worth a lot more money—if we leave them right where they are.

As Bud long ago noticed, there may be nothing that represents this New West any better than fly fishing. A wild trout, swimming free in a healthy, well-protected watershed, is a commodity too, and it's a very valuable one. Ever since I started reading Bud's catalog and visiting his shop in the early 1970s, I could see that he had a broader vision than most of us fishermen. That vision included not only his hard-earned expertise and his ability never to lose sight of the fun of fishing, but also the personal enrichment we could find in the environments wild trout need to thrive, and the personal responsibility we all have to protect the wild trout's world.

The Old West hasn't disappeared. There are still plenty of loggers, miners, cowboys, and others; in fact, many of them were fly fishing here themselves before it got so fashionable, and they are an essential part of Western culture. The New West is a fascinating combination of the old and the new. This book seems so special to me because Bud has a gift for finding the best in both the old and the new. If, for example, the latest miracle fly pattern doesn't work, he knows of a pattern from 60 years ago that just might. And if, for another example, you're baffled by all the hype and mystery of fishing in such a huge and famous country, Bud has a gift for remembering what that feeling was like when he started fishing, long before the West was new.

Paul Schullery
Yellowstone Park, Wyoming

A Western Fishing Life

Montana Beginnings

GUIDING SORT OF RUNS IN MY family. It began with our most famous and adventurous character, now remembered in this part of Montana as Granny Yates. Granny was born Mary Wells in Virginia in 1815. She was seventeen when she married her sister's widower, George Yates, after the family conducted a thorough search of the Bible to make sure it was okay for a woman to marry her former brother-in-law. After the wedding, they saddled up and rode the 1,600 miles to Jackson County, Missouri, where they settled, eventually adding nine more children to the widower's three. George died in the 1850s, and in 1863, when she heard about a gold strike in what would later become Montana, Mary took three of the boys (most of the children were grown by then) and joined a wagon train. They took six cows with them and used the rocking motion of the wagon to help churn butter, which they in turn sold to the other pilgrims.

Mary Wells "Granny" Yates, the family's matriarch, late in her long and adventurous life.

She made so much money selling the cows in Virginia City, Montana that she could afford a trip back to Missouri in 1864. She picked up some more of the children on this trip and also began to accumulate knowledge of the trail, so that eventually she organized and guided wagon trains of emigrants. The best estimate from the family is that she made the crossing between Montana and Missouri thirteen times (she ended up in Montana, which would account for the uneven number), the last time by rail.

My cousin, Dave Miller, who with his wife Norma now runs Bud Lilly's Angler's Retreat in Three Forks (see Chapter 33), has researched our two families, whose fortunes and fates intertwine into a great saga of the West. He recently provided me with the following summary of Granny Yates and the many adventures her family had, and I want to quote it in full here because it shows how all these supposedly ordinary people took part in one of the great epics of American history. It reduces an amazing number of pioneer experiences to a few sentences, each on the makings of a novel. It also shows why we not take our history, including the natural heritage of this region, so personally.

I was sitting here one day with my mind wandering. In front of me was my great-great-grandmother's 18K walking stick, a note written by Rev. Stateler to my wife's great-grandfather about a cash loan, and a pile of written material about several families, both mine and my wife's. The walking stick had been given to Granny Yates in the 1890s. This lady had made some 13 trips across the plains between Missouri and Montana after she was 49 years old. . . . She established a place called "Pilgrim's Rest" near Belgrade, Montana, building several log cabins to be used by pioneers as temporary quarters until they got established in their own places. Perhaps this was the first motel in Montana. . . . She was a legend by 1870, as a census taker noted while taking the census of other members of her family. Her son Zac was the only member of the gold-hunting Bozeman expedition to the Yellowstone to be killed in their many skirmishes with the Sioux. . . . On one of her journeys the wagon train included the same Rev. Stateler who wrote the note to the Williams family. Rev. Stateler was with her to bring six ministers to Montana, and his wagon rolled over an embankment. Granny's daughter owned the famous Belgrade Bull, which was sold to a wild west show and was said never to have been ridden. Alexander Williams (my wife's family) was with Joseph Smith in Illinois and then came to Utah with Brigham Young. They established the city of Provo, with the help of a son named Thomas and others. Thomas was killed by Indians in Arizona when he was running freight wagons from California to Utah. Alexander later (1864) either had a quarrel with Brigham Young, or because of fear of hoodlums left Utah with his wagon wheels wrapped in sheep skins, traveling at night so as not to be detected. He ended up in the Gallatin Valley. Another distant relative of both sides of our family, a James Shedd, built seven toll bridges at the headwaters of the Missouri and at Canyon House (later Logan, Montana), to provide better crossings of the many rivers and sloughs on the route from Virginia City and Bannack to Helena in the late 1860s and early 1870s. A member of this family also bought a ranch from Granny Yates on the North Boulder and turned it into a stage stop. He died in a fire that burned the place down. . . . The husband of one of Granny Yates granddaughters shot and killed the town marshal in Three Forks in 1915 during a stay in the red-light district. He was found not guilty because he had six children and was a good family man.

So many stories, so many characters both good and bad. Granny Yates bridged the years from the beginning of the Western pioneering period (when people first started to talk about a "new west") to the first years of this century, and she saw enormous changes in that period. On some of her Western trips the parties were threatened by Indians; one of her sons was wounded in an attack on the Yellowstone River in 1866, and she hid her youngest in a flour barrel for fear he would be discovered and taken by the Indians if they succeeded in capturing the wagon train.

She also displayed the sort of enterprise needed to succeed in the old territories. She once brought three barrels of apples to Virginia City from Missouri and sold them to the miners in that rough new town for a dollar apiece. She knew that everything she brought along had to pay its way, and it was said that the lineage of many horses in the Gallatin Valley could be traced to the animals she brought across, riding them sidesaddle. When she died in 1907, she was the matriarch of a large family, with more than sixty grandchildren and ninety great-grandchildren scattered throughout the country between Missouri and the West Coast. One of those grandchildren was my mother, born Violet Collins in 1903.

My mother's side of the family was dominated by big, strong women. They seemed to be in the tradition of Granny Yates, who was such a legend in the family that when I was young I sometimes wondered if she hadn't pulled the wagon herself. I grew up surrounded by these women, who ruled over most family get-togethers. It made me a fairly quiet kid because whenever we went somewhere, I just sat there with wide eyes while the women boomed at each other.

My mother's family were not sportsmen at all. They were ranchers, and even today, as the West continues to change, there seem to be a lot of ranchers who never hunt the wildlife that abounds on their land, much less understand the economic and social value of that wildlife. They were hardy, ambitious people, but I got my interest in outdoor sports from my dad's side of the family.

My father's mother had two brothers who were professional outdoorsmen. A.R. (Amos) and W.A. Hague emigrated from family farms in Nebraska to the Yellowstone area, apparently in the 1880s. Amos established himself in the Yellowstone Valley north of Yellowstone Park, and his brother settled in St. Anthony, Idaho. According to records in the Yellowstone National Park archives, both of them occasionally guided parties of tourists and sportsmen in the park, but so far Amos is the one about whom we have the most information. He was a tall, strong man, ramrod straight and of firm

Bud Lilly and friends, about 1930.

principles. There are letters in the park archives revealing that he and his brother both took considerable risk in reporting poaching activities they discovered near the park. Amos was known to have taken many parties through Yellowstone Park back in the 1890s and afterwards, including some important groups of dignitaries.

He was still alive in the 1930s, which was when I met him. My dad took me over to visit him in his cabin up in the hills west of Emigrant, Montana, in the Yellowstone River valley. He was a trapper and a professional hunter, and his cabin was a kid's idea

Violet and Walen "Bud" Lilly, Sr., about 1935.

of heaven, with furs and trophies all over the walls. I suspect that even then he was living off the land. He had a good many fine items that since have disappeared, including rifles and other gifts that were given to him by some of his more distinguished clients who, according to family tradition, included European royalty. I always thought I somehow inherited some of his characteristics in that I enjoy showing people the outdoors.

My dad was the son of a Nebraska corn farmer. He left a rough home life when he was twelve and apprenticed himself to a barber in Kearney, Nebraska, where his apprenticeship consisted of practicing on local jail prisoners. By the time he was sixteen he had his own barbering business.

He barbered around Nebraska until 1916, when he heard about a big dam project on the Owens River in California. This was the first big dam to be built in California, and he moved to Bishop that year. He was thirty-two at the time, and he made friends with an attorney in California who introduced him to fly fishing. He used to tell me stories of the fabulous fishing in California back in those days, when you could have some of the best trout streams to yourself. Those stories were part of the reason I was always so interested in fishing.

Dad had always been an avid outdoorsman even as a child. He had been a market hunter as a young man in Nebraska, shooting prairie chickens, ducks, and any other game that could be sold. He told me stories of going out with a spring wagon, his brother on one side of the wagon and him on the other, to hunt prairie chickens. One of his sisters would drive the wagon, and he and his brother would hunt the fields. By the end of the day, the wagon would be full of birds. He was a deadly shot, which was one reason I never got too excited about the shotgun. When we would go out hunting together, a bird would be dead as soon as it jumped up—before I could even swing my shotgun to it. He had no more mercy on me than he had on the birds; it was up to me to get off a shot first, and I hardly ever did.

As far as I knew, he was happy in California. He married there and had a daughter, but the marriage ended in divorce. Then, during World War I, he was a victim of the big flu epidemic that swept California, and the doctors suggested that he move to some place where he could convalesce and just do simple physical work. He had a relative near Bozeman, so he moved there and worked on a ranch for a year or two, doing as much fishing as he could in his free time.

Bud Lilly, Jr., age one.

He met my mother in about 1923 in Manhattan, Montana where he had just opened a barbershop. He was in his early forties, and she was about twenty. His name was Walen, but everybody called him Bud. I was to be Walen, Jr., and of course would be called Buddy. They were calling me Buddy even before I arrived.

So in 1925 they had me, and my dad announced that I was enough and he didn't want any more. That's how he was able to devote a lot of his free time to taking me fishing and hunting, really instilling in me a love of the outdoors. I was an avid Boy Scout, and I loved anything to do with being outside.

Chapter 2

An Angler's Apprenticeship

I STARTED TO FISH WHEN I WAS STILL A SMALL BOY, probably not even schoolage yet. Dad started me out in bait fishing, of course, and gradually got me involved in fly fishing. When I was about eight and could be trusted to ride a bicycle away from the house, I would ride down to the Gallatin River, which was only a mile from our house in Manhattan. On the weekend I'd often be there all day.

As long as I can remember, I was always engaged most by the instant of the strike. It doesn't matter how many thousands of trout I've taken since, I still have that same excitement whenever I put a fly over a trout and the miracle happens. I still react, in my mind and sometimes out loud, with something like, "Jesus! He took it! He took it!" There was a small creek called V Creek just on the edge of Manhattan, and just above the road bridge was a pool full of brook trout. The water was perfectly clear, and I could see those fish swimming around. I don't suppose any eight-year-old boy ever wanted anything more than I wanted to catch those fish. I would lie on the old plank bridge and feed a line down through a crack, staying as long as six hours to take a single fish. And when one would finally take it, I would be just amazed and thrilled. For me, at least, it's never changed.

Dad started me fly fishing as early as I could handle it. Having read all the outdoor magazines, I was familiar with fly fishing, but my exposure to it was limited to the old snelled wet flies until I got to West Yellowstone and opened my shop.

He wasn't influenced by eastern fishing at all. We got our tackle from South Bend and Horrocks-Ibbotson, and Martin and Meisselbach reels. For some reason Dad had decided that he liked automatics. My first was a Meisselbach, then I graduated to a South Bend Oreno-matic, then to a Perrine. My first fly rod was a telescopic Bristol steel rod. I don't know how heavy it was, but after a long, hot day of casting, it seemed to weigh about eight pounds.

On my thirteenth birthday my dad let me order a South Bend, nine-foot, three-piece split bamboo rod from Salt Lake City. It cost around twelve dollars. I've lost that rod, but I do have my first creel. You could put alligators in it. All I really needed for the summer was that rod, one of my reels, that laundry basket of a creel, and a few wet flies and snelled hooks. Heaven couldn't have offered a boy more.

Dad loved fly fishing, and was very good at it, but we were as open-minded as anyone at that time about tackle. We used bait or flies, depending upon the situation. If the water was fairly clear, we preferred flies, but if we had to use sucker meat, bullheads, worms, or grasshoppers, we didn't mind at all. We just loved catching fish.

Montana was not a place where you had to worry very much about what fly you were using, and I suppose that's why we developed such an independent set of flies. I doubt that I even knew that flies imitated certain aquatic insects; we used flies under some circumstances because they worked so well. The staple of our fly patterns was the series of flies developed by F.B. Pott. Pott had been a professional wigmaker, and he developed various techniques for weaving animal hair into fly bodies and hackles. I'm not sure he was the first, but of all the fly weavers in Montana, he was the most famous and successful, and we swore by his flies. I started with the woven-hackle Royal Coachman and the Mites—the Mr. Mite, Lady Mite, and Sandy Mite. Every now and then a new pattern would appear. I remember when the Graybacks were introduced; I thought it was a revolutionary event.

These were all just general attractor-type patterns. Pott apparently got the name of "mite" from "hellgrammite," which was a local name for the nymphs of the large stoneflies (the hellgrammite is actually the immature stage of the Dobsonfly, but that didn't matter to us). I don't know if Pott even knew that his flies often were pretty good imitations of stream insects; he just offered them all in about the same sizes and shape, so maybe it was just coincidence that some of the Mites were (and still are) excellent imitations of caddisfly larvae in their cases. He did offer a "rockworm" pattern that was pretty obviously an imitation of a cased caddis.

The Pott flies were expensive, usually about thirty-five cents each, at a time when most flies were ten cents apiece at most. I used to snag a lot of them in trees or on the bottom, and my mother would ask me, "Can't you find something cheaper to lose?"

I'm sure that I was unaware of dry flies until well after World War II. Our technique was pretty simple. We always fly fished with a double- or a triple-fly cast of snelled wet flies, and fishing was a matter of throw it out there, let it sink, and hang on. When I started, the limit was twenty-five trout, and whitefish didn't count. I could catch all the whitefish I could carry back when I was ten years old, and I often marvel at the amazing fishing we had practically in our backyard.

It was a common practice to poach. When I was small I often fished with an old woman who was a friend of my mother. Ma Wiedman just loved to fish. The two of us would dig a can of worms in her chicken coop and go up to the Gallatin, this ten-year-old and his older friend, and we'd catch our twenty-five each in the morning, clean them, and go home for lunch. Then we'd go back and get another fifty in the afternoon. It was my job to try to pawn them off on the neighbors. It got so that often when I'd knock, they wouldn't answer the door. We flooded the locals with fish.

We had a lot of great fishing, but I don't know if it was really that much better then than now. There were so few laws regarding harvesting fish, and so little protection for streambeds and habitat, that many rivers are probably in better shape now than they were when Ma Wiedman and I were at our peak. But one advantage it certainly had was lack of company. My dad used to take me up the Gallatin Canyon for some fishing, and we were so spoiled that if we saw another fisherman, we considered it crowded. I can imagine what he'd say if he were around today and could see the Henry's Fork during the green drake hatch, or the floaters on the Madison.

My dad introduced me to the Madison in the summer of 1935, when I was ten years old. We lived in Manhattan, where he was the local barber. One Sunday morning, we got up early, piled into our '34 Chevy, and went fishing. As on many later trips, we went through Logan, up past the old buffalo jump, and on through to where we would hit the river. That first time, we drove up as far as we could into Bear Trap Canyon. At the time, you could drive quite a ways up into the canyon, much farther than now. I don't remember much about the fishing on that first trip, but I do remember that the rattlesnakes were as thick as flies.

In fact, prior to World War II, the lower Madison was the only part of the river I was even aware of. I kind of thought the Madison was from Three Forks up to the Bear Trap. But it was all the fishing anybody needed.

Before the War we could drive way up into the Bear Trap. In about an hour's drive, we got to a place called the Shadoan Cabin, which was quite a few miles up, and a lot farther than you can go now. It was spectacular and exciting fishing, what with the huge rocks, big deep pools, and dangerous wading.

Our most memorable trips to the Madison before the war were during the salmonfly emergence. Whether in the Bear Trap or farther downstream, there were great salmonfly hatches. One of my favorite memories, one that I think is representative of the fishing experience back then, is of a trip we made in about 1939, when I was 14. As the local barber, my father knew everybody in the area, and had permission to fish from some of the biggest property holders, like the McDonald and Darlington ranches. Some friends of ours were camped over there, and we went over one evening to have supper with them, and to share the fishing. It would be the worst kind of behavior today, but in those days you kept every big trout you got, and put them on a string to show them off.

These fish were caught on the actual live salmonflies. As much as I may have preferred fly fishing when it was practical, we weren't troubled by too many refinements in tackle then, and with so much live bait just hanging off the bushes, it was easy to get into great fishing. The river was usually off color at least a little bit, so live bait seemed the obvious choice anyway.

But I suppose my best memories of those big fish on the lower Madison were from the first few years after the war. One of the first places I fished that first season after the war was the Madison. In June of 1946, just after I got home, I went fishing over near the Greycliffs. Imagine yourself there, back then, with hardly any other fishermen for miles. The salmonflies were dripping off the bushes, and you'd just grab them as you needed them. You'd put two on the hook, with a big sinker a little ways up the line, then throw it out there and let it bounce along until something big grabbed it.

We caught a lot of big fish, up to a few pounds each, but the thing that stands out in my mind now, almost fifty years later, is one fish I never even got a look at. I was fishing along when something grabbed my bait and without any hesitation just swam to the other side of the river and parked itself over near the far bank. I couldn't move it, even though I was using really heavy line, probably ten- or twelve-pound test. Whatever it was, it just stayed there until finally I pulled so hard I broke the line. There's no knowing how big a trout it was, of course, though obviously it was a whole lot bigger than the three- or four-pounders we were able to land pretty quickly. It wasn't uncommon in that period, particularly up in the Bear Trap area, for a good fisherman to catch a trout of eight to twelve pounds.

Nostalgia is a complicated thing, especially for those of us who've since abandoned some of our old ways. Many of us have gotten pretty touchy about bait fishing on today's trout streams, but those were different times, with different rules. I'd love to see that quality of fishing come back so we could try it with all the wonderful new fly-fishing gear and fly patterns we prefer now. We fished with the live salmonflies early in the season, and we often used sculpin, which were deadly, particularly up in the Bear Trap. We did do some fly fishing, but in those days, you just adjusted your methods to suit the circumstances, and had no twinges of conscience whatever method you used.

The times were much simpler, and the only goal was to catch a big one and then another. If fly fishing didn't seem practical, we'd sometimes start with a big gob of worms, fishing with it just long enough to catch a nice big sucker. Then we'd filet the sucker and cut out sections about an inch square. We'd leave the skin on those pieces, because it was strong and would hold the hook. We'd weight the line with a big sinker, throw it out there into a big hole and just wait. If you didn't hang up on the bottom sometimes, you weren't doing it right. Often, we'd use a fly rod, because if the bait is moving along in the current, your control is better with a fly line.

But fly fishing gave us plenty of great moments too, as flies were developed to match the local insects, especially the salmonflies. As a boy, when I wasn't fishing I was playing baseball on the local team. Once, around the Fourth of July in 1946, we had a game in Ennis. One of the guys on the other team was Jack Scully, who would become one of the long-time local fishermen and businessmen. During the game he suggested that as soon as the game was over, we should go down to the channels, just outside of town, and do a little fishing. So about four o'clock we went down, and sure enough the salmonflies were out. Jack had a new fly, one I'd never seen before, called the Bloody Butcher. I didn't really even understand about dry flies at the time, and I'm not sure Jack did, but we brought six of these and learned fast. The willows along the stream had salmonflies hanging down like bunches of grapes, so we would cast as far under those branches as we could and then hold on. We didn't worry much about keeping the fly afloat, and it certainly didn't matter to the trout. And that was what we thought of as a salmonfly imitation until we saw the Bunyan Bug.

Norman Means, a Missoula fly tier, had developed the series of flies he called Bunyan Bugs in about 1927. They were wood-bodied flies with horse-hair wings; the bodies were painted various colors, including those of the salmonfly. They recently became famous all over again in Norman Maclean's book *A River Runs Through It,* when Maclean described his first look at one: "I took one look at it and felt perfect." Well, so did the trout. I don't remember fishing with them until about 1943, when a teacher friend from Ennis and I stopped at the local tackle shop there and bought some. They floated beautifully, and the fish couldn't get enough of them. I know they've been tied and sold again recently, and it would be fun to give them another try, to see if they still make the fish feel perfect too.

Even in the 1940s, the Madison hadn't really been discovered by the visiting fishermen. Most of the fishermen were local. Another sign of the times was the way we looked at some of our fellow fishermen. There were guys that my dad referred to as "B.B.'s," which was short for "those Butte bastards." Apparently, he didn't like to see people leaving their neighborhood rivers and coming over and crowding "his" streams. The BB's, who of course had just as much right on the river as we did, loved the Jefferson up around Whitehall and through the canyon, but sometimes they'd leak down onto the Madison and would just make my dad furious. It might interest today's fishermen, who deal with much more crowded conditions, to know that half a century ago we didn't always welcome other fishermen either. My dad used to complain that he wouldn't fish the Gallatin on the Fourth of July weekend because he "didn't want to break off the tip of his rod in somebody's ass." My dad had a pretty strong sense of territoriality.

We also fished down below Three Forks, where all three rivers come together, and I'd fish the Missouri at Trident at night for ling and bullheads. The ling were so terrible looking they made you feel like you were eating a garter snake, but the meat was very flavorful. It just took quite a lot of bourbon to get you to try one.

Another of my home streams was Baker Creek, a tributary of the Gallatin that flowed right near Manhattan. Back then, nobody had any idea that it would someday be a famous spring creek; it was just another creek like all the others around the valley. When I was about eleven, my Dad and I went down to fish the creek one summer evening. It was still a good creek, not yet being dewatered for irrigation, and we knew it had good fish in it. Just about dusk, he hooked a fish on one of the Potts flies, and the fish was too strong for him to land. By the time it was dark, he was still fighting it, so he sent me running back to the car to get the flashlight. I brought the light back and aimed it at the fish so we could at least get a look at it, but he finally landed it, well after dark. It weighed about nine pounds, the first really large brown trout I remember. Fish that big weren't routine, but they didn't cause much excitement around town, either. Fishing was just something people did; it wasn't news.

My own first experience with a large trout came about that same time, in Central Park, a little community between Manhattan and Belgrade. My grandfather had a butcher shop there, and in the summer I made the trip over now and then for the local fishing. There was a little spring creek that paralleled the highway through Central Park before flowing into the Gallatin River near town. It was just the right-sized creek for a ten-year-old. It was lovely, full of watercress and perfectly clear, so clear that you could look in and see a batch of trout swimming around. If you pitched a grasshopper in, it would be a contest among the fish to get to it first; all you had to do was watch and set the hook. You'd yank back on the rod and they'd fly over you onto the highway, causing a good deal of confusion among passing motorists.

I was fishing it one September day, just after school had started, and I didn't know that in the early fall big brown trout would come up out of the Gallatin into the creek to get ready for spawning. I was used to hooking little brook trout, maybe ten inches long, but when I tossed a grasshopper out there, a huge brown grabbed it. The weeds were really thick in the creek by then, so I knew that if he burrowed into the watercress he'd be gone. We didn't use delicate equipment in Montana in those days—the standard snelled hook had a leader of ten- or twelve-pound test—so I just hauled back and tossed this four-pound brown trout out onto the highway.

It was some years after that before I really understood about spawning runs. I remember the day vividly. It was October of my sophomore year in high school. I had played football the previous fall, but my dad decided that I was going to be such a great baseball player that he didn't want me getting hurt playing football. It was okay with me because it gave me a chance to do more fishing. One day my dad came home and said, "I was talking to Hayes, and he said that some of those holes in the river by his house are just full of trout. Why don't you go down and try it?"

I went down to the river right after school, put on a couple of wet flies, and pulled some line off my Oreno-matic reel. As soon as the flies hit the water, it looked like I'd thrown a dead chicken to a bunch of alligators. I hauled back and found myself attached to two big browns, weighing three or four pounds each. This was a new experience for little Buddy. The trout were rolling around, pulling two ways at once, but as usual my leader was stout. So I got them up on the bank pretty quickly, threw my rod down, and jumped on them to wrestle them away from the river. I got them both, but when I tried to fish again I discovered I'd thrown the rod down too hard—the reel was bent and wouldn't work. I was so excited that I kept fishing anyway. I just pulled a whole lot of extra line out and kept it handy in case I needed it. I don't remember how many I kept except that I kept them all, big browns weighing up to four pounds.

Chapter 3

Other Loves

I HAD A SECOND LOVE AS A TEENAGER. I LOVED sports, especially baseball. Again, I owed my fondness for this pastime to my dad, who was an avid baseball fan. He was determined that I would become a major league ball player, which of course sounded like a great life to me, so whenever I wasn't fishing or in school, I played baseball. My dad let me just fish and play ball until the summer I was going on fifteen. Then I had to work and could play ball or fish only on Sundays and in the evening. I played on as many as three teams at once.

Manhattan had an independent baseball team that my dad more or less supported. He found a former pro pitcher who had a drinking problem and paid him twenty-five dollars a Sunday to pitch for us. The fellow was reliable enough that we won a lot and developed a reputation as one of the best teams in the state. Our biggest problem was finding a catcher who could hold this great pitcher, but once we did that we were hard to beat.

We didn't charge admission. We'd pass the hat, and though nobody had much money, we'd usually collect enough to pay the pitcher and a few other guys who demanded a little money. There was nothing in it for my dad except the joy of watching the game and placing an occasional bet. He'd bet on anything, even on whether or not little Buddy would strike out.

In the 1930s many of the great teams from the old black leagues did a lot of barnstorming, going through little towns all over the country picking up as many games as they could for a little money. I got to play against some of those great teams, and I always admired their spirit. Times had to be tougher for them than for the rest of us, and yet they'd show up at the big field where we played our games, park their cars under the trees, and have a picnic—they sometimes even had their families along—and just have a big time. I remember how I liked to listen to their talk, the women giving their men a hard time if they made an error, the kids running around and playing. It was our only exposure to a really different culture back then in Manhattan.

These were desperate times for the country, and some of the best ball players America ever produced were out on the road playing little local teams for a few bucks. These great black players had no chance to get into the majors back then, and so I suppose that the only good thing about it was that it did give a lot of guys like me the chance to play against really outstanding talents. I was playing on my dad's team of adults from the time I was thirteen, and besides our regular games against teams from Butte and Helena, we played the black teams whenever they came through.

I'm sure the high point of my baseball career was the day I batted against Satchel Paige. I don't even remember what team he was playing for, but I knew who Satch Paige was and had enough sense to be impressed. He would give me a big roundhouse curve and I'd almost fall on my face trying to get out of the way of it. I was only fifteen or so at the time, just a little over five feet tall, and his team thought it was hilarious that this team of Montana farmers had a little kid playing second base.

As good as he was, I did get on base. I suspect he let me hit because he thought I was cute, but however it happened, I ended up on first base with a ground ball single. I remember thinking that if I could get that far, maybe I could get farther, so after someone else advanced me to second, I decided to steal third. I guess I wasn't cute enough for that, because the third baseman was waiting with the ball when I arrived, and he just sort of scooped me up when I slid in.

We won enough games against other teams in the state and against the barnstorming teams that people started to hear about us in the cities. One Sunday two men showed up to see our team, and my dad didn't tell me that they were scouting us for the Cincinnati Reds. He introduced me to them after the game and told me that he would like me to take them fishing the next day. He was barbering and couldn't take the time off, so that was my first guiding experience. They were both fly fishermen from Salt Lake City, and they were really impressed with this teenaged kid who could catch so many fish. That seemed to impress them more than my ball playing.

About two years later they came back, and just as the war

was starting, I signed a contract with the Cincinnati Reds system. They wanted me to be on line to play for the Salt Lake City farm team when I got out of high school, but of course the war changed a lot of our lives. By the time I got back, I'd lost interest in baseball. I had always played on teams of people mostly older than I was, and I never got over being a little gun-shy against the big pitchers. I held my own and was a very good fielder, but I knew my limitations.

Meanwhile, my parents continued working hard. In 1939, my mother began managing the small railroad hotel in Three Forks, which she took care of until her death in 1994. Looking back, I can now see that hospitality was something I grew up with, and that it probably had much to do with my

More stories, all those lives intertwined, and Mrs Violet Lilly watching over them generation after generation. No wonder she became one of the leading forces in the local historical society.

The winter before my seventeenth birthday, the Navy was recruiting in our area. A friend came up to me at school one day and said, "Hey, let's go take this test—we can get out of school for two or three hours." I didn't even know what kind of test it was, but I took it. Soon after, I got notice that I'd passed the test and was invited to join a special Navy training program, which turned out to be the greatest thing that ever happened to me because it gave me the chance to get a college education. I signed up, and as soon as school was out I

1942 was a good year for collecting memories to carry me through the war.

interest in guiding and outfitting. The little salt-box hotel had been built in 1909, one of Three Forks' first buildings. It went up one room at a time, and each new room was immediately occupied by a railroad employee. It changed hands a couple times, finally becoming my parents' property in 1943. My cousin Dave Miller, who I quoted earlier about Granny Yates and other early family history, has captured the sense of legacy we share about this little hotel:

> Mrs. Violet Lilly ran the hotel from 1944 to 1994. She was a true pioneer of the Gallatin Valley. Her father, Frank Collins, was born in a cabin on the Jefferson River not far from Three Forks. Her grandfather, Christopher Columbus Collins, migrated from Missouri to Montana and was a toll bridge keeper for Jim Shedd just north of present Three Forks.
>
> During Mrs. Lilly's time at the hotel, the furnace was converted from coal to oil and then to gas. There had been several deaths among the tenants, five marriages, and one baby born. The hotel itself has withstood two severe earthquakes. One tenant occupied the same room for 20 years.

went to work for the Forest Service in the Cabinet National Forest out of Thompson Falls. I had worked there about three weeks, and was loving it, when my boss told me my letter had arrived—I was in the Navy.

I spent sixteen months at the old Montana School of Mines at Butte, getting an intensive introduction to engineering. Then I went to a midshipman's school at Throg's Neck, New York, an old Coast Guard school. I got my commission when I was nineteen and was sent to Florida for additional training in boats. There's more to education than class work, of course, and along the way I was learning about girls, and rental cars, and all sorts of things they hadn't been too talkative about back in Manhattan. I served for eighteen months in the South Pacific and was discharged from the Navy on June 12, 1946.

No sooner had I gotten home than my dad announced that we were going to fish the salmonfly hatch that weekend, and that was just the sort of announcement I wanted to hear. We fished right near Three Forks, using the naturals because the river was too muddy for fishing Bunyan Bugs on the surface. We used a two-fly cast—two Wright McGill snelled hooks with a couple of salmonflies on each hook. We'd put a big sinker on that rig, cast it out, and let it swing. To be back

The hotel Violet Lilly managed for many years in Three Forks is the flat-roofed building in the center of this photograph taken just as the building was being completed in 1909. The tent in the foreground housed railroad workers until the hotel was ready.

with the trout streams and trout that big was the greatest homecoming I could have imagined, and I spent about a month fishing until my dad, who didn't waste words, said, "Well, you've taken enough time off, now go to work."

About the middle of July I went to a barn dance down by Central Park. I had learned to drink fairly well in the Navy, so my friends and I were having a fine time when I saw this cute Irish girl dancing with some guy. I thought, "God, that's really neat." So I horned in and got a couple of dances. I found out that her name was Pat and that she worked for a doctor in Three Forks. The next day a friend and I drove down to Three Forks, hoping to find her. We pulled up and parked in front of the doctor's office. She later told me that when she saw us pull up, she decided that right then would be a good time to go across the street to the drugstore and get some cigarettes. When she came out in her cute little white uniform, we both affected a mutual show of surprise (sort of, "Well, hey, how are you?"), as if we both hadn't been trying to meet. We were married the following March.

In the late 1940s, when I was going to school at Bozeman, I very much wanted Pat to learn to fish. During the next couple of summers, we spent a lot of time fishing the Gallatin. There hadn't been much pressure on the river since before the war, so the fishing was outstanding everywhere.

But the income wasn't. I was on my way to becoming a teacher, but I knew that my salary wouldn't be good. I also knew that there was something else for me that I hadn't found yet. I also knew that it had to do with the outdoors.

Looking back now, it seems easy enough to see that I was headed in a certain direction. A few years before her death, my mother, who was very active in preserving local history, gathered up a lot of things she'd saved from my childhood and showed them to Paul Schullery and me. Among them were all the usual trinkets and souvenirs, lots of photographs, Navy mementos, and so on, and a little three-ring notebook that was my first fishing log. It started in April of 1942, not long before I went into the Navy, and it had the kind of title page that only a child's bright ambition could produce. Written in pencil on the first page, between tiny black-and-white photographs of me and my dad outdoors, was this:

> *This is a record of my excursions in the mountains and into field & stream.*
> *I like the good clean outdoors, wild game and all wildlife.*
> *My ambition is to always live in contact with wildlife.*
> *My hunting and fishing pardners, who are careful and considerate, are Don, Doug + Dad.*
> *This is from April 1, 1942 until Death.*

Well, actually, it was only from April 1, 1942 until sometime in 1943, but the spirit was what counted, and it still holds true for me. In fact, it was one of the things that got me through the war. While in the Navy, I did what I suppose a lot of men did, I diverted myself by making a plan for the rest of

Bud Lilly's Guide to Fly Fishing the New West

my life. I decided that if I survived, I was going to go to Alaska. I wanted to do something in the outdoors in Alaska, though I wasn't sure what. All the time I was in the Navy, I read everything I could find about Alaska. Marriage and school sidetracked that ambition, but my ambition "to always live in contact with wildlife" never faded.

I got my degree in applied sciences in 1948, and I thought I was a pretty smart man by the time I started my teaching career in Roundup, Montana, a small ranching and mining community. I was twenty-two, and my first duty was to register my teaching certificate at the courthouse. I arrived in Roundup, found the county superintendent's office, and announced, "I'd like to register for school." The superintendent looked at this fresh-faced kid and asked, "Well, what grade are you in?" It took a minute to convince him I was a teacher, and even at twenty-two I was teaching some "kids" who were older than I was. It seemed there were quite a few who just liked staying in school, which I suppose was a lot nicer than going into the mines like their fathers.

I taught biology, chemistry, general science, and physics, and I was assistant basketball coach. I had the feeling that I got all the courses that nobody else wanted, and I quickly realized that the teaching salary didn't stretch far enough. I

The original Trout Shop in the "off season," long before winter recreation was discovered in the West Yellowstone area.

also taught in Deer Lodge before settling in Bozeman in 1961, and by then I knew that I had to make more money.

A teacher friend of mine, Norm Hansen, told me about West Yellowstone one day. I don't know why it had occurred to him to tell me, or what had made him notice, but one day he pointed out to me that "Nobody in West Yellowstone will wash your car. They're all so busy pumping gas that you can't get a car wash. My mother has a little property there by the post office. Let's put up a little car wash."

So we went to West Yellowstone, cut a few trees for a tent, ran a garden hose from nearby, dug a drain ditch, and were in business. We'd wash cars from dawn until dark, and we eventually even put up lights so we could do it at night. One day I washed about eighteen cars and brought in more money than I was making as a teacher.

During that summer another friend said, "You know, there's a guy here that's a teacher in Billings who's going to be promoted to principal at the high school, and he'd like to sell his tackle shop. It's the one that Don Martinez started."

So I went over and looked at it, and I asked a friend to look at it. He said, "Well, you can buy it, but all you'll ever make is wages. It's just a little business." At that point, with my hands wrinkling up like prunes from all the car washing, wages sounded like a pretty good deal.

The shop was owned by Charles Borberg, who had tried to take over the Martinez reputation. Don still lived in California and still tied the flies for the shop, but he wasn't visiting much anymore. It looked like an interesting little business, but I had to agree that it didn't show much financial promise. I think I bought it for other reasons than the hope that it might make me a lot of money. I think I bought it because I could see West Yellowstone becoming a replacement for the Alaska dream; it would let me do what I wanted in the outdoors without even leaving my home state.

What I actually bought was the inventory, the sign, and a walk-in cooler. I paid $4,500 for the whole show. I had about $2,000 that I'd saved for a car, but right then it was hard to find a car, so I had that money just sitting. My mother loaned me the other $2,500. My dad had died in 1948, and my mother had some insurance money that he had said she could give to me if I looked like I was going to do something productive with it. He believed in results.

I talked it over with Pat, and she encouraged me by saying that "If you want to buy it, I'll help you." I don't imagine she had any idea that she was offering to work like she did for thirty years.

I wrote the man a check for $4,500, and he said, "Do you want a receipt?"

"Well, I probably should have something." High finance in West Yellowstone.

"I'll give you a bill of sale," which sounded pretty impressive to me. He took a little piece of paper and wrote out a bill of sale on it. I was in business.

Chapter 4

Five Dollars and a Clean Shirt

WHEN THE TROUT SHOP WAS OPERATING AT ITS PEAK during the great fly-fishing boom of the 1970s, we put in long days. I usually got to the shop at about 6:45 a.m. The first thing I did was make five gallons of coffee, and by the time I had done that, the line had started to form. We had the regulars, sort of the Trout Shop Coffee Klatch, who showed up when we unlocked the door for the early social hour, which seemed to last until about lunchtime.

The guides showed up at 7:00 a.m. Their clients had been told to meet them at the shop, and each guide's assignment for the day was posted, along with a suggested trip for that day. The clients and guides knew each others' names in advance. The guides had a checklist of what to make sure the clients had before leaving the shop, most of it routine, like making sure they had the right flies for that day's fishing. But within a few minutes after seven, we'd have eight guides and twice as many clients foraging here and there, picking out a few of this and a few of that, and the cash register would start to sing. The guides were trained as salesmen, and they knew our inventory and our prices; that isn't as mercenary as it might at first seem because the clients were generally pretty insistent that they be properly outfitted, and spending a little more after they'd already spent a lot to get there and to hire a guide didn't seem like a problem to them. We just made it as easy as we could.

We would have five or six people writing up the purchases and twice that many calling from various parts of the shop to put them down for six of this and ten of that. I had this old gas station adding machine on the counter that required pulling the handle every time you added a number. First thing in the morning, when all these people were milling around getting ready to go out, and the first early customers were drifting in, and the store staff was bustling around tripping over each other and a dog or two, someone would come up to me and ask how I kept track of 3,000 items in the store and all these people buying and renting. I'd tell them I had a computer. This was when computers were still pretty exotic, and they'd light up and say, "Really? Where is it?", assuming we had some kind of big electronic thing in the basement. I'd

give another yank on the handle of the adding machine and say, "Right here."

We'd have the clients and their guides. We'd have three or four people downstairs starting their day at the fly-fishing school. Mike might be getting someone ready to go backpacking into the Beartooth. Annette and Bonnie would be getting their ladies-only clients ready to go. Steve and Bonnie Billeb would be going over last-minute preparations for their headwaters camping trip group. I would stand in the middle of all that chaos and enjoy the cash flow, hoping we were getting receipts for most of it, at least.

The only disadvantage was that until all the guides cleared out about nine o'clock and the feeding frenzy kind of quieted down, the drop-in customer was likely to get neglected. There was just too much going on for us to handle any more.

The biggest challenge was keeping track of that much money being collected in a short time. Twenty or so fly fishermen fresh from the city and anxious to make the most of their fishing can be world-class impulse shoppers. If we had a full load of clients, we might have cleared $5,000 by nine o'clock in the morning. At that point, anything we took in during the rest of the day seemed like bonus money.

We worked both sides of the street; we had a good selection of spinning tackle as well as the fly-fishing tackle, and we always had at least one clerk like Chuck Johnson who was a whiz with spinning gear and could help the spin fishermen. We always had someone knowledgeable about backpacking, too, because we carried so much outdoor clothing and backpacking gear.

We kept the coffee and cookies for customers all day, every day. We fed every Boy Scout in America. They would pull up in big buses just for the cookies at the Trout Shop. I still don't know how they sniffed us out, but they didn't buy much tackle.

It stayed busy all day. There was no such thing as a reasonable break, and the business didn't arrange itself conveniently so that anybody could sit down and eat a civilized lunch. It seems to me now that during the years the shop was doing well, I ate about 9,000 hot dogs. Finding time for lunch was a problem.

Business did begin to taper off by four o'clock, and then about five we'd get an hour or so of rush from the guys who were going out for the evening fishing. After that, staying open was mostly a matter of doing the locals a favor by providing them with a place to come in and try on hats.

Late in the day, sometime after dark, the late shift of the coffee klatch would show up to talk over the day. It had been tradition in West Yellowstone to stay open until ten o'clock, but we gradually realized that we could close at nine, then at seven, with no harm to our business. But there were many evenings even then when I'd promise Pat we'd get out early, and at seven o'clock I'd still be standing there dispensing tackle and information like I'd just arrived.

I hated to close the shop in the evening. I'd just be about to turn off the sign and lock up when here would come some bleary-eyed guy who'd just driven three thousand miles and wanted to get an early start tomorrow and could he just pick up a few things and oh, by the way, how's the fishing been?

The guides would start dragging in between seven and eight to report on their day's fishing. I would have spent the day gathering random information from fishermen, so between what I had picked up and what the guides brought in, we had an unusually good idea of what the next day's fishing possibilities would be. That network of information gathering gave us a real edge over the other shops. The last few years, Greg was in charge of the guides, so he would check them all in and learn all that he could from them about fishing conditions. Then about ten o'clock that night, he and I would sit down at the kitchen table and go over all we'd learned that day about fishing in the area. Then we would plan the next day's trips, matching each client's personality, interests, and skills with the right guide and the right fishing. About ten-thirty or eleven we would call it a day. As I collapsed into bed, I would sometimes wonder if success was such a great thing after all. It had all been a lot simpler back in the beginning.

The early 1950s were still a time of pioneering in fly fishing around our part of the country. People had been fly fishing in the West for a long time, but as far as a commercial enterprise, it was only beginning to show its potential. Dan Bailey had opened his shop in Livingston some years earlier, and Bob Carmichael and Boots Allen and a few others were making a go of it in Jackson. West Yellowstone had a few shops and guides, but they catered to a much smaller and more exclusive crowd.

West Yellowstone, right at the west entrance to Yellowstone National Park, had not shown much sign that it would eventually become the western Mecca of fly fishing. The first real fly shop of which I know was Vint Johnson's, which was opened in about 1941. Vint started his shop in a corner of Fuller's Garage. The story goes that he opened up, went up to Billings and bought a pile of merchandise, came back, and sold it all on the Fourth of July. He had to go back to Billings for more.

His place was called the Tackle Shop, and though Vint was himself a fly fisherman, he knew enough to cater to all the interests he could. So he sold bait and lures, as well. Vint was one of the first West Yellowstone fishermen to get any national exposure. He had the good fortune to get written up by the great Ray Bergman (longtime fishing editor for *Outdoor Life*), who fished with Vint and who over the years wrote some wonderful things about fishing in the Yellowstone area.

But the first West Yellowstone fisherman to really establish himself as an important fly tier and authority was Don Martinez. Don was the original owner of the Trout Shop, the store I acquired in 1950, and for many years he ruled the fly-fishing scene there, especially as that business concerned wealthy and influential visiting fishermen. Like Carmichael down in Jackson, who was his friend, Don had become established as the man to see concerning fishing. He was only interested in fly fishermen, and he was one of the top fly tiers and fly-tying theorists of his time. It's a shame his skills aren't better remembered now because his flies were excellent, and his knowledge of the insect life of the Yellowstone area was extraordinary. He took entomology seriously and developed many excellent flies, including a series of mayfly nymphs, his multi-colored variant dry flies, some fine cranefly nymphs, and of course one of America's most famous flies, the woolly worm, which he refined from an earlier pattern and introduced in its present form. The Woolly Worm alone should entitle him to a front-row seat among angling history's luminaries, and it probably would if he'd had the good taste to develop it in New York or Pennsylvania where more people would have sung its praises in print.

As I said, Don was only interested in fly fishermen, and he had little use for other kinds of fishing. The crowd of regulars who fished the West Yellowstone area then was pretty highbrow by modern standards, sort of typified by the attitudes and writing in Howard Back's lovely little book, *The Waters of Yellowstone with Rod and Fly* (1938). They were few in number, they prided themselves on their fine tackle, and their circle was pretty much closed to newcomers or people who fished differently than they did. One of Martinez's most famous remarks was that the bait-fishermen came to town with five dollars and a clean shirt, and they didn't change either one. It wasn't a situation where it was easy to break in with a new tackle shop. The fly fishermen knew where they would spend their money, and the bait fishermen didn't spend enough to make any difference.

The first man to make a significant dent in the Martinez hold was Pat Barnes, who by the time I arrived had to a great extent replaced Don as the reigning expert in town. He had a lock on the fly-fishing business, at least among the affluent clients. Pat's father and uncle both had many connections in Chicago, and they had done a lot to help connect Pat with

Lefty Kreh was one of many leading fishing authorities who visited the Yellowstone waters regularly and became a good friend.

sportsmen from the Midwest and East. Pat taught school in West Yellowstone a year or two and worked in the summers for Don Martinez before going on his own. By the late 1940s he was way ahead of any other guide in the area.

Where I grew up, if you wanted to fish, your father or a brother taught you, and you went fishing. I had no idea that there was more to it than that, so it took me awhile to get used to the idea that people would actually pay to be taken fishing. Pat Barnes was about the only really busy guide in West Yellowstone when I got there, and I could see that guiding was something we would have to do. During most of the 1950s I was the Trout Shop's only guide, just as Pat Barnes did practically all of his guiding himself. His wife Sig ran the shop while he was out, and my wife Pat did the same for us. I started out at twenty-five dollars a day, whether I was taking one fisherman or a dozen.

Among other things, Pat should probably get the credit for first bringing the McKenzie boats to our part of Montana and thus popularizing that kind of float trip. The McKenzies didn't take over instantly, and they still share the river with rafts and johnboats. Merton Parks, who came out to Gardiner, Montana from Minnesota, was a real booster of the johnboats, and he gave me my first lesson in them. I asked him if he'd show me how he floated with them, and he said he

would if I'd give him a tour of the Henry's Fork at the same time. One pretty day in early June we put in at Last Chance, Idaho and spent a lovely day floating along. The fishing was slow, but we were too busy marveling at how we had the river to ourselves to notice. When we floated up to the Osborne Bridge we saw a big sign that said: "Fishing Season Opens June 15." Suddenly we understood why we had the river to ourselves.

Anyway, when I first opened the door to my shop in 1950, I could see that the competition wasn't going to do me too many favors. There wasn't much business to go around, and it took many years to slowly break in to those exclusive circles and gain the trust and respect of the fishermen. In the meantime, I spent a lot of time sitting on the fence outside my door gossiping with the man who owned the little curio shop next door. This man was so fatalistic about business that he really wasn't too interested in being bothered by customers. If, while we were sitting there, someone would come by and act like he or she were going to walk into his shop, he'd say, "Wait a minute; don't go in there! Tell me what you want; maybe I don't have it." He wasn't the most inspiring role model for a new merchant.

We were all looking for ways to attract attention. In Jackson Hole, the Humpy (now usually called the Goofus

Bug), a fly based on an earlier pattern called the Horner special (developed by Jack Horner of San Francisco), became all the rage. In order to sell more of them, the shopowners introduced them with different-colored bodies, which probably made no difference at all to the fish. It was a great fly pattern, whatever color you made it, and they were sold by the millions. Boots Allen used to put them out in nail kegs—a keg full of green-bodied Humpies, a keg full of red-bodied Humpies, and so on—and people would just grab a handful, saying, "I'll take these." Western fishing was still fairly short on theory, despite the best efforts of Martinez.

It's hard to imagine, now, just how little was known about fishing in the area. I suspect that the competition between the shops and guides had a lot to do with the rapid pace of progress we've made since then. For instance, when I cam to town, many of the serious visiting fly fishermen still followed the British approach of fishing only the rise. They would go out to the rivers, and if they saw no fish rising, they would come home. They might all be back in West Yellowstone by noon. "Well, the hatch is over," they'd announce, and they'd take a seat until that evening or the next day. Many of them wouldn't use nymphs or streamers. Some of them probably didn't even know about them.

That changed dramatically in the 1950s, as more and more dry-fly patterns, streamers, and other flies were developed or brought in and as technological advances, especially the popularization of spin fishing and the advent of the fiberglass rod, made trout fishing more accessible to more people. Coupled with that was our constant effort to attract attention to our businesses, and I guess that's where I found I had an edge. I seemed to have a knack for figuring out ways to make customers happy and keep them coming back.

I could see that Martinez and Bob Carmichael, over in Moose, Wyoming, were very successful with a personal approach. Selling fly-fishing tackle wasn't like selling pharmaceutical products; people wanted to talk, and they wanted to get to know you. I made an effort to talk to everybody who came in, and because I was blessed with a good memory, I accumulated a lot of information about just where the fishing was good, and what flies or techniques were working, and all of that. In that way the shop became a real

Symbol of a fading era in western trout fishing, when big fish were killed without hesitation, the Trout Shop's Lunker Club was a center of attention for customers in the 1950s and 1960s. We posted many photographs of the biggest trout.

clearinghouse of information, which benefitted us and the customers. It may have benefitted my son Greg most of all because while I was standing in the shop talking all summer long, he was out guiding and fishing every day, putting all those ideas into practice. That's one reason he is a much better fisherman than I am today. He has an adjustability that few other fishermen can match; he can find a way to solve the problem.

Of course, the other good thing about having that kind of memory was that it was great for customer relations in general. There was a Baptist minister who came to West Yellowstone as part of a revival, and he loved to fly fish. He often came into the shop when he wasn't working, and though I'm sure he didn't know it, he was very easy to remember. He had a hat covered with flies and an accent you could cut with a crosscut saw, so he stood out like the proverbial turd in a punchbowl. Then, about ten years went by, and one day he strolled in the shop again. I looked up and said, "Could I help you, Reverend?" He almost fell over.

During the early 1950s, I began to keep a record of anyone who caught a trout weighing three pounds or more. We called it the Lunker Club and encouraged customers to sign it. We'd record the date, the species of fish, where it had been caught, and what had been used to catch it. Unlike Dan Bailey's very famous Wall of Fame up in Livingston, we didn't differentiate between methods. To qualify for Dan's Wall you had to take the fish on a fly, and if it was taken from a stream, it had to weigh at least four pounds. We accepted fish for the Lunker Club if they were caught on bait, lures, or flies, and if they were kept or released. The interesting thing was that the people who took time to register a big fish were usually fly fishermen. The bait fishermen and lure fishermen didn't bother, being interested mostly in meat in the first place.

The Lunker Club was such a useful promotion because we had a little pennant that was awarded to the most recent entry. The fisherman could put it on his car aerial, but most of them let their motel have it to display for their customers. That was the best we could hope for because it got the motels involved, which in turn meant that their guests would be hearing about the Trout Shop.

Of course, we were always looking for promotional ideas, and many of the best were provided free by various tackle manufacturers. Their representatives came to town regularly to put on demonstrations, which were always good for gathering a crowd even if it was only the local boys with nothing better to do. One summer a man named Warden came around giving demonstrations with a reel that was detached from the rod. You wore the reel on a harness that was strapped around your body. The reel was a free-spooling model that was mounted in the middle of your chest, with line running to the rod, which you held in your right hand. Warden got himself all trussed up in this rig and gave a demonstration in the street in front of my shop one day, and it was true that he could practically throw a casting plug out of sight. He was really impressing the crowd; quite a few tourists had gathered to watch this expert, who was all outfitted in his waders and everything. In fact, his show was a big success until someone called out, "That's a great outfit, but what do you have to do if you want to take a shit?" That really dampened the spirit of the group, and we didn't get any orders for Mr. Warden's outfit.

I guess our biggest and most effective promotional effort in those early years was our map. We reprinted Don Martinez's little fishing map for the Yellowstone area and distributed it by the thousands. In 1960 I revised it, and with the help of Dave Bascom (better known to fishermen in the 1960s and 1970s as Milford Poltroon, editor of the *Wretched Mess News*), designed a new map more to our liking. Dave was a successful California advertising executive who loved fly fishing and who was an able copywriter. The entire map was littered with the most wonderfully silly remarks, like:

> For years now, writers in Field & Stream, Outdoor Life, and Sports Afield have been bragging so loud about the terrific fishing hereabouts, it's sort of inspired the fish, given them something to live up to. And around this neck of the woods, The Trout Shop is generally acknowledged as offishal fishing headquarters. In fact, FISH KNOW if you've been here first, and if you haven't, they're likely to fin their noses at you.
>
> So first thing to do when you arrive in West Yellowstone is visit The Trout Shop. Get your license (no license required in Park), get free current fishing regulations, swap lies, etc. NOTE: I will listen to all your fish stories with a straight face. No other tackle shop can make this claim. I promise not to pressure you to buy a single doggone thing. You're welcome if all you want is free directions, advice, or to escape from a charging moose. (No moose can charge in The Trout Shop, and neither can you. Cash only.)

Those maps traveled far, and by 1970 we were giving away 10,000 of them a year. They were handy for use in the shop because we could make notes on them for the visiting fishermen, showing them which general areas were good. They were great also for sending to people who asked questions by mail. We didn't have a handier educational tool until the catalog came along, but that's getting a little ahead of my story.

I had been teaching at Deer Lodge for nine years by 1959, and the tackle business was picking up, so I decided to try to make a complete living from it. I quit my teaching job that year, but as practically everyone from our part of the country knows, Providence took a hand in the local economy that year. The famous earthquake of 1959 killed many people in a campground downstream from Hebgen Lake. The landslide created Quake Lake by damming the Madison River, and the quake messed up the fishing in many parts of the region. Even if people weren't too scared to come and fish, they might not find much worth doing when they got here. Business in West Yellowstone was bad for a few years before it gradually recovered, but at the time of the quake I'd already sold my house in Deer Lodge. So I was lucky to find work in Bozeman at the university, working as a biological assistant for professors doing research. I grew very tired of Petri dishes.

In 1960 I tried a year in Scottsdale, Arizona, teaching high school. That came about because of my son Mike's health problems. His doctor suggested we try a drier climate, but it turned out to be unnecessary for Mike and unbearable for the rest of us. So then I came back to Bozeman and taught for nine more years at Bozeman Junior High School, retiring in 1970 as it became clear we could develop the shop into a year-round business. Everyone who fished through the 1970s knows that it was the first decade of real growth in fly fishing, and we were ready when it started.

Chapter 5

Glory Days

BY 1970, THE YOUNG LILLYS HAD GROWN UP AND were able to take a share of the business of the shop, and we older Lillys had twenty years of experience under our belts. It was an enormously exciting time, exhausting and fulfilling at once. Suddenly there were writers appearing who had spent the sixties patiently studying insects and trout and who were now ready to publish their results. New fly patterns, new rods, new reels, and new ideas appeared regularly. A lot of what happened was hype, but much of it was important, too, and it was a great time to be running the Trout Shop.

In 1967 we had moved from our cramped quarters in the little shop in what is known as the "Eagle's Corner" of West Yellowstone (the Eagle family have been storekeepers in town for many years) to the shop's present location in a much larger, more roomy building. This gave us the room to meet all the new needs of fly fishermen in the new era that dawned about the time Swisher and Richards' *Selective Trout* was published, in 1971.

So much was happening. The campaign for special regulations was gathering force, the park was rewriting its regulations, the Federation of Fly Fishermen (now the Federation of Fly Fishers, FFF) and Trout Unlimited (TU) were gaining a national audience, and local fly-fishing clubs were springing up everywhere. Swisher and Richards, Dave Whitlock, Ernie Schwiebert, I, and many others began to make speaking tours, talking about western fishing and inviting people to come try it. It all fit into my various schemes to

Swapping fish stories in front of the Trout Shop.

promote fly fishing and do some business at the same time.

Our guiding, gradually increasing through the 1960s, really took off. We started our guide trips in May, and we would be busy until late October. More and more people were visiting our area in the off-season. In the fall we were especially busy. There was no break in our traffic after Labor Day, as many of the regular visitors knew that was when the tourist traffic eased up and the fishing started to improve in the cooler weather.

We were lucky to have some really great guides working for us, but I always felt that Greg and Mike and Barry Schaplow (who became Annette's first husband) were probably the best. There were others who were as good at guiding, but my two sons and my son-in-law were really loyal and became the most popular with the clients. People practically fought over them—who was going to go with one, and who was going to go with another.

We reached the point in the 1970s where we dominated the guide business in West Yellowstone. Pat Barnes had his own very good, carefully chosen clientele, but we had such a demand that we'd book all our own guides, eight or ten of them, and then we'd call around and book everyone else's with our overflow.

But it seemed as if there were more opportunities for us and for fly fishers than just the guiding business, and it was here that I think the Trout Shop really set itself apart. We organized the second set of fly-fishing schools in this country

We worked with Berkley to sponsor fly-fishing seminars; here, Greg demonstrates casting to a group beside the old Union Pacific building that eventually became the International Fly Fishing Center.

after Orvis had started theirs in 1966. I could see that Orvis had a good idea, and that there had to be a market for something similar in the West. The first schools we set up were in cooperation with Phil Clock of Fenwick in 1969. We had Jimmy Green and Lefty Kreh, two of the greatest casting instructors in the world, running the classes, and it cost only about twenty-five dollars. It had to be one of the great bargains in fly fishing.

The schools were an incredible opportunity for people to learn a lot from the best fishermen. We had various representatives from the tackle companies (Lefty Kreh and Ben Silkknitter from Scientific Anglers, and Hugh Reilly, Jimmy Green, or Phil Clock from Fenwick), and they not only were outstanding fishermen and instructors, they were great salesmen. If you watch Lefty cast for about five minutes, you're ready to buy anything he's got. I think a lot of people didn't realize how much expertise they were getting for their money, though looking back now we can see how rare that kind of gathering of talent is. The tackle companies participated for the promotional aspects of it, and we all benefitted. We'd have a school of thirty or thirty-five people, and we'd do five or six thousand dollars' worth of business in tackle before the school was over.

Of course, eventually Fenwick set up its own schools on the edge of town, and gradually other competition developed, but we had a lot of fun anyway, getting all those great fishermen together.

After the schools were going, I began to cook up more specialized sessions. We offered what we called angling rendezvous, where a few advanced fishermen would pay for an intensive fly-fishing session with some well-known angler. We

had Doug Swisher and Carl Richards, Ed Koch, Ed Shenk, Charlie Brooks, and Ernie Schwiebert, which gave people an opportunity to spend a day or two with their favorite authors and get a firsthand experience with their expertise. That was a very popular program, though not especially successful financially because there were just too few customers involved to bring in enough money to pay everybody who needed to be paid. But I think of the opportunity it gave fishermen to attend a clinic with an acknowledged master, or several of them, and it seems like it was worth a try. The students certainly thought so.

Then we developed the clinic, with Berkley and other companies. It differed from the schools in that it was a one-day intensive program where several companies would send their representatives and they'd all introduce the people to a variety of techniques and tackle.

When Charlie Brooks's book, *Larger Trout for the Western Fly Fisherman*, came out, it occurred to me to have a sort of "show-me" trip, where the author would take a few people out and show them all the things that they'd read in his book. That didn't work out as well as some of the programs because the people didn't catch as many trout as they must have expected; Charlie was trying to concentrate on acquainting them with the stream ecology aspects of fishing and didn't get them into fish the way they wanted. We got a few complaints from people who felt they'd not gotten the fishing experience they wanted, so eventually we abandoned that program.

But despite how some people reacted, the show-me trips were a great bargain for the customers. The chance to spend a day with Charlie, or Dave Whitlock, or Ernie Schwiebert, for only the regular guide fee, was a rare gift in fly fishing, and a lot of people found it very rewarding.

My daughter Annette and Bonnie (Greg's wife at the time) ran the ladies-only trips, where a woman was able to go out with a woman guide, with no husband looking over her shoulder or screaming at her. It provided the woman fly fisher with several things, including a lot of good instruction and the chance to see a woman who had mastered fly fishing and become an accomplished angler. A few other guides worked for us in this program, including Lynn Corcoran who now operates the River's Edge shop in Bozeman with her husband Dave. They'd start with a short session in the shop, demonstrating knots and talking a little about flies, depending upon the client's experience, and then go to the Firehole or the Madison or some other stream for some fishing.

Mike and Barry took people on backpacking trips, and I think we were among the first in the area to offer trips of that sort. We specialized in high-country lake fishing in the Beartooth region northeast of Yellowstone Park. It's some of the wildest, most beautiful country in the world, with hundreds of small lakes with cutthroat, golden, and brook trout fishing in a spectacular setting.

We also had some very successful trips to the headwaters of the Yellowstone. This involved a boat and canoe trip to the southeast arm of Yellowstone Lake in the Park, one of the most isolated parts of the Park. We'd precook a lot of things and then take steaks and other fresh food packed in dry ice, so that the whole five days was very comfortable. We'd have the guide bake biscuits in a reflector oven, so all the rustic touches were there.

We'd establish a base camp along the lake, then make short trips up into tributaries of the lake for some of the wildest fishing imaginable. These were all cutthroat trout, part of the greatest remaining pure cutthroat fishery in the country. The fishing was sometimes very easy, which it can be with wilderness fish. There was a cutthroat in Mountain Creek that they marked the first time they caught him, and in the course of a five-day camp, they caught him a total of twelve times. Fishing doesn't get much more pristine than that.

I sent a man and wife team to this camp, Steve and Bonnie Billeb, both of whom were trained naturalists. Steve was a botanist, Bonnie a zoologist, and both had taught on the university level. The people got a great all-around experience, not only the fishing but everything about the place was shown to them. There was a doctor from Bakersfield, California who enjoyed the trip so much that two years in a row he bought the whole trip for himself and his wife. He would pay the cost of guiding six or eight people just so he and his wife could enjoy all that service, attention, and grandeur.

We had a twenty-seven-foot trailer that we would use to take three or four people for four or five days and move around to different rivers. I'd send along a cook, and it was

very popular. We'd do it only in the fall, when other things were kind of slow. Usually those trips were booked up a year in advance.

What we developed out of this program was a broader approach to western fly fishing than was being promoted by anyone else. We made "Western Fly Fishing—The Total Experience" a sort of informal motto for the shop, and we firmly believed in convincing people that this wasn't just a place to come and catch trout. We sold field guides, backpacking gear, and many nonfishing items, but this was never just a matter of finding new ways to make money. Our whole family loved the West for many reasons not having to do with fishing, and we wanted to share those things. It's amazing, for example, how many fishermen come to Yellowstone Park for twenty or thirty years to fish and after all that time they still know practically nothing about the park and all its natural

Night-time visits by grizzly bears reminded us that West Yellowstone is surrounded by some of the finest remaining wilderness in the lower 48 states.

wonders. We wanted to change that, and to persuade people to take some time out to enjoy the surroundings of western fishing as much as they did the fishing. I think we had some success.

The new part of the business of which Pat and I were probably proudest was the art gallery. We opened the gallery in the early 1970s. By the time we sold the shop, it was pretty well established. That was a fun part of the business. It wasn't a great money-maker, but it paid its way, and we enjoyed broadening the business. Pottery was usually what sold best, and people bought hundreds of those rocks painted like animals. We concentrated on local artists, getting to know some wonderfully talented people, some of whom have gone on to earn national reputations. These were unusual directions for a western tackle shop, but they brought us a lot of joy, while substantially broadening the business. That's a hard combination to beat.

But our biggest business adventure was our catalog. Mail order was old news in 1969, but we saw some great opportunities for our little shop in catalog sales. So we embarked on what was a completely amateur program that turned into a more successful business than we ever would have dreamed. We were pretty conservative. I imagine that if we'd jumped into mail order, we could have grown faster than we did. If we'd gone to professional procedures and the buying of lists and all of that, we could possibly have done more. But what we did we seemed to do well.

The first catalog came out in about 1969. I had no experience in catalogs whatsoever. All I knew was that it was time to publish a catalog. So I started cutting pictures out of other people's catalogs, sticking them on a piece of paper and writing a little copy. Peter Alport's handbook from his Wyoming Outfitter's shop was more or less my model. It was a mix of products and useful information, and that was always the idea with the Trout Shop's catalog. Every year I'd write up some short items about the fishing and the new flies and such to mix in with the products. We cultivated a very hospitable and conversational tone in the catalog, and many people told us how they looked forward to it each year.

We started with a small list of about 3,000 names gleaned from fishing license sales and the Lunker Club book. Somewhere I had heard that I needed to get a bulk mailing permit, but I didn't know anything about sorting. We simply addressed 3,000 catalogs, threw them in sacks, and hauled them over to the post office. The post office people had fits, and we had to drag them all back and presort them by zip code, just like real mail-order outfits were expected to do.

The catalog became our official voice. It let us keep people up-to-date on the rivers, on developments in our family, and on all the new products that were flooding the market. I went out of my way to include lots of pictures that had no real product orientation: fishing scenes, insect photography, and so on. Just the other day I heard that early copies of the catalog (its full name was Bud Lilly's Tackle Catalog and Handbook for Western Trout Fishing) are appearing in used angling-book catalogs, being sold for actual money. I should have kept more of them.

I suppose I knew we had really arrived when Arnold Gingrich praised the handbook in *The Joys of Trout* (1973):

> *Bud Lilly's Trout Shop for the past twenty years has been a virtual gateway to paradise for fly fishermen... His tackle catalog and handbook for western trout fishing is the best I know. But send for it at your own risk, as it's highly infectious. Don't say I didn't warn you, that you'd better be prepared, before you open its covers, to be lured into a trip to Montana. Few better fates, however, could befall a fly fisher.*

It didn't take too much of that kind of talk to make the catalogs even more popular. By the time I sold the shop in 1982, the mailing list was up to 30,000 names.

Being in a retail business is a great course in human nature. If you don't like people, you probably have no business standing behind a counter selling them stuff. Fly fishermen are interesting, and knowing them, meeting them in the shop all those years, was a great experience. Oh, sure, some people demand too much, like the guy who wants to get you over in the corner for an hour or so and get detailed instructions on how to tie a fly, or the person who wants to debate the qualities of different hackles for two or three hours. Once in a great while I had to get pretty rude to get someone to let us get on with our work and help other people.

Perhaps the most surprising tackle shop characters were the people who hardly ever seemed to fish. They'd come to town for a couple weeks and spend the first few days just getting ready. This is no exaggeration; they might spend a day or two just tying up leaders in the motel. They'd come in to all the shops, gathering information about the fishing. I suppose they wanted to know exactly what it was they weren't doing. They would go from tackle shop to tackle shop, asking the same questions so they could compare information. I'd go through my spiel, answering some fishing question, and they'd nod happily and say, "Yes, that's what they told me at the last place."

For others the tackle shop was a social gathering place. They seemed to get up in the morning, put their vest on, and then just wear it all day. They were attracted to fishing by the society of it, which is something most of us are interested in, but most of us kind of like to fish, too. This sort of person would get to the tackle shop and just hang around until a conversation started up in which they could get involved. One conversation might be good for two or three hours.

I didn't really mind this type, because I'd also get people who wanted to spend an hour or two going over their fishing that day on a minute-to-minute basis. When I could see I'd been captured by one of those, I'd say, "Wait a minute; I've got

The end of another long day at the Trout Shop.

a friend over here who knows all about that," and I'd call the conversationalist over and introduce him to the detail man. It was sort of like introducing a sadist to a masochist; here were people who could really satisfy each other. Two hours later they'd still be deep in their discussion. It was almost a community service I performed, getting these people with common interests—one wanted to talk, one wanted to listen—together. They'd just about wear out our wall map with their fingertips, following various streams here and there.

But people like those were the exception. Most of the time there was really no telling the customers from the friends. We always got our greatest satisfaction as shopowners, and our greatest pleasure as fly fishers, from being able to put someone in the right place for some good fishing. There's nothing more rewarding than to have people come back voluntarily and go out of their way to thank you for putting them on to some good fishing. We loved it when someone would come in and say, "Thank God for you; you just saved our whole trip—we'd had four days of no luck at all and you sent us to a great spot."

Possibly the nicest testimonial I ever received came from Reverend Dan Abrams, a fine gentleman and fly fisherman from Jackson Hole. He moved to the West some years ago and came into my shop for some advice. A story like the one below (which was part of a column he wrote for one of the Jackson newspapers) goes a long way in convincing me that the early mornings and the late evenings were more than worth it.

When the family and I finally got to make the long-planned trip, one of the first things I did was to drag them off to the Lilly's Trout Shop. After I told Bud I had driven over 2,000 miles for a taste of his famous waters, I thought he would send me immediately to the Madison, suggest the Firehole, or at least point me in the direction of the Yellowstone. He courteously answered all my questions about these well-known streams, but then, looking at my two young boys and travel-weary wife, he advised me to consider another possibility.

"Look," he said, "my wife and I just returned from a two day stay at a tiny Forest Service campground containing but three sites along the Gallatin between here and Bozeman. It's a great place for the whole family to relax and enjoy. The scenery is impressive and the fishing is interesting."

"Interesting?" I asked. "What do you mean by that?"

Bud just smiled and said, "I think you'll find it to your liking. Here, I'll draw you a map showing you exactly how to find the spot."

We left the shop, grateful for the tip and amazed that anyone would share one of his favorite fishing holes with a friend he'd known for only fifteen minutes.

Chapter 6

A Fly-fishing Family

IT WAS ALWAYS THE FAMILY THAT MADE THE TROUT Shop matter. I don't mean that the shop mattered because it helped support the family, though that was also true; I mean that the Trout Shop, with its long hours and all the rest, became such a central part of our lives because we were all involved. We did it together, and I can't imagine a finer thing a family could say than that.

Greg was born in 1949, and Mike and Annette came along after the shop was in operation, Mike in 1952 and Annette in 1955. I don't know now how we found time to run both the shop and the family, but I do know that we were lucky things didn't get really busy in the shop until the kids

*Greg, age eight, and Mike, age six,
on a successful fishing trip.*

Mike, age six, shows off his catch at the Trout Shop.

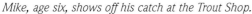

were older. Those first few years were pretty slow-going for the business.

But life could hardly be called routine in West Yellowstone, even for such a small town. For one thing, there were the bears. There were grizzly bears using the dump north of town every night until the early 1970s, and they were often seen in town at night (they still are), as were the smaller black bears.

The black bears would get especially bold during the day, and sometimes we'd have to chase them away. I sold wrist rockets (very powerful slingshots) in the shop, and if you hit a black bear once or twice with a rock or a marble, it would usually go away. I remember one day the kids were out playing in the yard, and a black bear climbed a lodgepole pine right next to the yard. He just sat there watching them. There aren't many things that would make a parent more nervous, so I gave him a few rounds with the wrist rocket and he left. It wasn't a matter of hitting any vital part. You just sort of aimed for the bear.

A far more frightening incident occurred one night when Pat and I were working late in the old shop. It was a hundred feet or so from our little cabin, in an area that the bears used as a highway all night long. We'd left the kids with a babysitter, who foolishly went outside to talk to her boyfriend. Somehow Mike, who was just an infant, got out of his crib, opened the back door, and crawled through the night all the way to the back door of the shop, where we heard him trying to get in. That babysitter had a very short career with us.

I started the kids fishing when they were small, but I was careful not to start them too soon. If children aren't ready and don't have quite the patience, coordination, or enthusiasm needed to stick with fishing, you can ruin them forever by not waiting another year or two. They sense your frustration, and that can kill their interest.

I started them where my dad started me, on the Gallatin, with its quick little rainbows that weren't too choosy about lure or fly pattern. The most important thing for new fishermen, no matter what age, is action. You can show them the fine points any time, and if they're enthusiastic they'll pick them up themselves. But if they don't catch some fish and see the fun and excitement of it, all the lectures and instruction in the world won't help. At first the kids used spinning outfits because they're almost instantly easy, and they had a chance not only to catch fish, but to learn something about wading and reading the water. By the time they were ten or eleven, they switched to fly fishing, and they all loved it and still do. It got easier with each new child, too, because Greg took on a lot of the teaching himself, taking Mike and then Annette out fishing once he was old enough to go by himself.

When they were small I did a good bit of mulework, hauling one or two of them on my back across the water that was too deep for them. But very quickly they all had their own hip waders and were competent enough to get along. Annette was so small as a child, and only five feet two inches tall as

Young Annette on a local stream.

an adult, that we had Marathon make a pair of custom waders for her. She wore them until she was about thirty, and she modeled them beautifully in our catalog. Waders often leak before you get them out of the box, but hers lasted forever.

Mike, left, and Greg, right, were both veteran guides with tremendous river savvy by the time they were twenty.

It was also when the children were still small that we started teaching them to release their fish. This was before such practice was popular, and their friends used to look at them like they were crazy, but it was a good thing to teach them early. It seems to be something that is somehow harder for older people to learn. Greg, Mike, and Annette of course passed along their enthusiasm for preserving the trout in the stream to thousands of customers and clients, and the shop became our little forum for discussing trout conservation with the public.

Meanwhile, Pat generally took care of the money, and she was largely responsible for our success. She worked with the accountant, kept track of all the receipts, paid all the bills, and supervised all the help. She was always taking advantage of discounts, which often boosted our profits. We called her the shift boss. She set up all the shift schedules and assigned duties to people, made sure the shelves were always stocked and inventories were all up-to-date, and made sure that nobody stood around while working. Anytime anyone stood still, she'd find something for them to do, even if it was just to make sure no dust had settled anywhere.

That attitude kind of went against the old tradition of tackle shops, of course, which were usually somewhat gloomy little places where nobody would dream of dusting. There used to be a good-natured joke in the business that if you went into Dan Bailey's shop on a windy day, the dust would be so stirred up you couldn't even see Dan. Earlier generations of fishermen kind of liked it that way, and there isn't anything like the atmosphere in an old tackle shop, but we saw that fly fishing was changing, and new kinds of people, including more and more women, were getting interested. We knew that although the Trout Shop needed atmosphere, it needed a fairly clear one.

It was Pat who kept things running. I didn't have that kind of latitude to pay attention to all those things every day because people pretty much expected me to be available just to answer questions. I became the focal point for all the information that came in from the guides, the clients, the other customers, and various friends, so I was also the main distribution center for that same information. The way I saw it, they'd just prop me up somewhere and keep feeding me people with questions.

It was an interesting division of labor, and I know it's happened with other shop owners who get well known. People just insist on talking to that certain person they've heard of. It's important for business, too, because when the well-known person is in the shop, sales will often increase significantly. My family used to try to take the heat off me sometimes when people would start lining up to ask me questions, and eventually there were more and more people coming in looking for Greg, or Mike, or Annette specifically, but that took time. One day a fellow came in and waited very patiently while I worked my way through some other customers. It was late in the day, and I was just about worn out. Finally I got a minute so I could say, "I'm sorry, I'm just not going to be able to talk to you. Why don't you talk to my daughter?"

"Oh, no, I have to talk to you; everybody said I had to talk to Bud Lilly, and I want to get the straight dope."

"But she can help you as well as I can."

"Well, okay, but I'd really rather talk to you than that little girl."

I got busy again, and pretty soon he came over and tugged on my arm, saying, "Gosh, I'm glad I talked to her! She knows a lot more than you do!" I don't know, maybe she did. Annette's disadvantage was that she always looked like she was about fourteen years old, so I had to insist sometimes that "Either you talk to her or you don't talk to anybody." Once they talked to her for a minute, they realized she really did know fly fishing. She was sharp, she listened well, she was a good fisherman, and she was always up-to-date on what was going on in the area fishing. It was a good education for customers, especially the crusty old types who had never taken advice from a woman in their lives. Eventually there were a lot of people who would come in and say, "Where's that little girl? I want to talk to her."

When I started, I did all the guiding myself. Then I hired a guy from Connecticut, Chip Smith, and then I hired Al Troth. Greg started guiding when he was about sixteen, and by the time he was eighteen he was doing full-time guiding in the summer, which means that now he's got more than thirty years of experience on these western streams, and has floated many thousands of miles.

In the fall I'd have to go back to Bozeman to teach at the high school, but we'd keep the shop open, with Pat and Greg pretty much running things. Mike was still in high school and Annette was still in junior high school, but Greg was about to start his freshman year of college, so he was able to work later at the shop. I went up to West Yellowstone one weekend and Pat took me aside and said, "You know, Greg is getting awfully tired. He's been carrying a full load, and I think he's coming down with a cold. We'd better give him some time off. Besides that, he's about to start school, and he needs a couple days to rest up."

So I found Greg and said, "Greg, you're going to have to

Poppy, for many years official greeter at the Trout Shop, patrolled the floor while Pat was busy behind the "computer."

take some time off. You've guided for twenty-six straight days without a day off."

"Well," he said, "I'll take a day off if I can go fishing." So we gave him two days off so he could go fishing before he went back to school.

Both the boys started their guiding work as soon as school was out, the very next day, in fact. They both worked all their summers, paying for most of their college educations that way. Annette also worked like crazy all summer and at school, so none of the kids cost us much in education, and all were a great help with the shop. It made us proud and very happy to see our children not only taking part in the business, and not only succeeding, but sharing our love for the fly-fishing life. Both Greg and Mike developed reputations as superb guides, and as the Trout Shop got more publicity, so did they. Mike was the central figure in a story in Nick Lyons's book, *Bright Rivers,* and Greg was featured demonstrating fly casting in many photographs in Joe Bates's big book, *Fishing.* The boys and Annette became polished public speakers, giving many talks at fly-fishing meetings. They were our best spokesmen.

Annette was one of the first women in Montana to get a fishing outfitter's license. She took her first ladies-only trips, guiding women clients, when she was eighteen. Soon after that Greg's wife Bonnie began guiding too, which gave us an unusual edge on the shops with no women guides.

The year that Greg graduated, he and Barry Schaplow and Jim Ahrendes were all in the same class, but we couldn't give any of them time off to go to graduation; as soon as school was out, they all came up and went right to work. So the school mailed their diplomas to the Trout Shop. That night, when the boys came dragging in after dark from a long day of guiding, we waited until they were settled down by the fireplace before I announced, "All right, tonight we're having graduation exercises," and Pat and I presented them with their diplomas. They sat there kind of glassy-eyed, too tired to care one way or the other.

Greg and Bonnie got married that same summer. They had met at Montana State, where she was studying business education and was a basketball cheerleader. Bonnie was from Lewistown, Montana, so we had to arrange to get up there during the summer season for the wedding. Barry and Jim were in the wedding party. We left the shop in the care of Will Godfrey, who was working for us at that time, and the Lillys all took off for Lewistown.

There's a terrific spring creek that runs through Lewistown, and back in those days there were some enormous fish being taken from it. So the morning of the wedding, the boys decided there was just enough time for a little fishing. They pulled up in front of the church about ten minutes before the ceremony was to start, frantically trying to change out of their fishing clothes into their wedding clothes in the car. The wedding went just fine, and as Greg and Bonnie drove away on their honeymoon, Barry and Jim went back to the spring creek.

This kind of energy and enthusiasm seemed to drive all of us. Mike met his first wife, Karen, at school at Pullman, Washington, and she worked a couple of summers at Mammoth in the Park. Mike would guide for twelve or fourteen hours a day, then drive forty-five miles to Mammoth, stay there half the night, and then drive back and guide the next day.

Barry worked for us for several years, and eventually Pat, who noticed these things better than I, said, "You know, I think Barry has his eye on Annette." One summer he had to go to National Guard camp, and he was gone quite a while. When he came back for a visit, all the boys thought he'd come back to see the guides, but Pat said, "Nope—he came back to see Annette." She was right, as usual, and Barry and Annette eventually married. He earned his M.A. in wildlife management and went to work in Dillon, Montana, where they spent two years. Barry eventually let that job go and came to work at the Trout Shop full time. He was a trained fisheries biologist, and he gave the Trout Shop's credibility one more boost by being on the staff because he was also an excellent fisherman and guide.

When Annette was married, Pat decided that we would have a family get-together, and she wanted to serve fish. We had a kind of family policy that we didn't keep any fish, so whoever was the youngest member of the family was always the one required to kill fish if we wanted to eat some. It turned out that the youngest member of the family was Barry, Annette's new husband, so there he came sneaking in with six trout out of the Gallatin River.

We had some other family members that were an important part of our lives and of the Trout Shop. We've had several dogs, but none made the Trout Shop his territory so aggressively as Sam. Sam was a big black lab with a couple of unusual characteristics. One was that he loved rocks. If you took him to the river, he'd dive in and bring up a rock in his mouth. Some labs will do this sort of thing, but Sam eventually wore his teeth down so badly that in his later years he could hardly eat.

But what got Sam and us in the most trouble was that he loved Dairy Queen ice cream. The Dairy Queen in West Yellowstone was right across the street from the Trout Shop. Every day when the crowd would start to gather, Sam would stroll over to the Dairy Queen; whenever someone wasn't looking, he'd lose his ice cream cone. He was especially effective with small kids, who tended to gawk all around while they were eating and who, being short, held their ice cream cones just about at the level of Sam's nose. He had no mercy. Finally, the owner of the Dairy Queen called me up and said, "Bud, I know we're good friends and everything, but you're going to have to call that lab home. He's eating all my patrons' ice cream, and they complain, and then I have to replace whatever he ate."

So I apologized and promised to keep Sam home. For a while, every time he'd head across the street, one of us would

Our family in the late 1970s, from left: Annette, Greg, Pat, Bud, and Mike. This picture was taken during an FFF Conclave, and we were all exhausted from guiding, giving talks, hosting visiting friends, and running the shop. Poppy maintained her usual calm.

Sam ruled the Trout Shop the same way. Once in a while someone would make a mistake and bring their dog in. Then we'd have rods and reels and waders and things flying in every direction. When he got old and lost his ability to fight, he became more peaceable. One day a friend came in from Livingston and let his young lab out of his car. The dog came in and jumped on Sam and was just chewing the hell out of the poor old dog. This guy thought that was the funniest thing he'd ever seen, but I went over and kicked his dog about thirty feet out into the street, which ended the friendship. Sam was family.

This was during the years when we were boarding several of the guides in the shop basement. It wasn't the Ritz and had no ventilation, but it was cool, and Sam would go down there and spend the day. It smelled of old socks and Sam. I don't know how those guys stood it. They'd have to kick Sam out of someone's bed every night before they could go to sleep.

One February, when he was thirteen, Sam just went out and found himself a nice place under a tree and laid down and died. Greg found him in the morning.

By 1980 the Trout Shop was becoming less and less of a family business. Greg, Mike, and Annette had all gone out on their own with careers. Pat had been having health problems for a few years, and the long hours at the shop were pretty hard on her. So in 1982 we sold all the related businesses—the shop, the schools, the guide services, the catalog business, and so on—to Fred Terwilliger, a fellow Montana native who had worked for many years at Dan Bailey's shop. Things didn't work out for Fred, and in 1987 the shop passed into the hands of Jim Criner, former football coach at Boise State University. I worked closely as a consultant with Jim, who is doing well with the shop, but I'm out of the shopkeeping business. It was an exciting, exhausting, and fulfilling thirty years, and I think my dad got his money's worth out of that original $2,500.

holler at him to come back. We kept him in the shop a couple days that way, but then we got another call from Eileen over at the Dairy Queen.

"Bud, you still got Sam over there?"

"Yeah, we've been watching him."

"Let him come back. He keeps all the other dogs away."

Sam was a real fighter, and I suppose he was just keeping all the spoils for himself at the Dairy Queen. Eileen decided it was easier to deal with one Sam than with a whole pack of local dogs.

Clients and Other Challenges

AFTER I GOT USED TO THE IDEA OF what I was supposed to do with a client, we were always looking for ways to find more of them, especially before the shop became well known. One of my brainstorms was to develop a partnership with a travel agent in an effort to keep a steady flow of customers coming in. I went to California and met with the travel director for Western Airlines. He was a fisherman, and we set up these "Western Tours," out of San Jose, that sold the fishermen a room at the Stagecoach Inn in West Yellowstone and some fishing with my guides. It sounded great.

I must have been insecure, because I set the price too low, drawing mostly non-fly fishermen: very nice people but hard on the guides. Our guides were hard-core fly fishermen, and when these Californians would come in with their little green canvas creels and their spinning rods, I could just see the guides cringing, hoping they wouldn't be called for this one.

This went on for an entire summer, and though any good guide is prepared to handle an occasional duffer, we got a new load of these guys with their salmon eggs and sinkers every few days. One group spent their first two days drinking and couldn't fish, so Barry took them horseback riding. I've never been more grateful to the guides for being creative and finding ways to get difficult clients into some good fishing. But it did bring a new phrase to the Trout Shop lexicon. Any time after that when a client arrived with all the earmarks of not knowing anything about fly fishing, I'd hear the guides mumbling, "Uh-oh—Western Tour."

Clients can be wonderfully generous at times. I was fishing with one client on the Madison when we saw the fish starting to work in the heavier riffles. I pointed them out to my client, whose name was Max, and he said, "I'm sorry, Bud, but I just can't wade out that far. Could you wade out and reach him?" So I waded out and put a fly over the fish, who took it and headed

Our logo, a trout with a lily in his mouth, was created by one of West Yellowstone's many unforgettable characters, Dave Bascom. An advertising executive by profession, Dave was for many years proprietor of the Wretched Mess store, and was editor, under the pen name of Stanley Milford Poltroon, of the Wretched Mess News.

downstream a few hundred yards, where Max netted it for me. This was in the old days, so we hit it over the head; it was a four-and-three-quarter-pound brown. We went back upstream, and Max pointed out to the same riffle, saying, "Bud, I think there's another one out there."

"You want to try it this time?"

"Oh, no, I couldn't get out there."

So out I went again, cast the Sofa Pillow again, and took a near twin of the first trout. It took me back downstream where Max netted it, a four-and-a-half-pound brown trout.

These two fish were within ten feet of each other, and each was an outstanding trophy. Thanks to a client who just loved to see fish taken, I had the chance to take them within a few minutes of each other.

On the other hand, some people had some amazing ideas about what was appropriate to ask of the guide. About the time the West Yellowstone area began to get a lot of publicity in the 1970s, fly fishing became very fashionable, much the way skiing had some years earlier. For us, this was probably the beginning of the New West, which suddenly seemed to attract a different crowd with a much higher percentage of urban people who knew practically nothing about the outdoors. There were many people who got into the sport almost overnight, and they wanted to move right to the top and not mess around with all the things the rest of us went through, like practicing and learning and getting experience. A surprising number of people came in and announced, "Now, we don't necessarily want to catch a lot of fish; we'd rather just have a few big ones." I think they really believed they were doing us a favor—Don't knock yourself out worrying about getting us the numbers, just put us on to a couple of those monster trout you have out here.

That's a fairly innocent mistake, of course. It's like the folks who would call up in January and ask me what the weather was going to be like during the third week of July, and if such and such a stream would be having good hatches right then. They didn't know enough to know what they didn't know. But other people simply had no sense of what was appropriate behavior when dealing with a professional guide, and even less sense about what was simply poor taste. One gentleman who had no shortage of money came into the shop one day and explained that he didn't really need a guide, that both he and his son were accomplished fly fishers. They even had their own rubber raft. But they would kind of like to know what stretch of water to fish, so would we mind if they followed one of the guides out to where he would put his boat in the water? They'd just put their raft in there and kind of drift along behind and not get in the way or anything.

There was another old gent who would hire a boat for the day. The man's son would put his raft in right behind the boat, and at lunchtime the father and son would trade places so that they had to pay the price of having only one person guided for the day.

What is curious about these incidents is that they almost always involved people for whom a little more expense would not have made any difference. They were willing to let their bad manners show in order to save a little money. In my experience, the guy who slaved and saved to make a float trip did all he could to have the full experience and didn't try to flimflam the guide or the outfitter. And those were the people we would work our tails off for, because they knew what it all was worth.

It's surprising, though, how many people would not follow the guide's guidance. There they were, paying $175 or more for the day of fishing with a guide who is presumably the person who knows most about the water they are going to fish that day. As I've explained, we spent a lot of time getting the best possible information on each stretch of water each day so that the guide would know what the best runs were, which flies to use, and so on. The guide wasn't just along to row. But many clients would refuse advice about the proper fly pattern, or the best places to cast, and sometimes they would ruin their chances by doing so. It's a shame to waste a good guide's knowledge that way, but people have their own notions of what to do.

But I must admit that there were times when we didn't want the client to make too good use of the guide's knowledge. If we had reason to believe that the client might be a little too talkative about an especially good spot we'd shown him, we had some tricks for throwing him off. This was important if the client happily announced that he was going to bring his whole club back here tomorrow, and if "here" was some fragile place that couldn't take that kind of pressure. I think Greg developed the technique for getting the people turned around just enough so that they couldn't find their way back. If, for example, he was taking them somewhere on the Firehole (which is pretty much a roadside stream most of its length), Greg would drive past the turn he wanted to take, find some other road to turn onto, and make

a loop back. Then he'd approach the important turn from the opposite direction. The Continental Divide runs right through the park, and people are always getting confused with so many different watersheds so close together, so Greg's simple maneuver was usually enough to confuse them, even along a relatively short and highly visible river like the Firehole. This kind of maneuvering wasn't necessary very often, but with some fishermen it was our only choice.

But fly fishermen are generally wonderful people. We practically never had anyone make trouble, for example, over the inevitable slow day. There are days when you just can't buy a client a fish, even if the client is pretty skilled. In fact, we probably had more people get upset about a bad guide than about poor fishing. We would sometimes get a guide who either had a bad day or was an independent we had used because ours were all busy, and if he didn't perform well, people had a right to get upset. If the guide didn't give them a full day, or fished too much when he should have been helping the client, or in some other way didn't live up to the bargain, he truly had failed the clients, and I'd occasionally have to take it out of his pay.

People were reluctant to complain to me. They were trying to be realistic about fishing, I suppose, and keep in mind that nobody makes any guarantees that you'll catch fish. Some of them may have been embarrassed that they caught so few, which they should never be. Nobody catches them all the time, and nobody is testing them out there. They should just do their best and have fun. The last thing they should do is worry about what the guide thinks of their abilities; no matter how bad you are, he's seen worse, and his goal is to make the best of your abilities, whatever your skills or limitations.

The toughest guide trip we ever had was when we spent several days guiding a man who was totally blind. He insisted on fishing with flies, and he insisted on bringing his three children along and that they fly fish too. This was a very brave man who was determined that our guides could be brave too.

I sent two guides with him, and when they came in at the end of the day, the fly rods were tangled up in a hopeless rat's nest. It seemed like it took hours to get everything disentangled after those three nursery-school-age kids had spent the day with it.

The man could cast just fine, and so one guide, George Kelly, would get him into the stream and spot a fish, then tell him where to cast. As the casts got close, the guide would advise him, "about three feet farther," or, "a couple feet farther to your right," or whatever was necessary. Together they would zero in on the fish, and when the dry fly went right over it and it rose, the guide would yell "There!" and he'd set the hook. It was sad, and happy, and beautiful all at once.

In the meantime, the other guide was putting in a less fulfilling day, with three kids climbing all over him. Jim Ahrendes, a blocky, good-natured guy, got the assignment to watch over the kids, and he spent his day wrestling these kids up and down the river. One of them bit him, though Jim never did know why. Maybe the fishing was too slow.

Celebrities and Experts

IT WAS INEVITABLE THAT AS THE SHOP GOT BETTER known we would begin to see some genuine celebrities coming in for a trip. Chet Huntley used to vacation up at the 320 Ranch north of West Yellowstone for some years before he got the idea for Big Sky, the development he created between Bozeman and West Yellowstone. Chet was a native Montanan and a serious fisherman who usually came in August because he loved to fish hoppers. He got in the habit of stopping in the shop and became sort of a regular visitor. In fact, I believe it was Chet who introduced the Rappala to the West Yellowstone area. He came into the shop one day, I suppose it was in about 1965, and said, "I was over in Finland and they have this interesting lure—why don't you try it out?" He handed me this thing, and, not being much of a lure fisherman, I passed it along to a friend of mine who was a well-known fish hog. He tried it out on Hebgen Lake and announced that it wouldn't work. Of course, eventually it became one of the most successful lures of all time.

It was through Chet that a number of other media personalities became our clients at the shop. Dan Rather was visiting Chet at Big Sky when Chet was just getting the development off the ground, and Dan and I fished together one day. We also got to know Robert Pierpont and Charles Kurrault through Chet.

You have to keep in mind that this was pretty heady stuff for a boy from Manhattan, Montana. I had a lot to learn about famous people and their world. Charles Kurrault used to stay at the Parade Rest Ranch near West Yellowstone, and one of his visits gave me a lesson in how peculiar fame can be. One day Ted Trueblood and Peter Barrett, both very well-known writers for *Field & Stream*, wanted me to take them fishing. Ted was one of the best known of all outdoor writers and an important conservationist down in Idaho, and I'd been reading his articles for many years. I really admired him, so I was just thrilled to take him and Peter fishing. Then at the last minute I got a request also to take Charles Kurrault out that day. That sounded like a pretty big deal to me too; how could I pass up a chance to fish with Charles Kurrault?

So I teamed them up when we met at the shop, going through the motions of introducing all these famous people to each other. But as I was making the introductions, I noticed the blank looks on all their faces as they shook hands. They all looked like perfect strangers look when they meet each other—polite and genial, but nothing more. It turned out that Charlie had never heard of Ted and Pete, and they had never heard of him. And there I stood, beside myself that I was taking all these household names fishing.

I suppose that of all the famous clients we've had, though, the one whose fishing style most suited my own was the great sportscaster Curt Gowdy. Curt is an old-western-style fly fisherman, the kind who may not have classic form but who knows how to get results. He's a lifelong fisherman, a western native, and like many western fishermen I know, he's not a fancy caster or a hatch-matcher. But he understands the water and knows where to find fish. He's got a great deal of enthusiasm, and he's absolutely charming to be with, partly because his voice is so familiar. It's fascinating to hear that voice we've all heard for years on television sports broadcasts, except that now it's talking about fly patterns and trout.

Curt called me up one time and told me that the network was interested in making an episode of a popular television program at the time, "The American Sportsman," around West Yellowstone. After explaining the plan to me, he asked, "Would you mind helping us out with this?"

"Why, Curt, I'd be delighted!"

"Great. Let's see, first, I need two helicopters, and...."

"Uh, I don't know if I can arrange for two helicopters." Eventually the project fell through, and I still don't know how to arrange for helicopters.

Curt, Yellowstone's superintendent Jack Anderson, and I were fishing together in the Park one day, a tough one. Not only was the fishing slow, the wind was high. Jack was doing most of the guiding, so we were going to all his favorite places, and he also had brought along a fancy lunch. So in terms of everything but the trout—food, companionship, scenery—it was a great day. But we wanted some trout, too. There was a photographer following Curt around for something or other, and his day was a lot slower than ours.

Jack even brought along a bottle of "Old Yellowstone" bourbon, and he and Curt managed to just about finish that at lunchtime. Finally I suggested we try a spot I knew on the Firehole. When we got there, for some reason I suggested that we put a Bitch Creek nymph on the point, and then put another fly on the dropper. It was illegal to use a rig like that, with two flies, in the Park, but Jack didn't say a word. At the time, I didn't even think about it. I was just getting desperate to get some action from the trout, and this was a good technique.

Immediately Curt announced, around the big cigar he had in his mouth, that "By God, now we're doing it the way I learned to fish!" and we hoped that finally the photographer

Curt Gowdy was our kind of fisherman: practical, skilled in western basics, and great fun.

would get some action. Curt winged a good cast out and almost immediately hooked about a three-pound brown. It was a beautiful fish, and the cameraman was running up and down the bank trying to get a picture of this fish, which was jumping and putting on a great show before it finally broke off. It was the only fish we hooked all day, and the photographer never did get a decent picture of Curt with a trout. The interesting thing was that we'd spent the whole day doing the proper Firehole River sort of fishing, with small flies and hatch-matching and so forth, then finally went back to a basic old technique and hooked the only fish of the day.

I never considered Jack a client, even though we fished together a few times. We were sort of in the same business,

dealing with the public, though he had a lot more pressure on him to produce than I did. He was superintendent of Yellowstone in the late 1960s and early 1970s, one of the most controversial periods in the Park's history. Though he's gone, he won't be forgotten by fishermen, because he set the Park on a management course that turned it into a world model of good fisheries management. That example has inspired good all over the country, and it was the best thing to happen in our area in many years—both for business and just for those of us who loved fishing.

I talked to Jack almost every Sunday. That was a fairly quiet day for him, and he'd drive down from his home at Park headquarters, at Mammoth Hot Springs. I think he liked that beautiful forty-five-mile drive early in the morning. He'd come in and we'd drink coffee and talk. Sunday morning was a quiet time in the Trout Shop, too, and it gave us both a chance to unwind a little. We'd swap stories, compare notes on fishing, and talk about the future of the area's natural resources. We supported his programs at the Trout Shop, and I like to think that we may even have had a little influence on his thinking. Western fly fishing has had a lot of heroes, but few of them have done as much good for the actual fishing as Jack did.

One of my most memorable experiences with guiding a prominent person occurred after Jack had retired and John Townsley, now also deceased, was superintendent. John spent a lot of time politicking on behalf of the Park by inviting various dignitaries to visit, and it was because of one such visit that Greg and I went into the headwaters of the Lewis River in Yellowstone Park to guide the British Ambassador to the United States, Sir Peter Ramsbotham. Sir Peter was, as you'd expect, a gentleman in every sense of the word, and as this was a specially arranged visit involving the State Department and who knows how many other agencies and people, John wanted to give the Ambassador a good chance to catch a trout. We were pleased and honored to be asked to help out, and it was really a lesson in how luxurious and well organized a camping trip can be.

Sir Peter was an enthusiastic fisherman. He hadn't had all that much experience with this kind of fishing, though, and we happened to hit one of those periods in the late fall when the fish in Lewis channel weren't easy to catch. Late fall is when the spawning browns and lake trout move up to shallow water, and sometimes they're thick and aggressive in the channel. Almost any fly will take them. But this time they had no regard for diplomatic standing, and the fishing was pretty slow most of the days.

The Ambassador did hook one big trout. He hooked it in the channel on a Montana nymph, and it was a good piece of fishing because it was a bright day and the fish, like many spawners, just weren't interested. They were spooky in that shallow water and weren't showing much interest until after sundown, when nobody was able to get good pictures. On the first day, he caught several fish late in the evening, but the

Guiding the British Ambassador on the Lewis Channel, Yellowstone Park.

action was so good and the light was so poor that nobody thought to bother with pictures. The next day we were all set to have a big day of catching fish, and it got very tough. From that point on he only hooked the one big fish, which got off after a brief fight.

The pressure was really on because they wanted to have a fish fry, so Greg was fishing like crazy to accumulate enough trout for a fish dinner for eight. He caught enough fish, but it wasn't as easy as wilderness fishing is advertised to be.

It couldn't have failed to be a great experience for everyone, though. John Townsley wasn't the kind of host who would take chances. The arrangements were made with military organization. Everything was always just so—the wood stacked just right, everything clean and perfectly organized. The food was superb. A helicopter had shuttled in everything, including a huge iron cookstove. We had fresh salads, all kinds of good things, throughout our four days there. The Ambassador and his wife were charming people; as so often happens when the fishing is slow, other parts of the outdoor experience—good cooking, good setting, and most of all, good company—take up the slack. And in a note to me afterwards, Sir Peter made sure I knew that he had enjoyed himself immensely, and he concluded by singing the praises of that wonderful fly I'd introduced him to, the "Manitoba Nymph."

Experiences like these don't go away. Bob Haraden was an assistant superintendent of Yellowstone back then and

went on to become superintendent of Glacier National Park before retiring here in Bozeman. Like me, he has fond memories of the trip with the Ambassador, and recently sent me an exchange of letters between himself and another member of the party. In the photograph we have of the whole party, there was an unidentified young man standing between Greg and me in the back row, and we'd never been able to recall who he was. But Bob tracked him down, which wasn't that hard considering that he is now Sir Jeremy Greenstock KCMG, the United Kingdom's ambassador to the United Nations. Bob recently wrote him, and got this response:

> *I remember with great clarity the fishing trip with Peter Ramsbotham on Shoshone Lake in October 1975. I recall hauling our canoes up the top end of Shoshone River and completely failing to catch any fish myself. I also remember making a fool of myself in thinking that a bear had raided our camp in the middle of the night, when it was probably my Ambassador leaving the tent for a middle-of-the-night necessity.*

There is one famous fly fisherman with whom I look forward to fishing some day, and that's Jimmy Carter. He fished the West Yellowstone area in 1981, having then just recently gotten interested in the sport, which is now apparently one of his favorite pastimes. We were able to persuade him to come

Bud Lilly's Guide to Fly Fishing the New West

and speak at the groundbreaking of the International Fly Fishing Center, which was a wonderful boost for publicity, and he did some fishing with Dave Whitlock and Charlie Brooks while he was there.

His fish and game director when he was governor of Georgia was a guy that I had gotten to know, and so the director had told him that if he ever got to West Yellowstone he had to go and see Bud Lilly. He was also a friend of a law family in Atlanta, Jack Izard, the oldest law firm in the south, and Jack also had told Jimmy the same thing—you gotta see ol' Bud Lilly.

I knew he was still in the area, and I had been warned that he might be dropping in on me, but it was still a little surprising when he did. It was early on a Sunday morning, probably the day he left the area. I'd opened the shop and it was still very quiet when I looked out and here was a parade of big black limousines surrounding the Trout Shop. People were piling out of them and running here and there, and a heavily armed guy came in the door—I was wondering by then if maybe the place was on fire—and walked up to me with a walkie-talkie in his hand.

"Are you Bud Lilly?"

"Yes." There was no denying it.

"President Carter would like to see you."

"Tell him to come on in."

So he came in, with some more guards, and we had a nice chat. Knowing that he was probably going to visit me, we had prepared a little presentation for him. I had a plaque made up with some flies and a peanut on it. There was a little inscription that said: "These flies are just like peanuts to the trout." We talked about fishing and mutual friends, and after he got back to Georgia he wrote me a nice letter telling me that he would like to go fishing with me next time he comes out. That would be just fine with me.

I did arrange for Jimmy to write the foreword for *Fly Fishing Always,* the little book published by the Federation of Fly Fishers in 1984. I called him up and told him that this was a good project, one that deserved the help, and he was more than glad to do it for us. He's a friend of fly fishermen and could help us in many ways if invited to do so.

Another friend of fly fishermen is a man I met just a few years ago, the great Olympic basketball coach from Indiana, Bobby Knight. Bobby has become an avid fly fisherman who has zeroed in on Montana fishing. He spoke at the International Fly Fishing Center, at our big banquet, a few years ago, and he returns to the area regularly to fish.

Bobby is of course a very popular speaker in America today, an outspoken advocate of good sport and American

The Ambassador's camp on Shoshone Lake. Front row, left to right: Mrs. Townsley, Mrs. Ramsbotham, Sir Peter Ramsbotham. Second row: Greg, Jeremy Greenstock, Bud, Yellowstone Park maintenance supervisor Bill Hape, Assistant Superintendent Bob Haraden, Superintendent John Townsley, Assistant Superintendent Vern Hennesay.

values. I think he has great promise to be a good force for fly fishermen because he has such a large audience and such a commanding personality. I've fished with him a few times and intend to fish with him more; he's great company for his sense of good sport and his enthusiasm, and he's one of the great storytellers.

Nothing is more uncertain or difficult to pin down in fly fishing than the notion of the expert. If you say the word "expert" to most fishermen, they immediately think of some person, either someone they know or someone they've heard of, who always seems to catch the big fish. If you say the same word to someone in the fishing tackle industry, they're liable to sneer and make a smart remark about "instant experts," or quote Lefty Kreh's comment that an expert is a guy with his own slide projector, more than fifty miles from home.

Admitting right away that I wouldn't be writing books if at least a few people didn't consider me an expert, I have to say that the problem of sorting out the genuine authorities from the phonies is real. When the fishing around West Yellowstone started to get a lot of attention from the fishing writers in the late 1960s and early 1970s, those of us who lived there noticed a surprising increase in the size of fish being reported (but not seen or photographed) from some rivers.

I'd been keeping records in the Lunker Club book for many years, and I knew how rare a real three-pounder was. I knew that only once in a great while could the Firehole, for example, produce a fish in the six-pound class, probably only once every few years. We fished the rivers hard, and we measured and weighed those fish; the Trout Shop was the closest thing they had to an official record-keeper.

Then suddenly we started to read about four-, five-, and six-pounders being caught like fingerlings. I fished with some of those writers, and when there were witnesses around, the fish they caught looked pretty much like anyone else's, sometimes a little smaller. There was a lot of poetic license in those weight estimations, and there's no real harm in that except that it put those of us who ran tackle shops in an awkward position. People would come out having read so-and-so's book and expect to start hauling in the five-pounders from streams we knew had very few fish weighing over three pounds. We really knew, not only from our own experiences but from electroshocking studies that management agencies did.

So I'm sure I can't give you a simple definition of an expert. It isn't just a guy who knows more than most of us. The late Ted Trueblood was one of the first writers whose stories really stuck with me, but I don't think it was just because he obviously knew what he was talking about. Ted had a quality beyond expertise. Ed Zern, who has never pretended to be a great authority on anything, and whom I have always considered the greatest outdoor humorist, is also my idea of a real expert because he knows how to enjoy himself and his companions and good fishing and because he doesn't ever take himself too seriously. What expertise often

Lefty Kreh's almost magical ability to cast a fly line always drew a crowd. His zesty sense of humor didn't hurt, either.

is confused with, or replaced by, is the image of expertise. Consider, as I often have, something that seems very inconsequential at first but actually is very powerful. Consider the fishing hat.

People are pretty easily impressed once they get out of their own territory. We had a tackle shop owner in West Yellowstone for awhile who wore a western hat with a huge fleece hatband, the kind you could load down with flies. He had a real menagerie on that hat, and it became part of his trademark. People would come into the Trout Shop after they'd been visiting with this fellow, and they'd say, "Boy, that guy down the street, he knows a lot; he's got that terrific hat, you know, all full of flies...." And I'd say, "Did he tell you about that hat?" acting innocent and honest.

"No," they said, all ears.

"Well," I'd wind up, "he was down on the Madison the other day and he fell in, and he got three strikes before he could get out."

I've thought about the hat for very good reasons myself, also having to do with image. I always wanted to popularize the western hat, partly because I was concerned about giving us a distinct image at the Trout Shop. I figured it was better than just wearing the Irish wool hats that have always been so popular among fly fishermen. So I started wearing my hat all the time, even in the shop. Some of those hats would get a lot of character over the years; I still have most of the ones I finally had to retire because distinctiveness was being replaced by seediness.

Well, it worked. The hat became a part of our image at the shop, I became very accustomed to wearing one, and people would sometimes look at me strangely if they saw me without it, like they weren't sure who I was. I didn't realize how successful I had been at developing the image until one day a fellow came into the shop and wanted to buy the hat right off my head.

"Jesus," he said, "I'd like to buy that hat. Is it for sale?"

"Everything is for sale in here except my wife."

"Well, I'd sure like to have that hat."

So I quoted him a price for it (there were a good many flies on it, as I recall), and he took it. I wore a western hat for twenty-five years in the store, though I finally had to quit because in the last few years I had a little trouble with skin cancers. I like to think that we had something to do with the popularization of western hats among fishermen and guides in our area, and I was glad to see it. I was glad partly because we sold Stetsons and Resistols in the shop, but also because it was part of the developing image of western fly fishermen. Easterners had their tyroleans and little tweed hats and all that, but there was no clearly identified western style.

The other hat that became closely identified with the shop was the one we'd advertise as "Greg's leather hat." When Greg and Bonnie were on their honeymoon in San Francisco, he found a wide-brimmed leather hat that had been made there. He came back wearing it, and I immediately announced we could make a fortune on that hat. We didn't really make a fortune, but we sold thousands of them over the years. I visited the factory once, down on Third Street, the same street where the Winston Rod Company was located for many years. It was a rough section of town, and Pat and I took a bus down to the address we had; there was the building with the windows all broken out, no sign, all boarded up. But the number was right, so I knocked on the door, and a little Chinese man peeked out. I asked him if this was the Winfield Cover Company.

"Yup."

"May we come in and look around? We're one of your customers."

"Okay." So we went in and I introduced myself. "I'm Bud Lilly from Montana."

"Oh, God, have we wanted to meet you! We've been wondering who those crazy people were in Montana who were buying all those hats!" There you have it. One man's expert was another man's sucker.

I was fortunate to start fly fishing with the help of an accomplished fisherman, my dad, and to grow up in a neighborhood where being a good fisherman was as natural as it could be. There were unlimited opportunities to fish, and experience really is one of the best teachers. I fished so much that I gradually came to recognize the good water in a stream without even consciously thinking about it. It's a slower way to learn than from books or professional guides, but what you learn you learn very well. I came to the Trout Shop with a lot of fishing experience for someone my age, and enough sense to know that I had a lot more to learn. Luckily for me, the Trout Shop was a great place to do that learning.

I learned a lot from a man named Irving Strong. Irving was an excellent fly fisherman, though I got the impression he was one of those people who had been put out to pasture by a wealthy family back East. Irving really taught me most of the fundamentals of dry-fly fishing. I knew nothing about how to pick a fly off the water with a roll cast. Irving knew a lot about how to read rises, how to tell a caddisfly rise from other kinds, for example.

The first fishing book that had any effect on me was Ray Bergman's *Trout,* the book that so many fishermen still consider their Bible. Bergman fished the Yellowstone country and wrote about it in *Trout,* including telling about fishing with Vint Johnson, one of my early competitors in West Yellowstone. Vint Johnson had shown Bergman how effective a big Royal Coachman bucktail was on trout in the Park, and after reading that, I began to promote not only that fly but a number of other bucktail and squirrel tail patterns.

Sid Gordon's book *How to Fish from Top to Bottom* had a big influence on me. It contains so much information on the character of streams and lakes, and how fish go about their lives, that I still recommend it to people all the time. What he did was reveal to me how important it was to be aware of the conditions on any given day. Having all the famous fly patterns and knowing a lot of fancy casts wouldn't really do you much good if you didn't understand the influences of sunshine, water temperature, air temperature, shade, and other factors on the fish and their world. I still find it best to concentrate more attention on those conditions rather than on having a fly with just the right shade of hackle in the tail. By spending many years observing those environmental conditions, I got a reputation for being able to predict fishing conditions. Paul would like to add a note here, too:

Charlie Brooks was probably the person most responsible for alerting fly fishermen to Sid Gordon's book, which had been published in the 1950s but wasn't available when fly fishing became so popular twenty years later. When I was getting started in fly fishing Bud loaned me his copy of the book, and after a few years I found one of my own. Luckily for all of us, Stackpole recently published a new edition, for which I was pleased to write a foreword. As Bud and Charlie both emphasized, the book is just packed with information about how streams and lakes work. There is now a huge scientific and popular literature on aquatic ecology, but How to Fish from Top to Bottom *is still one of the most accessible introductions to it all, perhaps because Gordon himself was both an angler and a professional in fisheries management and had so much sympathy for how we think and what we need to know.*

I suppose the reason we got so sensitive to these environmental conditions was that we were right on the edge of Yellowstone Park, where there is a unique range of such conditions in trout streams very close together. The Firehole, Gibbon, and Gardner rivers all have significant geothermal influences that dramatically affect their fishing, and they flow into larger streams that also are influenced. There's no place else in the world where you have trout streams of such ecological diversity so close together. If you know the streams, and are aware of how environmental conditions are influencing them, you can almost always find at least one place where the fishing is promising.

Before I got to know any of the really famous fishing experts, I naturally got to know some of the behind-the-scenes people who have a great deal to do with the success of the experts. I had the pleasure of meeting many of the leaders in the industry, often just when they were getting started. We were able to work with Leon Martuch, when he was getting Scientific Anglers started. Leon had involved Ted Trueblood in his company, and Ted was a creative guy who deserves a lot of credit for some of the Scientific Anglers projects. I know he was very involved in the development of the first sink-tip lines. I didn't really see good fly rods in any appreciable number until Paul Young came out from Detroit in about 1955 looking for someone to open a dealership. He called on Dan Bailey, who somehow got crosswise of Paul, so Paul approached me. I was delighted to carry the rods. Paul Young built beautiful rods that were great fishing tools, and I still use a couple Young rods now and then for fishing smaller waters.

Of course, one of the modern western fly-fishing masters was Dan Bailey, who always will be remembered not only for his many contributions to fly fishing, but also as one of trout fishing's staunchest conservationists. Dan and I were competitors, but we often found ourselves next to one another in some battle to protect the streams from some idiotic dam or diversion project. This was an endless fight, and Dan had started fighting it virtually alone, well before the rest of us got involved and a system of fishermen's organizations was developed.

In 1986 Charlie Waterman published a tribute book about Dan, called *Mist on the River*, and I can't think of anyone more deserving of Charlie's skillful attention than Dan. Most fly fishermen who remember him know all he did for western fly fishing—helping develop the Wulff flies, popularizing the modern version of the Muddler Minnow, and much more—but they should remember him also as one of the original western trout crusaders. His son John still runs the shop in

Livingston and they have established a memorial award in honor of Dan, given every year to some deserving conservationist or group.

One of the first really famous fishing writers whom I got to know was Ed Zern. I first took Ed fishing in July of 1963. There were four of us, including Sam Radan, Ray Rhoades, Ed, and me, and for some reason I was using a big eight-man Air Force surplus raft. I was not known as an expert in raft management and for some reason had brought along only one paddle rather than the customary two oars, so Ed and the others spent much of the day fending us off banks as I furiously switched the paddle from one side to the other. He

Greg with Pennsylvania limestone creek expert Ed Koch during one of our clinics in the 1970s. Specialists like Ed brought a world of fresh thinking to western fly fishing and made the Trout Shop a crossroads of new ideas.

had just returned from Scotland, where his hosts had presented him with a beautiful hardwood wading staff with a staghorn handle and a brass ferrule on the end. He was a great sport about the extra duties, but eventually he poked this gorgeous wading staff into a bunch of willows that kept it, and I had to pile out of the raft and fight my way back upstream through the brush to retrieve it.

The salmonflies were on that day, and the fishing was outstanding. Ed had never caught a brown over eighteen inches long in all his years of fishing, and as this was his first trip to the Madison, he was probably unprepared for the kind of day you could have during the salmonfly hatch. We put in at Varney Bridge and, thanks as much to the others keeping us out in the current as to me paddling like mad, we found our way to a good run where we could see trout rising. We beached the raft, started casting, and immediately were all into big fish. Ed hooked a twenty-inch brown that he landed after ten minutes of jumping and running (by both Ed and the trout), Sam took a twenty-one-inch rainbow, I took a twenty-two-and-a-half-inch rainbow, and Ray lost a fish bigger than any of ours. It was like that all day. We caught several fish weighing more than three pounds, and I caught a rainbow that weighed five pounds two ounces. Ed caught one rainbow over four pounds that we photographed and released, the largest rainbow he'd ever caught.

A few years later, in 1968, when I was putting together my first catalog, I asked Ed if he would write a little foreword and let us use the photograph of him with the big rainbow. He immediately agreed, but he had a sad story to tell about the photograph, a story he related in his foreword:

> *Writing forewords to somebody else's book is a chore I usually avoid, but I volunteered for this one. Not because it's likely to win a Pulitzer Prize, but because Bud Lilly is a guy I've known since before I was senile, for whose knowledge of Western fishing and of proper tackle for it I have immense respect, and whose skills as a trout man I envy and admire.*
>
> *Also, there's the fact that one of the photos that should be in this book, perhaps even on the cover, isn't there. I took it one day just after I had beached just under four pounds of wild brown trout that had taken a fly Bud had given me a few hours earlier, and while I was admiring it Bud came whooping down the river with a rainbow of just over five pounds on the other end of his line. When he had netted it and brought it ashore and weighed it I broke out a Pentax camera and spent*
>
> *ten minutes photographing Bud with that picture-book rainbow. Then, dammit, I lost that roll of film, and even today have hopes of finding it in an old fishing-jacket pocket or some dark corner of my tackle box (on the same roll I had my only photos of the largest brown trout I had ever caught). So in a way, this is a poor substitute for a photo that might have said more about Bud and his expertise than any mere words can do.*
>
> *Buying tackle from a catalog, of course, isn't as good as buying it from Bud's store in West Yellowstone, where you can paw through flies and lines and reels to your heart's content, and watch a lot of famous fishermen come by to pick up oddments of tackle or the latest dope on the fly hatches or just to gab a bit with Bud. But a lot of us live a long way from the Trout Shop, and this is the next best thing to actually being there, leaning on a counter and arguing about the proper monstrosity to imitate a natural salmonfly. So until we meet there in person, good fishing.*
>
> —Ed Zern

My business gave me the opportunity to meet and help some of the best fly tiers in the world. We helped develop the careers of some superb new talents, and allowed some well-known talents to broaden their audience and market. Dave Whitlock, Al Troth, and Jack Gartside, all enormously talented guys, got their commercial start through the shop. It was a matter of importance to us that besides the full selection of flies tied by professional tiers who were more or less anonymous, we offered many specialties—flies by Darwin Atkins, George Grant, René Harrop, and others. It was an exciting time for us, keeping in touch with these highly creative individuals, seeing what they developed, and testing some wonderful new fly patterns just as they first appeared from the vises of their creators.

We did the same thing with blossoming artists. The Gallery introduced us to many fine young artists who needed a boost. We never took credit for their success—if they hadn't been good artists, it wouldn't have mattered how much we

Bud, Charlie Brooks, and Doug Swisher, in mildly uncomfortable weather during a clinic.

Our clinics were an incredible bargain for the fisherman, who was surrounded by expertise, but on this occasion, my ability to remember the names of customers has failed me completely. From the left, unidentified woman client, Carl Richards, Bob Jacklin, unidentified man client, Bud, unidentified man, Doug Swisher, Dave Corcoran, unidentified man client, Barry Schaplow, Jim Ahrendes, and Mike.
Photo by Dr. James G. McCue, Jr.

promoted them—but we did feel good about helping them while at the same time helping our business.

Dave Whitlock had gotten started as a commercial fly tier in the Oklahoma-Arkansas area, but I was pleased to help him get started in the West. He came to my shop in the late 1960s with some of his flies, and they were extremely impressive. When our first catalog appeared in 1969, I had three pages of Dave's flies. We continued to offer them, and he kept coming up with new ones. We were sure from the start that this man was going to be an extraordinary influence on fly fishing, and he has been. I'm not sure anyone has influenced fly tying since World War II more than Dave. He has become one of the most adept public speakers on fly fishing, he's published some excellent, practical books, he's championed his well-known Whitlock-Vibert box for stocking trout eggs in streams, and, more than practically any of the other modern authorities, he is versatile. He's a great all-around fisherman, able to do well with anything from the smallest nymphs to the largest streamers (his Multi-colored Marabou Muddlers are among the most effective streamers since the Muddler itself appeared forty years ago), he has adapted fly fishing to many species of fish not usually taken on flies, and he's the kind of sportsman who is never too busy to help another fisherman.

Until the last thirty or so years, we didn't have any nationally known fishing writers who specialized in the Yellowstone country. There were various local guidebooks now and then, and there was an occasional little book published by some fisherman from another part of the country. Howard Back's beautifully written little book, *The Waters of Yellowstone with Rod and Fly,* published back in the 1930s, was about the most you would find about this area unless you collected the articles in outdoor magazines for years until you had a good file. But part of the boom in publishing in the 1970s was the appearance of more local writers, and I'm sure none of them have been more closely identified with our area, or have been more successful in writing books about it, than has Charlie Brooks. After his first book, *Larger Trout for the Western Fly Fisherman,* appeared in 1970, Charlie became the leading fly-fishing writer of this area. It's been an interesting change from the old days, when only outsiders wrote about our fishing, and even though Charlie died in 1987 after a long fight with cancer, his influence will last many years. Many later local writers, such as Craig Mathews, who has written and co-written a series of fine books on fly fishing this area, are happy to acknowledge how much Charlie's work meant to them.

Books sometimes have funny effects that you wouldn't expect. When Charlie started publishing his very popular books, he moved into a vacant niche in fishing writing. There was nobody really paying full-time attention to the big weighted flies, and Charlie was a great proponent of those flies. He had the strength of his convictions to carry the principle of the weighted fly to a logical conclusion, and one reason his flies work so well is that he wasn't shy about making them heavy enough to reach the fish. In a way he was challenging traditional perspectives, and he took some criticism for promoting flies that are as heavy as lures. Those of us who use the heavy flies believe we're not doing anything unsporting, and Charlie did a lot to give those flies more credibility.

On the other hand, his books tended to create fishermen who believed they could learn it all by just reading a book. There was something about Charlie's way of writing that seemed to bring that out in people. As much as he encouraged people to do their own studying of streams, and to think for themselves, the biggest effect I saw of his books was that crowds of people would show up at certain spots, just as the books told them to, and expect to catch big fish almost automatically. People went through his books page by page, and more or less thought that was all that was necessary. Charlie talked a lot about the Barns Pools, a series of runs on the Madison just a few miles upstream from the Park boundary. These pools are great for migrating trout that move out of Hebgen Lake to spawn in the late fall, and Charlie told of his exploits with those fish. All summer long people would come into the shop and complain that they couldn't catch those fish that Charlie claimed were in those pools, and I'd have to explain that the fish weren't there yet, that the fishing only got good in October.

Charlie's books generated a lot of enthusiasm for fishing in our area, and he earned a lot of credit for that. He was an avid conservationist and always stressed releasing fish. But he was also the most controversial fishing writer the Rockies has produced. Many people I know out here felt that their confidence had been betrayed when his books included information they had given him, because they'd worked hard to learn things about the local fishing that they didn't necessarily want published. One fellow came into the shop shortly after Charlie's book *The Trout and the Stream* came out and said, "I think I'll buy six copies and burn 'em." That's a lot of hostility for a fishing writer to generate.

The most frequent complaint I heard at the shop about his books was that they ruined this spot or that spot by exposing the good fishing in a specific pool or stretch of water. It was Charlie's right to publish what he wanted, of course, and the Trout Shop sold hundreds of his books and thousands of his flies, but my own approach to telling people about fishing has gone exactly in the opposite direction. Over the years we've had to get away from telling people exactly where to go and behind which rock to cast. But that's not the way Charlie saw it, so we just agreed to disagree. I'm sure that some of the people we guided over the years at the Trout Shop went out and revealed good spots we'd shown them; anyone who guides shares some responsibility for spreading the word about a good fishing spot. The difference between Charlie and me is that my approach is to try to spread that use around, letting it move with the seasons and changing conditions, while Charlie's approach, whether intentionally or not, tends to concentrate fishermen in a few spots.

The nice thing is that the rivers themselves will eventually make a lot of this debate academic. Anything you publish will start to be wrong almost immediately as the river changes its channel, as the silt moves around, and as the fish subsequently find new lies. The more specific a book, the shorter its useful lifespan. The really important things about Charlie's books, such as his introductions to stream ecology and his recommendations on fly patterns, will be useful for a long, long time.

From left, TGF members Pres Tolman and Arnold Gingrich with Bud during Arnold's last visit to the West.

Drawing a map for some friends during an FFF Conclave. From left to right: Yellowstone Superintendent Jack Anderson, Doug Swisher, Joan Wulff, Lee Wulff, and Bud.

Charlie's books were part of that great surge of fishing book publishing in the 1970s that brought so many new names to the attention of fishermen and that brought some of the old masters back into print. The various seminars and trips we arranged at the Trout Shop gave me a chance to meet some of these very talented people, and others I met through the Federation of Fly Fishermen (now the Federation of Fly Fishers), which started holding its annual conclave in West Yellowstone every year or two in the late 1960s. This was an especially important experience for me; no matter how good you think you are at something, you can always learn by watching someone else, whether that person is just as good or better.

Ernie Schwiebert was one of the great fishermen I met in the 1960s just before we started developing our various special seminars, and Ernie is really an exceptional fisherman, a classic in his style. He follows all the proper procedures, all the good manners, and he's had a very broad experience that has taught him more than most people will ever have a chance to learn. Fishing for giant salmon in Norway, big brook trout in Argentina, and many kinds of fish elsewhere has turned Ernie into a great angler.

He wasn't an early starter. The first big challenge was to get him out of bed. If you're going to fish with Ernie, we learned, you start your day around twelve or one o'clock because Ernie likes to stay up late and celebrate the previous day's successes.

Ernie, for all his experience and expertise in catching huge fish, wasn't really a fisherman for the brawling, stony,

big rivers. His special interest was in streams where he could practice his wonderful skills with aquatic entomology and delicate presentation. We took him floating on the Madison a couple of times, and he didn't really enjoy it much. He preferred rivers like the Firehole and the Henry's Fork.

And there is no question that of all the people with whom I've fished, none of them could identify what difficult fish are feeding on and match it any quicker than Ernie can. He is a master. He's also a master at using emergers. I've watched him make extraordinarily long casts, straight across the Madison in the Park, using extremely long leaders in the eighteen-foot range, and take large browns on #20 emergers. He is an excellent caster, accomplished at handling a line in tricky currents and fishing a dry fly in any direction, upstream or downstream.

Ernie is so well known on trout streams that people often recognize him, which must get tiring sometimes. One day Ernie and Dan Callaghan, an outstanding fly-fishing photographer whose pictures have appeared in a number of books and magazines, and I were fishing the Madison in the Park, a section right along the highway. I saw these people pull over into the parking area and watch us for awhile, and I figured Ernie's notoriety was catching up with him again. Finally they came over closer to us, walked right past Ernie, looked at me, and said, "Oh, you're Bud Lilly!" Ernie enjoyed that, too.

Ernie has been in the enviable position of fishing every-where in the world and getting paid for it. Shortly after his first visit to the shop in 1965, I wrote to thank him for the publicity a story of his had given us. His response was a quick glimpse into what life was like for fly fishing's jet set at the time.

> Dear Bud:
>
> Am pleased the Firehole story brought you some business, and that some of the people I personally sent your way actually showed in West Yellowstone. You have a fine shop and deserve the business, so no thanks is necessary.
>
> Have been to Argentina since I last saw you. Best fish were a 16 pound brown, 18 pound landlock, 12 pound rainbow, and 9 pound brook. This winter I have been busy here, so am only thinking about it unhappily! Last July I fished salmon in Norway and killed a 51 pound fish with a 9-1/2 foot Young Parabolic, WetCel Wf-11-S High Density, Hardy St. Andrews, 12 pound tippet and 2/0 Dusty Miller. Once in a lifetime!
>
> Sorry to miss your fishing in past months, because I really love early fall in the Rockies.
>
> Cordially,
> Ernie

Among the leaders of the new generation of scientific anglers that appeared in the late 1960s were Doug Swisher and Carl Richards. We announced the forthcoming publication of their book, *Selective Trout*, in our 1970 catalog, with a few of their remarkable photographs of mayflies and a picture of Doug and Carl. They are among the outstanding modern trout-fishing technicians, of course, and we involved them in some of our special seminars.

Some of what I thought of as the most characteristically western fishing didn't interest them, though. Like Ernie, they weren't interested in fishing the fast, turbulent streams, the sort of water where the whitefish have to hold hands. They were specialists in accurate identification and imitation of stream insects, and the way I learned to fish, with general fly patterns that served lots of purposes, wasn't like that.

I fished with Doug and Carl down on the Henry's Fork one day during one of our clinics. The fishing was terribly difficult and nobody was doing well, which always looks a little embarrassing for the experts. After awhile we spread out and lost sight of each other, and when we joined up again Doug made a remark that was destined to add another expression to the sarcastic lexicon of the Trout Shop guides. He reported that he'd caught and released a good one, "over on the other side of that island." My guides latched on to that and soon were talking about "island fish," those being the ones that nobody else saw and that were always several inches bigger than anything anyone else caught that day.

For all the good that Doug and Carl did with *Selective Trout*, I think that in the long run their most important

contribution to fly fishing will not be their no-hackle flies or any of their other developments. Those things have been accepted by a lot of people, but I think more important is that Doug and Carl have made us all think about things we took for granted and have shown us the importance of experimenting. Those beautifully clear photographs of trout-stream insects opened a window for us onto a world about which we really didn't know much.

On the opposite end of the spectrum were the nontheorists, people like Nick Lyons and the late Arnold Gingrich, who bring the best of fly fishing's other side—the warmth, the fraternity, the foolishness—to life for us. Arnold was master of ceremonies at several FFF conclaves in the 1970s, and he was truly a master. He was so articulate and well-read that he could synthesize and coordinate and review and summarize and placate and bullshit, and he loved being associated with the great fly fishermen. I think fishing was his idea of a great vacation from his other work, and he portrayed the brotherhood of fly fishing beautifully. I enjoyed being in any party of which he was a member because the banter was several levels above what we usually encountered in West Yellowstone.

Arnold came out to a conclave in West Yellowstone just a year or two before his death. He wasn't in great health, so we went to some fairly quiet water on the Firehole. Arnold was devoted to very small rods, and so he spent most of his time untangling the fly from the grassy banks behind him. That was the last time I saw him, and fly fishing lost one of its best friends when he died.

Arnold was a central part of a very exciting period for fly fishing, and it was exciting partly because we were discovering all these experts, who were almost like heroes to the average fly fishermen. Fly fishing has probably never had a more satisfying social life. One of the early Federation of Fly Fishers conclaves in West Yellowstone was held before they would allow liquor at the Convention Center, and so I hosted a cocktail party in the Trout Shop. I invited about one hundred and fifty people, and the night of the big dinner we closed early, about six o'clock. We set up a bar, and I had Mike and Greg and Annette and all the guides packing drinks and peanuts to everybody. Arnold had a few martinis and settled into a comfortable spot on the stairway, where he signed books and held forth on many subjects. Ernie Schwiebert and all the others were there, talking and drinking and having a big time; the atmosphere of the Trout Shop, with all the tackle and outdoor clothes and art surrounding the people, seemed just perfect for this kind of get-together. We were having so much fun that we forgot all about dinner. Finally, they called us from the Convention Center and said, "Would you please close down the party so we can get everyone back here and serve them dinner?" For me, times like that were when fly fishing's experts were at their best.

Tackle and Techniques for Western Fly Fishing
(with some thoughts on attitude)

Chapter 9

So You Want to Fish the West

Western Rivers come in all sizes, and so do the fish; keep your expectations realistic.

PAUL SCHULLERY

"I KNOW A LOT," THE OLD COWBOY SAID, "I JUST CAN'T think of it." Unlike him, I'm not willing to come out and announce that I know a lot, but I will allow that I've seen a lot, and that in almost 70 years of fly fishing and 50 of guiding I've had a chance to get to know western fly fishing as few people have. I'm going to tell you what I know, or at least, in those many cases where there is no surefire advice to give, what I suspect. I hope to deflate some old myths, and not to create any new ones.

Western fly fishing has been a central part of my life, I'm going to try to see to it that you don't miss the best it has to offer, but the one point I want most to make is this: after all the planning, the practice, and fly tying, and reading, and travel, and talk, when you finally get out on the water along the Fryingpan or the Firehole or wherever, the part that matters most depends not only on how good a fisherman you are but how open you are to the experience. It comes down at last to you and the river, and how good you are at understanding and appreciating it. As much as I want to help you prepare for the practical details of western fishing, I am going to treat you pretty much the way I've treated thousands of clients who have hired me as a guide. We're not in this just to catch fish, but to have a good time in some of the finest country in the world. For me, and I hope for you, fly fishing is the best way of all to do just that.

I am going to tell you how, but I'm not going to tell you where, at least not too specifically. I'm far more interested in helping you to find fish on your own than I am in telling you about "secret spots" that I know of. There really aren't that many secret spots in western fly fishing anymore, not compared to the great amount of public water that anyone can find. Many parts of the West, including my own home area in southwestern Montana, have already been the subjects of very specific books, some of which are so detailed that they practically tell you which rocks to cast behind to catch a 19-inch trout named Sam.

I am not going to take that approach, partly because I don't approve of it (I'd rather you learned to catch your own fish rather than some writer's fish), and partly because I don't want to limit myself to a small part of the West. You will see that most of the examples I use are from my fishing experience in Montana, Wyoming, and Idaho, but I've fished the rest of the Rockies enough to know that the same rules apply there. What I want to do is get you ready for fishing anywhere in the Rockies. Then it's your choice how you proceed, whether you buy local guidebooks, or hire a guide, or just head out on your own and look for a likely river. Whether you are a native of the region or a newcomer, this is great trout country, with more water than could be fished in a lifetime. But knowing you could never fish it all won't in the least discourage you from trying to.

Chapter 10

Great Expectations

A LOT OF PEOPLE NEW TO WESTERN picture it as something you do in a certain place. You fly into Bozeman, West Yellowstone, or some other trout town, and from the plane you step immediately into any of your favorite trout streams. The streams are all big, brawling ones, and the fish are huge and fairly easy to catch. It may seem inappropriate to start on a negative note, but before I can tell you what western fly fishing is, I ought to tell you a few things about what it isn't.

The scale of western fishing is grand. So often people have called me up and said something like this: "we have a week to spend, and we'd like to fish the Yellowstone and the Bighorn the first day, then move to the Madison and the Big Hole the second day," and so on. These are big rivers, and they are draining a big, dry country. Eastern fishermen especially are surprised by the distances between them, even after they've studied a map. There are rivers out here that drain tens of millions of acres, and are separated from the next big valley by major mountain ranges. The hardest expectation for many people to reduce is that they can somehow fish everywhere. They may be able to make a few casts at five different rivers, but they'll spend most of their time in the car.

Western fishing is as diverse as any other fishing. A few years ago, John Randolph, editor of *Fly Fisherman*, was shown the spring creeks of the Gallatin Valley where I live. John has fished all over the world, and is no stranger to the West, but he expressed surprise and pleasure at the sight of one of the wonderful little spring creeks just a few miles from my home here in Bozeman. "This is just like the Letort! Those

Every now and then the dream of a really great fish comes true: California angler C. A. Van Nice with an eight-pound, nine-ounce rainbow from the Henry's Fork.

weed beds with the deep channels between them there—that's exactly how it is in the Letort." He also discovered that the fishing was just as challenging, and the fish just as large. That's just one example of many. The Rockies have slow-moving rivers in the valleys, rivers with a huge volume of flow—the upper Missouri, the Snake, the Yellowstone—that have very few counterparts in the East. We also have tiny glacier-fed ponds at 10,000 feet where summer doesn't come until August. If anything, western fishing is more diverse than eastern fishing, partly because there is such a variety of fish: the native cutthroat, the rainbow, the brown, the brook, lake trout, grayling, Dolly Varden, golden trout, bull trout, and an assortment of hybrids and subspecies.

The diversity carries beyond the fishing. In a matter of hours from my home I can travel through several climate zones, through a variety of major wildlife habitat types, and through some of the most glorious mountain scenery in the world. To me this has always been an important part of western sport. My way of fly fishing requires these things as much as it requires eager trout and a good fly rod.

Some time ago my son Greg was guiding an experienced fly fisherman from another part of the country. They were fishing the Madison from shore, when Greg saw the rise of a good fish. He immediately pointed it out to the fisherman, who put his fly over it. The fly was taken, the man set the hook, and the largest brown trout that Greg had ever seen came out of the water in a jump that so surprised the fisherman that he wet his pants right there. He also lost the fish.

Some years earlier, a group of saltwater fishermen came out from Florida for their first taste of trout fishing. We took them to the Box Canyon on the Henry's Fork, and in the morning one of them caught a seven-pound trout. In the afternoon, another of them caught a thirteen-pounder. The evening, as we sat around talking about the day's fishing, one of the men calmly asked me, "Do they all run about that size?"

Western trout have a larger-than-life reputation. It is based partly on the experiences of people who really do hook huge fish, partly on the exaggerations writers and other visitors make, and partly on the general mystique of the American West as a place of legends and wonders. Greg's client that day on the Madison certainly knew there were big fish in the river, but just knowing that is no guarantee you'll react calmly when you hook one. On the other extreme, the saltwater fishermen were used to catching much larger fish in Florida, routinely, so a thirteen-pound fish didn't seem all that unusual. I don't suppose they will ever know what an amazing first day they had at trout fishing. Many knowledgeable western fly fishermen would have considered even the seven-pounder to be the fish of a lifetime.

Fishermen arrive here from other parts of the country with certain expectations. If they saw a stream the size of the

And sometimes the dream gets even better: Florida angler John Dillin and his fourteen-pound, nine-ounce rainbow, also from the Henry's Fork.

upper Madison back home, they would never expect it to have the size of fish they assume are in it out here. Wherever it is, a trout stream is a trout stream. We have some outstanding ones here in the West. But we don't have magic water that makes fish grow bigger than in other places. In fact, when I think of how short the trout's growing season is at this elevation, it surprises me how many really large trout we do have. We're lucky.

In many parts of the West you can catch a really large fish, but they are not typical. Though the typical fish on many western streams is larger than in some other parts of the country, don't let anybody kid you. If you catch a three-pound trout during your week in the West, you've caught an outstanding fish.

Not all western streams, even the famous ones, produce fish over four pounds. Every stream can harbor a very few such fish, of course, but even a stream as famous as the Firehole River in Yellowstone Park rarely yields a trout of more than three pounds. When it does, that one fish will get more publicity than the thousand smaller fish that everybody else caught. People naturally hope they will catch the biggest fish. That's fine, but don't let it ruin your trip if you have to settle for a few 18-inchers or smaller fish.

Another myth, one that has grown less popular in recent years, is that western fish will not be selective. Any species of western trout, including the cutthroat, can be very hard to take. There are even times during the famous salmonfly hatches, which everybody thinks of as hog heaven for trout, when the fish get terribly difficult to fool. There you are, in the middle of this great feeding frenzy, with fish wallowing all around you and you can't hook them. That's the kind of defeat that will make your trip, and will bring you back again.

There are some serious adjustments the non-western fisherman ought to be prepared to make. You can bring most of your skills with you, but some of the rules you've learned may not apply. As we'll see later, time of day, holding water, and many other factors are likely to be different in western fishing. You may have to open your mind on subjects you thought you had all figured out. I've been fishing western waters for half a century and I'm still learning. As frustrating as the lessons sometimes are, I hope I never stop learning.

One common misconception is that the best fishing must be the most remote fishing. With modern regulations, that is usually not true. It was once true in many parts of the country that only the remote waters were unfished enough to be good, but we learned that even roadside fishing can be kept good. The most famous streams here in Montana—the Yellowstone, the Madison, the Gallatin, and so on—are all bordered almost continuously by roads. Fishermen have come to me with all their backpacking gear, excited about getting to those "really good spots" that they imagine must exist up over the mountain. There are such places, especially in terms of high-country lake fishing, but my response is usually "Well, do you want to hike or do you want to fish?"

Of course part of the definition of good fishing is the occasional opportunity for solitude, and that alone may make you seek remoter waters.

The good news is that even if the fishing isn't supernatural—even if most people don't catch the five-pounders that rise so regularly in the pages of the magazines—western fishing is still very good, and at times sensational. And it's getting better. It's time I tell you how to enjoy it.

Chapter 11

Tackle Basics

PLENTY OF BOOKS WILL TEACH YOU THE BASICS OF tackle, and there are a lot of excellent videos that will give you the basics of how to cast. I'm going to assume that you either know a little about those things or can find them out easily enough, and I'm going to concentrate instead on helping you be prepared for western fishing conditions with the right tackle and the right related gear.

Rods

When it comes to fly casting, there is one overriding factor on western waters that most seems to differentiate them from fly fishing waters in the East. It isn't the size of the rivers, or the size of the flies. It's the wind. My approach to fly fishing tackle, especially fly rods, is more the product of my experiences with wind than with any other part of the fishing. I don't think it's possible to overemphasize to the newcomer just how much of a presence wind will be in western fly fishing. Our western geography is often a blessing and often seems to be a curse, but it has given us a lot of very fast weather, and the fly fisherman needs to be prepared for that.

I like graphite rods for most fishing. My favorites for most western fishing are a 9-foot rod for a 5-weight line and a 9 1/2-foot rod for a 6-weight line. I use the 5-weight for everything from small dry flies to large streamers, and I use the 6-weight as an all-purpose rod that will handle even heavily weighted nymphs. If you enjoy carrying several rods to use for different purposes, that's fine too, but I have found that for practically all my fishing it's unnecessary to switch to anything beyond these two rods.

I disapprove of shorter rods because my line control is much better with a long rod, because the long rod keeps heavy flies a little farther away from my ears, and because I happen to enjoy casting the longer rod. For many years shorter rods were quite fashionable, and many people still swear by them, but the fishermen I guided who showed up to fish the Madison on a windy day during the salmonfly hatch with a 6-foot rod had to do a good imitation of a man having an epileptic fit just to get the fly into the water. The long graphite rods are such forgiving instruments; they will cover

a multitude of casting problems, and generally make life easier for most casters. For a third rod, for really large waters and the very largest flies, a 9 1/2-foot for a 7-weight will do the job.

Yet I do think that the smaller western waters, or waters where delicacy of presentation is so important, are just perfect for a bamboo rod. As I mentioned earlier, it was my good fortune back in the 1950s to have a dealership for Paul Young's rods, and since then I've often fished with a beautiful little Paul Young bamboo rod, a 7 1/2 for a 4- or 5-weight. On the spring creeks, such as Armstrong, Nelson's, the many creeks in the Gallatin Valley, or Silver Creek, there is nothing more exciting than hooking an 18-inch rainbow with a fine tippet and a responsive, light bamboo rod.

Reels

In the past 20 years or so, the fly reel has undergone a technological advancement kind of like the fly rod did in the 1970s. There are a couple big changes. One is that the top-end prices are astronomical compared to the best reels of earlier days. The other is that some very talented engineering specialists have come along and developed a whole batch of new machinery. There are a number of incredibly sophisticated, beautifully engineered new brands on the market, and even the low-cost reels are on the average much better than the bottom-end reels were a few years ago.

What all this means is that whether you're on a tight budget or are an enthusiastic recreational big spender, you have a great many choices and most of them are very good.

On the top end, you can spend what my dad might have spent for a car and get a truly superb piece of engineering and beautiful design in a reel from Abel, Marryat, Orvis, Peerless, Hardy, Steelfin, Tibor, ATH, and other companies. Some of those same companies make more modestly priced reels, too, like Orvis's Rocky Mountain or the Orvis Clearwater (both of these are made in England). With such a wealth of models out there in such a broad price range, the best advice may be to stick to well-known brands, whether the most expensive ones as listed above, or the more affordable ones from Sage,

Fenwick, Scientific Anglers, Martin, Berkley, and a variety of other well-known firms.

Watch out for extremes in size; don't get a reel that has little room for backing. If you're going to be fishing for trout in the West, you want a reel that can hold 150 or so yards of backing and full fly line, but you don't want something so large that it will make casting clumsy.

The question may be, how necessary is a really good reel? There was a time when most people fishing freshwater would have said that all the reel does is store the line and balance the rod, but those days are gone. Now that fly fishing has stretched so many of its boundaries, and now that we're fishing for large fish we couldn't reach before, and doing so with finer and finer terminal tackle, we need a reel that will respond correctly to difficult situations. You need a smooth, adjustable drag.

Actually, the saltwater fly fishermen led the way in developing better reels. They took on huge fish, with fine leaders, under difficult conditions, and forced reel manufacturers to upgrade and continue searching for better and better ways to build and engineer reels with the necessary guts and sensitivity to do the job.

But brace yourself when you go shopping. When the clerk says, "This one's $400 and that one's $600," remember what you're buying, and all it can do. It can be a lot of fun just to have a really great piece of gear like that. Also remember that you don't have to pay that much to get a good, trustworthy reel. And keep in mind that the fly-reel market will bear some hefty markups, and that the most expensive reels may be better, but after a point the improvements may be meaningless for your purposes.

This reminds me of the man who came hurrying into the shop one day and asked, "Do you have a five-dollar fly reel?"

"You bet we do," I said.

"God, that's wonderful," he said. "I've been all over town looking for one."

"Well, we've got one," I said. "It'll cost you fifteen dollars, but it's a five-dollar reel."

Reels, like most good equipment, have to do a basic job, but after that your choice is mostly a matter of personal taste. I'm very happy with the Hardy reels that I've been using for many years. You must have a single- or double-action reel, not an automatic. I use Hardy reels partly because they're such a joy to own. For heavyweights I use the Perfects, and for lightweights I use the L.R.H. and the Princess. But the old Pflueger Medalist, those made in the U.S.A., is still the best buy for a lifelong stream companion with no space-age metallurgy or finicky gearings or subtleties that might not stand up under rough use.

Lines

One of the reasons I prefer the lighter lines, even with very large flies, is that they allow me to keep in better contact with the fly, especially if I'm fishing a dead drift. If you can cast the big flies with a five-weight, you've got a better chance to detect the strikes. You have a finer touch. Another advantage that is especially helpful with those deeply fished flies is that once you've hooked a big fish, the smaller diameter line has less water resistance and gives the fish just that much less leverage against the hook. And of course though there's no question that a nine-foot graphite rod with a five-weight line

A strike indicator made all the difference with several fish on this bright afternoon on the Gallatin.

can handle a big trout (guides are using similar outfits for baby tarpon in Florida now), the lighter outfit does make the fight more exciting, even though it may tire the fish more than is wise if you're going to release it. It's sort of like trading in a Greyhound bus for a sports car. You're using sports car equipment but you're getting Greyhound bus results.

I usually use weight-forward lines, and for practically all situations in which I need a sinking line I use a sink-tip, with about ten feet of sinking line. It is difficult to control more than ten feet of submerged line in many fast, turbulent streams, and you can't keep in good enough touch with the fly if you are noodling around with twenty or thirty feet of sunken, curling fly line between you and the leader.

About the only time I ever use a double-taper line is with my light bamboo rods. I find it's part of the fun of presenting a fly with those bamboo rods to use a double-taper line for increased delicacy.

We've all been spoiled by modern fly lines because they need so little care. But they do need some, and most people don't give them enough. If the tip of your floating line starts sinking it will affect your fishing in important ways. One way that most people don't think about is that if the last several feet of your line has sunk several inches, each time you pull your dry fly from the water it's going to follow the path of that sunken tip and get soaked. More important, if that line sinks it can drift right through the fish you're trying to fool and ruin your chances. You should clean the line regularly. I dress mine with a flotant periodically, and clean it with detergent. There is a good bit of argument over whether detergent will eventually harm the line's finish, but I haven't had any trouble and I've been doing it for many years.

One last recommendation on lines: use a strike indicator. Those bright little plastic sleeves that you attach to the end of your line will make an amazing difference in the number of strikes you detect when you're nymph fishing. You'll get so you can read the slightest little jump in the end of the fly line, and you'll catch more fish. It's one of the simplest, most reliable new pieces of tackle to come along in many years. It's like using a bobber when you bait fish.

Leaders

Recently it's become popular to use extremely short leaders with wet flies, leaders only three feet long. I differ from that approach most of the time. The leader isn't there just to convince the fish that the fly isn't attached to something. It's also there to permit the fly to move right. On a short, thick, heavy leader the fly moves through the water like it's on the end of a stick. I'm convinced, from having watched such flies and how trout approach them, that a leader like that does not drift naturally enough. Even using the heaviest, largest flies, I try to use as light a leader as I can get away with. Presentation is everything.

This may be less important with a big streamer, because the fisherman provides the action by working the fly through the water in what he hopes is a lifelike manner. But with big nymphs, or any big fly that you want to act like something being tossed around by the current, the lighter the leader you use the more lifelike it will be. Leaders as strong as 0X are often recommended for big nymphs, like a #4 Woolly Worm.

I have found that about the finest leader that I can use with the big flies is 3X. In really fast water a big fish can easily break a 3X leader off on the strike, so when I have to I will go to 2X or even 1X. The only real exception to this rule for me is in the fall when I'm fishing the largest streamers, some of which are four or five inches long. That time of year, with a fly that size, I know I have the opportunity to hook a really large trout. Then I will use 0X, or even heavier.

On the other extreme, we've been blessed in recent years with stronger leader materials in the fine sizes. Often you will see fishermen, especially on the spring creeks and other waters famous for selective and finicky fish, using 7 and even 8X tippets. Sometimes they will even land the fish they hook on those tippets. But really accomplished fishermen can present practically any small fly well enough using 5X. I use 6X sometimes, but I don't even carry 7X. I must admit, that has something to do with the way I learned to fish, which was with heavier leaders and larger flies than are now common.

Besides being an excellent and knowledgeable guide and instructor, Annette was a good role model for aspiring women anglers because she was a great model for the newer, better-fitting gear being produced with women in mind.

When you hooked a fish, you hooked it well, and I've never completely overcome those reflexes. I break off a lot of fish when I use the finest tippets, but by not using them I've learned that they aren't really necessary most of the time, and I'm not going to try to do it just because it's fashionable.

Leader size is important with all western trout, by the way. The browns and rainbows are the ones you hear most about being selective, but the cutthroat has gotten a bum rap as a dumb, easy-to-catch fish. There are times, I know, when you can catch them fairly easily, say on the Yellowstone River in the Park where it's catch-and-release fishing, but those same fish can be very choosy and demand fine leaders at other times.

Paul always offers a dissenting opinion when we discuss leader length and thickness, so, even though I'm the expert, I'll show how open-minded I am by letting him talk here for a moment:

> *I'm the first to admit that Bud outfishes me every time, and so his advice is the most trustworthy, but I encourage you to give very short leaders a try. I've often used leaders of less than two feet in length. They're not even leaders, really; I just loop a couple feet of monofilament on to the fly line and fish with it.*
>
> *I sometimes do this with small flies and fine tippet material, say 4X, but mostly I do it with big flies and strong monofilament, tied to really large streamers and nymphs. Bud is right that a short leader affects the action of the fly, and it's also true that a short leader seems to spook fish because the fly line itself is too close to them. I don't use really short leaders in quiet streams, or in lakes. I only use it in fast water, or in water where the visibility is fairly limited— when it's almost dark, or when the water is turbid during spring runoff. Under those conditions, the fish doesn't have nearly as much time or ability to look the situation over and decide there's something wrong. Most of my streamer fishing is with flies I am actively moving through a good current, and so a very stiff leader doesn't make much difference in that situation.*
>
> *Watch for opportunities to use very short leaders with small flies, too. For example, if you're fishing to quiet pockets behind rocks in fast water, the chances of the fish seeing the fly line (or caring about it if they do see it) out in the fast water are pretty slim. If you want to put a fly deep into such a pocket, a foot of light tippet material, 4X or 5X, looped directly onto a Hi-D sink-tip fly line, might be just the thing.*
>
> *Now back to Bud, and the voice of reason.*

Waders

Unless for some reason you are physically unable to wade, you must have chest-high waders. That seems to be frightening to a lot of people, especially older people, to put on a pair of high waders and step into a big fast stream when they're accustomed to much smaller waters. Felt soles are also essential. There are several styles of gripping devices that can be attached to your wader foot. Korkers are very popular on west coast steelhead rivers, where felt is almost worthless, and I've also used the low galoshes with the metal bars on the sole. There are many occasions on slippery, rocky river bottoms where felt is just not enough.

I use both stocking-foot waders and boot-foot waders depending on the circumstances. The stocking-foot waders are often more comfortable for extended wear, but in the fall and winter those laces freeze up while you're wearing them, and the boots themselves become difficult to work with after they've sat and stiffened in the cold all night. Boot-foot waders are not always as comfortable as stocking-foot ones, but they are much easier to get on and off. Take your pick.

You will probably be glad if you also bring some hip boots. A lot of the smaller streams need no more, and I wear them whenever I can. They are much cooler, more comfortable, and a lot easier to maneuver in.

In my guiding I have found that women, especially those new to fly fishing, are often much more enthusiastic about the sport if they've been fitted out with a good pair of hip waders. Most chest-high waders are still made with no sympathy for the differences in shape between men and women, and a woman who has never worn waders before and suddenly finds herself encased in these awkward things can be intimidated. Wearing the hip waders may limit the number of places she can fish, but it may also help her feel more comfortable about fishing at all. I don't say this to patronize women, or to suggest that they are less adventurous. It's just the truth that most men are likely to have some past experience with waders whether they've ever fly fished or not, and a lot of women won't have had any such experience. If wearing hip waders will ease their entry into the sport, I think they ought to start that way. I'm sure it would be a good start for many men, too.

At one time Hodgman made a waist-high plastic wader that was inexpensive and tough. They were ideal, and versatile, and were very useful for shorter people. Someone ought to bring them back.

I grew up in the heyday of the Hodgman Wadewell wader. It was the first bootfoot wader with high-quality piano-felt soles. In my early days as a guide, I would run into well-heeled anglers who had Hodgman's they'd been using hard for ten or fifteen years, and they loved those waders. Then we moved into a long era dominated by import waders; Hodgman seemed to almost drop out of the wader business, but the imports were all cheap imitations, badly cut and horribly unreliable. They didn't fit, they didn't last, and there was a long period that some fishermen still remember, well into the 1970s, when it just seemed impossible to get good waders. Everybody had a story about putting on their new waders, stepping into the stream, and feeling the icy water sluicing through the seams. It didn't seem to matter if they were imports or made in the U.S.A. It became one of those things that everybody said we should be able to do if we were able to put a man on the moon, but nobody seemed able to make a decent wader any more. There were exceptions, of course; stocking-foot waders were available from a couple of companies—the reinforced Seal-dri and the Royal Redball—that were very good, and still are.

The advent of neoprene waders was a shock to us old-timers. Not only did it completely change the way fly fishermen looked on the river, it required a whole new attitude about how we looked to ourselves. They still look like ballet tutus to me, even though they've been around for years now and are certainly the most popular type of wader. They're hot, they require a lot of wrestling to get in, and they get more expensive all the time, but they're one of those items that have caught on and everybody must have.

Probably the welcome news we've had about waders in recent years is the new "breathable" wader. Some of the most reputable firms, including Orvis and Dan Bailey, are offering them. In our hot, dry climate, a wader that allows a little more air circulation will be a real blessing.

There are some very good, very comfortable boot-foot waders out there now, waders that are roomy without making you feel like you're standing in a collapsed tent. But the price you pay, and one of the big disadvantages of almost all boot-foot waders, is that the boots themselves are very generally sized for a generic fit. Most fishermen who prefer a boot-foot wader for some reason (they're a lot quicker to put on than stocking-foot waders with wading shoes), tend to adjust for the generic fit by adding or subtracting layers of socks or adding insoles. That means you'll never have the kind of perfect, snug fit you need for the most difficult wading, but that's just the tradeoff you have to make.

On the other hand, if you wear stocking-foot waders, there are many excellent new wading shoes. Several companies make sturdy wading shoes that give you excellent traction and control, which you absolutely must have on the bigger rivers in the West. I recommend spending as much as you can afford to on the shoes. The lighter, flimsier ones just aren't worth the risk you take in having poorly fitting boots on slimy rocks.

I still prefer boot-foot waders, for comfort and for appearance, and especially for colder weather. One of the big disadvantages of the stocking-foot waders and wading shoes is that once the weather gets cold, unless you're traveling in high style and can take all your gear into some warm place every night you're in for trouble. When you get up for your second morning of fishing, and it's colder than a mother-in-law's kiss, and you reach into the back of the car for your wading shoes,

you'll see what I mean. They'll be frozen up like bronzed baby shoes.

In the 1990s, waders have finally appeared that are made for women. They haven't priced them out of sight, and they are much more appealing to women. In fact, the innovations for women's fly-fishing gear have probably outrun the innovations for men, whether it's vests, gloves, or all sorts of other accessories.

Wading Socks

For many years, the quality wading sock I like best has been made by Wigwam, a Midwestern company that has maintained the same quality and reasonable prices all that time. There are other excellent socks, but I'll make a pretty straightforward recommendation on this one; I count on Wigwam socks. They don't call any of their socks wading socks, but in their variety of styles you'll find plenty of good, heavy or light as you prefer, wool socks that work.

Wading Staffs

Some of the more recent collapsible wading staffs are reliable, but a sturdy ski pole works just fine. It surprises me that more people aren't selling a really fine staff; there is no widely available high-quality staff on the market. If you enjoy shopping, you might start looking in every tackle shop you visit for locally made staffs, and find a nice custom one that suits your needs.

Accessories and Clothing

After your rod, reel line, and fly, the most important piece of gear you can have is a pair of polarized fishing glasses. If you've never gotten into the habit of using them, you're in for a thrill the first time you look into water while you're wearing them. There are many on the market, including some with side panels along the temples.

You need a good hat, for protection from the sun and from your weighted flies. I wear a western hat with a three-inch brim. Much of the summer I wear a western straw hat with a chin strap so I don't spend my day chasing the hat down the stream. A lighter hat, like the modern long-brimmed hats popularized by saltwater fishermen, can be just fine but it isn't quite as "bullet-proof" as the harder formed hats. A weighted #4 Montana Nymph has a mass about like a .45-caliber bullet, with the difference that the bullet doesn't have as sharp a point.

Good raingear is essential. If you can afford the new Gore-Tex outfits, they're terrific, but have a good raincoat in any case.

You will often be fishing at elevations between 6,000 and 10,000 feet. Summer lasts about an hour and a half on some of these streams, and you've got to be prepared not just for chills but for anything up to a blizzard. Bring long underwear, no matter what month you fish. You may want to wear them even on days that are just cool because the high-country streams are sometimes painfully cold. You may find yourself fishing a stream in the mountains where even in June you have to wade through snowbanks to get to the river, and you can see as you're fishing that some of that river water had to be snow just a few hours ago.

Bring at least a light down or fleece jacket, even if you're going to be fishing in summer, and be prepared to add or subtract layers as you need. In the fall, I sometimes use sweatpants to add a layer on cold days. You can make your own choices about what you wear—whether it's wool or cotton chamois or flannel—just be sure to bring enough warm clothes. Sweaters are essential on cool mountain evenings. My own impression is that people from the East, and from the

*The scenery is so great that you
sometimes forget to keep your eyes open for surprises.
How many places could you hide a moose in this picture?*

West Coast, are much more likely to underestimate than overestimate how much warm clothing they need.

Have a pair of fishing gloves. Some of the new ones give you the choice of which fingers you want to have exposed. Nothing stops me from enjoying fishing faster than cold hands.

The Rockies have a dry climate. Be prepared for chapped face, hands, and lips. Besides all the well-known commercial preparations, the old farm treatment called Bag Balm (an ointment used on cows' udders) is a great soother of chapped hands. High-altitude sunlight can be harmful too, so bring some sunscreen. You can get a mean sunburn just from the light reflected from water.

Be prepared also for voracious insects. The mosquitoes can often be kept off with one of the strong repellents; my favorite is Muskol. But nothing seems to deter some of the biting flies that take a hunk of meat rather than just blood. If you have allergic reactions to biting insects, get some good advice on how to handle it before you get here, and if you have a guide let him know about your problem.

Almost everybody wants to bring a camera. At the shop, we always encouraged people to bring an automatic camera of some sort, just a little one you can slip in a vest pocket. Those are getting so sophisticated now that it's almost impossible to mess up the picture, and they're really quick. You can catch things you might otherwise miss, and if you are releasing your fish you can get a picture of a good catch without keeping it out of water a long time while you adjust half a dozen settings.

Other accessories will depend on your interests. Field guides, binoculars (the light, pocket-sized ones are all you'll need), pocket knives (who can get along without a Swiss army knife?), picnic equipment, and all sorts of other items may come to mind. Most of us tend to overpack and bring too much, but it's usually cheaper to bring it along than buy it after you get here.

The West Is Still Wild

One July day in the 1950s, a client of mine from Kentucky said, "You know, I'd sure like to fish that Bear Trap I've heard so much about." So we drove over from West Yellowstone, and in Ennis I stopped and bought one of those Cutter snakebite kits, just in case. We drove up as far as we could go, which by then was not very far, and got out and walked another three miles or so, where we started fishing. He was a pretty self-sufficient fisherman, so I let him walk a little ways from me. I'd just started fishing, when here he comes, limping down the road toward me. He said, "Bud, I think a rattlesnake bit me." By the time I located the bite and determined that it was from a snake, the sweat was beginning to pour off of him and he was getting a little weak, so I had him lie down in the shade while I read the instructions on this snakebite kit. I got the razorblade out, made the big X's on the teethmarks, and used the little suction cup to try to get the poison out. After a while he said, "You know I think I'm beginning to feel better. I think you got it." As if it worked that simply. We're three miles from the car, it's two o'clock in the middle of a hot afternoon, and that was a long, hard walk for him.

We finally got back to the car, and I told him I should take him to a doctor in Ennis, but he said, "Nah, I'm feeling fine." Well, luckily he was staying at Yellowstone Park headquarters, at Mammoth Hot Springs, which has a clinic, because about midnight his leg just exploded. I'd gotten just enough of the venom out so it took a while to get started. He was permanently injured, and could hardly walk. His leg just dried up.

Here and there in this book, I make a point of asking you to be careful about something, whether it's getting in and out of a boat or wearing sunscreen. This isn't a book about safety, so I try not to overload it with motherly advice about not getting hurt. But don't ever forget that you're fishing in or very near some of the wildest country in the lower 48. Be aware of where you're going, and where you walk or sit. Tune in to what's going on around you. Paul has spent a lot of time learning about these dangers, so here are some of his thoughts.

I've lived in Yellowstone National Park about half of the past 27 years, and I am almost never surprised by the ways that people will put themselves at risk because I've seen or heard of so many different ones. On the other hand, I never get used to it; it's so easy to be careful, and yet so many people aren't.

The safety problems we hear the most about out here are wildlife-related. For some reason, people just have to get close to animals. In the park, bison, which seem so stolid and cow-like, injure a lot more people than do bears; bison can turn on a dime and accelerate instantly to cruising speed. But any animal, whether a deer, a coyote, an elk, or a moose, can hurt you very badly and very quickly. Just telling people not to get close doesn't seem to be enough, because people don't know what "close" means. For example, I would not knowingly approach a moose within 200 feet, and would consider that distance too small. You should never get within 100 yards of a grizzly bear. Think of it this way: if you're within casting distance (using your best long-distance rod and line) of any of these large animals, you're too close. If you're that close to a grizzly bear, you're nuts.

I know, I know, you'll see a bunch of other people getting much closer, and that might make you feel foolish staying back. But trust me: they're the fools. If you don't get yourself hurt (and these animals are amazingly tolerant

most of the time), you'll eventually drive the animal back from the road and no one else will get to enjoy it.

Wildlife can cause other complications in your trip than the risk that one of them might run an antler through you. With the national increases in deer populations, more people are familiar with driving carefully around wildlife, but there are still states where cars kill more animals than do hunters. During the summer season, cars account for about one large animal every day in Yellowstone National Park. Even bison, who are almost panoramically huge, and visible from miles away, die regularly in front of unwary drivers. Slow down, and be extremely careful at night. All over the West, elk, deer, pronghorn, and moose are depending upon your consideration. And remember that hitting something the size of an elk or a moose (much less a bison) can kill you, too.

Bears are the animals people worry most about, especially if they're hiking any distance from the road. Grizzly bears are found in only a few places in the lower 48, and you should always check in with the local warden or ranger for more information if you're concerned. Black bears, too often seen as always timid and harmless, can be very aggressive, and require vigilance. The presence of bears should not keep you from using an area, as long as you do a little homework. In fact, they're one of the most exciting parts of the experience, even if you don't see them. For more information on bears, read Steve Herrero's Bear Attacks: Their Causes and Avoidance, *or Gary Brown's* Safe Travel in Bear Country. *They offer expert advice of the highest order. Now back to Bud.*

Common Problems — One More Time

There are a few things visitors tend to do in the West, things so common that they bear repeating. Visitors tend to underestimate the distances between the places they want to visit, underestimate how wild and variable the weather can be, and overestimate how much they can do. They aren't accustomed to how cold it can be at the higher elevations, and what that can mean in terms of how you should dress, or how you should drive when there might be frost or even snow in mid-summer.

I ought to add that some of the same things can be said of resident westerners, who seem to forget now and then just how quickly this country can surprise you with cold weather and hard storms.

Chapter 12

Flies

CERTAINLY ONE OF THE MOST SERIOUS STUDENTS OF fly-fishing theory whom I ever met was the late Vincent Marinaro, author of one of the great modern fishing books, *A Modern Dry Fly Code* and *In the Ring of the Rise*. Vince came out one summer in the late 1960s before the Federation of Fly Fishers conclave, and he stayed with Pat and me. The Federation officers asked me if I would take him around the area and show him some of the streams. We got ready to go fishing in the morning, and I was loading my gear in the car when I noticed that Vince didn't seem to be bringing along a rod or anything. I asked him, "Aren't you bringing any tackle?"

He said, "No, I want a rake and a bucket."

"Don't you want to fish?"

"No, I just want to take a look at all the insects."

So we went out to Thompson Spring Creek, one of the fine little creeks in the Gallatin Valley near Belgrade, where he collected insects to his heart's content. Then we went home and he discussed insects until three o'clock in the morning. He really liked to talk, and I must have been a good listener. Fly fishing is a complex passion, and it brings out different interests in different people. We're lucky to have thinkers of the caliber of Vince, but even at the end of the Twentieth Century, a lot of veteran western fishermen still tend to view entomology with a little skepticism, especially when it replaces the fishing.

Hatch-matching theory is of course one of the biggest topics in fly fishing. It's amazing how determined some fishermen will get in defending a certain hypothesis or approach to fly patterns. I do know that there are times when having the right fly is terribly important; I've been skunked often enough by very difficult fish to understand that sometimes you have to pay close attention to fly choice. But the quest for the "only good fly" has a tendency to get out of hand. When I was still running my shop in West Yellowstone, I got in the habit of keeping track of these good flies.

For example, let's say there was a very good day on the Firehole River, with lots of fishermen. Over the course of the day I might have talked to fifty or more fishermen, all of whom wanted to come back and tell me about their success.

"How was the fishing?"

"Oh, God, it was fabulous, fabulous!"

"Was it tough, or easy?"

"Oh, they were selective, very selective."

"What were you using?"

"The only thing they would take was this little beauty here...."

Of course, by the end of the day I'd seen about fifty different "only things." I went through this time after time. I should have developed a series of flies called the Only Things.

Though this is less true than it used to be, there is a common attitude about western flies, one that oversimplifies them. We all joke about it. Western flies, in stereotype, are big, bushy, and don't really look much like anything. There is an answer to that attitude, that says "But they catch fish!" And that's true too, and usually that's about as far as the conversation goes. Most people are content to have flies that work, and will overlook any theoretical complications that may puzzle them too much. A lot of people who are into hatch-matching won't use Humpies or Royal Wulffs because they don't look enough like anything. Other people won't use no-hackles and other attempts at close imitation because they aren't bushy enough.

I think that we need to be more open-minded than either of those viewpoints. We know the big flies work, and we know that materials like rubber and bead chain work. If we're so interested in understanding trout feeding, and in triggering their feeding activity, we ought to be trying harder to understand just why those unusual materials do it so well. Something is making that fish come up and eat that Royal Wulff, even though it resembles nothing we can imagine. The fish has recognized it, and that's the most important piece of information we can get about a fly. We just don't know enough about how trout see things and how they understand them. But if the trout is impressed by a fly, then we ought to be very curious about why. I think that it would be useful for future students of fly fishing to devote a little more attention to answering questions like that, now that we've devoted so many years to learning the hatches.

I think it was about 40 years ago that some guy in Deer Lodge, Montana took some rubber from a girdle and made some legs for a fly he tied. It was like a revolution. What is it about rubber legs that attract trout, even so-called selective trout? For all our entomology, we have a lot to learn about trout, and these western fish are asking us some very interesting questions when they take flies we like to call "unrealistic."

The nice thing about matching the hatch is that, in the West at least, you can participate to whatever degree you like or are able. If you are a really accomplished fly fisher and can handle the special demands of fishing the Swisher-Richards no-hackles and other delicate patterns, you can be deadly on the most difficult fish. But a lot of the fishermen I have met or guided simply aren't that advanced, and the good news is that they don't need to be in order to catch fish. It is often unfair to the newcomer who goes into a western tackle shop for advice to load him or her down with no-hackles, for example, and send him down to the Henry's Fork. He'll cast one of them out there, it'll sink, and that's the last he'll see of it.

Matching the hatch is great sport. It gives some people a great thrill to do everything as exactly as it can be done. It gets results. There are many people who get a great deal of joy from it, and it has spawned a multitude of patterns that are fascinating and often quite effective. For many other people, however, following the sport to that degree of detail would be too much, and if they had to do it that way they would quit fishing. I've been lucky enough to see most of the important new patterns either while they were still being tested or as soon as they were announced to the fly-fishing world. At our shop we made every effort not only to carry the new patterns but to try them out. But you don't have to do it if you don't want to. You can still catch fish a lot of the time with a general assortment of standard patterns. There may be those times, on certain hard-fished waters, where the hatch-matcher will have a clear edge. Those times are a kind of invitation, I think, to people who haven't gotten interested in serious hatch-matching but might enjoy it.

But don't forget that this is the West, where the Goofus Bug and the Sofa Pillow and the Woolly Worm were all popularized. Discussions of hatch-matching always remind me of a day on the Henry's Fork a few years ago. I was fishing down on the Railroad Ranch, and here they were, 9,000 experts hunched in a group crouch, trying to catch those fish. Things were tough, and the fish were almost uncatchable for the fishermen I could see, when here comes a guy sloshing along just yanking fish after fish from the water. Of course he was greeted by "Whatcha usin'?" and he answered "Renegade." The saying goes that in Idaho they don't care what it is as long as it's a Renegade. If the fishing is really tough they'll switch to a double Renegade, or for very selective fish they switch to a jointed Renegade and fish it wet.

Western Flies: A Basic Selection

What follows is as good a general assortment of fly patterns as I can recommend. If you live in the West, this selection will handle practically all of your fishing needs. If you are planning a visit, it will serve as a guide to give you an idea of what to expect, but you may not need to have them all, depending on when you visit. If you visit in October, for example, you won't need to bother with the salmonfly dry-fly patterns, and if you visit in May you won't need the hoppers.

I don't mean to suggest that there are no other good flies, or that you shouldn't experiment on your own. There is probably nothing more important you can do when selecting flies than to get up-to-date information either right before you arrive, or as soon as you get here, about local favorites. There may be a hatch on the river you plan to fish that is not covered by this selection. And part of the fun of fly fishing is playing around with new patterns anyway.

A great example of how new fly patterns can change things, at least here in Montana, happened not that long ago on the Bighorn River. The Bighorn has spawned fly patterns that just aren't seen elsewhere yet. Some may only be good there, but they probably will spread to other rivers. The San Juan Worm has been all the rage on the Bighorn. Though this is a pattern that was developed in the Southwest, it has become closely identified with the Bighorn River, where it has been almost unbelievably successful. Fishermen are now discovering that it works great on spring creeks, too. We've always needed a good worm imitation, and here it is, though I think that its effectiveness may already be starting to fade a little.

Another recent development that has changed the way we fish here is the advent of the bead-head flies. This started with a few nymph patterns, but now there are all kinds of bead-heads, including many deadly streamers with "conehead" weights on the front. These take some careful casting, especially in the larger calibers, but they've allowed fishermen yet another way to get the fly where you couldn't get it before. Most of the nymphs and streamers listed in this chapter are improved for certain situations by adding the bead, and the bead isn't toxic, so you don't have to worry about doing harm while you're doing good.

Another example, and in a way a change that is very similar to the bead-head, is the appearance on flies of cul de canard feathers, from the rump of ducks. It may seem odd to say that these delicate feathers are somehow similar to bead-heads, but what they have in common is that they are a significant innovation that can be applied to many situations. Unlike inventing a single new fly pattern, the people who introduced bead-heads and CDC feathers instantly changed our approach to dozens, even hundreds, of fly patterns, having a sweeping effect throughout the sport. It is amazing the breadth of application you will see with these simple materials—bead heads, CDC feathers, even rubber legs—and how big a change they have brought to our sport.

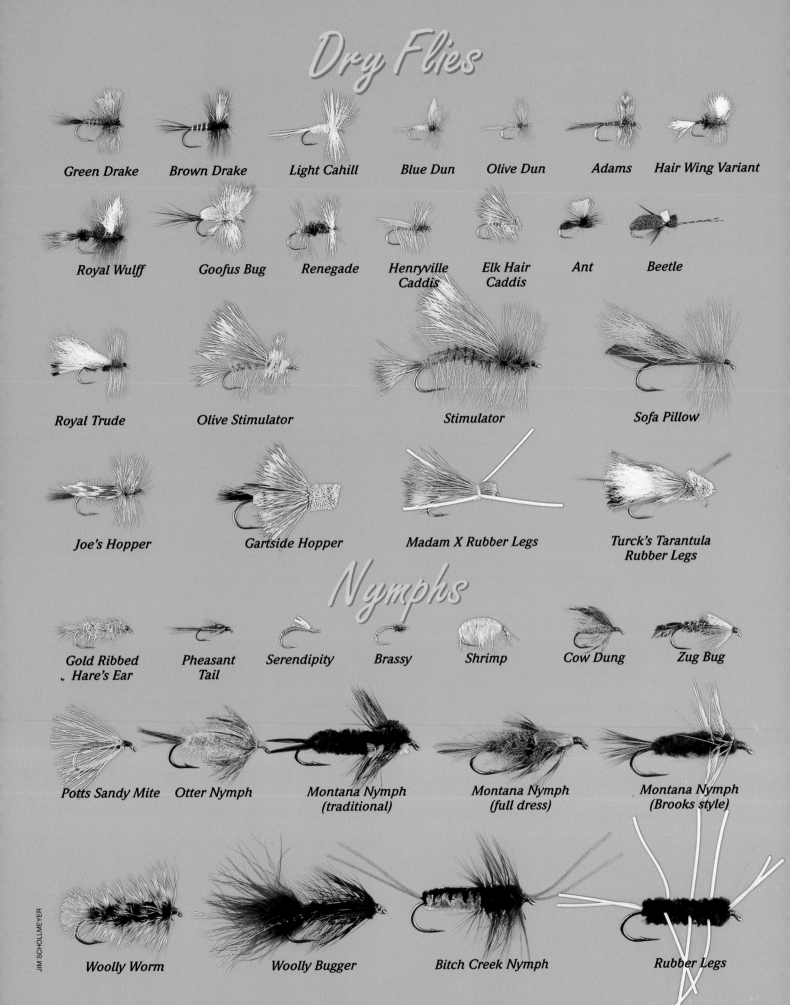

Dry Flies

Green Drake   Brown Drake   Light Cahill   Blue Dun   Olive Dun   Adams   Hair Wing Variant

Royal Wulff   Goofus Bug   Renegade   Henryville Caddis   Elk Hair Caddis   Ant   Beetle

Royal Trude   Olive Stimulator   Stimulator   Sofa Pillow

Joe's Hopper   Gartside Hopper   Madam X Rubber Legs   Turck's Tarantula Rubber Legs

Nymphs

Gold Ribbed Hare's Ear   Pheasant Tail   Serendipity   Brassy   Shrimp   Cow Dung   Zug Bug

Potts Sandy Mite   Otter Nymph   Montana Nymph (traditional)   Montana Nymph (full dress)   Montana Nymph (Brooks style)

Woolly Worm   Woolly Bugger   Bitch Creek Nymph   Rubber Legs

Streamers

Light Spruce

Dark Spruce

Muddler Minnow

White Conehead Marabou Muddler

Black Conehead Marabou Muddler

White Zonker

Olive Zonker

JIM SCHOLLMEYER

All flies were tied by Josh Stanish, of Bozeman, Montana, except for the following patterns which were tied by Dale Greenley, of Myrtle Creek, Oregon: Light Cahill, Goofus Bug, Rubber Legs, Montana Nymphs, Cowdung, Pheasant Tail Nymph, Otter Nymph, and Sofa Pillow.

Driven by the energy of its spawning urge, a large brown trout negotiates a rapids in a small Montana stream.

PAUL SCHULLERY

Random casting is rarely productive in a big lake. Look for springholes, shoals, inlets, outlets, weed beds, submerged trees, and other places where trout might find cover or food.

A beautiful summer day on the Big Hole, and the long-awaited thrill of a good fish in open water.

PAUL SCHULLERY

*Spring creeks are rare and special little ecosystems, as rich in terrestrial life
as they are in aquatic life, and they need our help to survive.*

A big brown nearing the net is a study in greens and golds.

Left: Esther and Bud Lilly.

DAVID KUMLIEN

*Overleaf: A small
meadow stream may
double back on itself
again and again,
creating miles of
excellent trout
habitat in a very
small space.*

Bud Lilly taking advantage of the last light, closing day on the Madison in Yellowstone Park.

On a bitterly cold day, a mountain stream steams and rolls like something alive.

Western trout rivers originate in some of America's last great wilderness lands.

The point is that wherever you fish you will probably run into some special local patterns that are worth learning about. And the rate at which successful new fly patterns appear reveals just how many more options await development. Many years ago, when my son Greg and I were studying the insect life in some of the Montana streams, we did some seining on the Beaverhead, a stream famous for its huge brown trout. We discovered heavy densities of large cranefly larvae, fat nymphs almost the size of the last joint of your little finger. Sometimes the seine was almost solid with them. Now the guides have developed some good imitations, but it seems like there's always something new.

Even if you don't take hatch-matching seriously (and you will see that I often don't either), always try to know what the fish are feeding on, even if you choose not to imitate it exactly. A lot of westerners don't consider themselves hatch-matchers, but if they see the fish feeding on a small gray mayfly they won't hesitate to tie on a #18 Adams.

So here's a basic list of patterns I would want with me in most parts of the West. Where it seems helpful, I'll add some notes on the pattern's history or the best ways to use it.

Dry Flies

Adams, #12-20

The Adams, created in Michigan, has changed as it traveled. It went east and became a much lighter fly than it originally was, tied like the other Catskill-style dry flies. But when it came west it got the opposite treatment. The original was big and bushy, and the tiers in the Yellowstone area, such as Sig Barnes and Martinez, tied it with an extra hackle, and used hackles that were variant length. In a lot of the shops today the Adams is tied more neatly than that, probably because of what fishermen expect it to look like more than because of what works best.

Blue Dun, #16-18

There is no end of complication in the language of fly tying, and the Blue Dun illustrates it as well as any pattern can. I can remember once in the 1970s when Paul came into the shop looking pretty perplexed. He was learning to tie flies at the time, and was struggling with what must have seemed to him an impossible set of words that really didn't describe anything very well. As I recall, he complained that one of his fly-tying books told him to use a hackle that was, as he put it, "a kind of a medium grayish blue." To which I, adopting an expression of knowing recognition, responded, "Oh, you mean a pale watery dun!" He laughed, relieved to discover that other people saw what a mess we'd made of the language by trying to describe these delicate shades and tints that could completely change if the sun came out.

All of this is to say that when I say you should get some Blue Duns, or Olive Duns, or any other standard patterns, I'm counting on you to understand that there are Blue Duns and

Blue Duns, and like a lot of other patterns they vary from shop to shop, just as the insects they imitate vary from stream to stream. Blue Duns may serve to imitate a lot of small mayflies, just as the Adams will. By suggesting you have some, I'm not telling you only to use them when an official blue dun hatch (whatever that is) comes off. I've tried to tailor this list so that each pattern has a number of possible uses.

Olive Dun, #16-20

Light Cahill, #16-20

In a lot of places, what fishermen used to call Cahills they now call sulfurs. In either case, there are many sizes and kinds of light, cream, or yellow mayflies, so Light Cahills are mighty handy, whether in the traditional "Catskill-style" dry fly or in a parachute or thorax pattern.

Royal Wulff, #10-16

The Royal Wulff in a #12 is good all year long, even though that size is larger than most of the insects you will encounter. Later in the summer you can switch to a #14 or #16. Late in the season we often use #8 and #10, and some fishermen even overtie in these bigger sizes, so that the wings on their #10 are really the size of #8 wings.

The Royal Wulff isn't just an attractor pattern; it has served well imitating the western March brown. I've used a #12 Royal Wulff with great success during the March brown hatch on the Henry's Fork in Idaho and the Gibbon in Yellowstone Park.

It is true that flies like these are not quite as effective as they were ten or twenty years ago, much less further back. For a variety of reasons having to do with increasing fishing pressure, it is not as easy as it once was to bamboozle a western trout even on a big, fast stream. But it's still hard to beat the Royal Wulff, day in and day out, through the season. The trout still take Wulffs larger than the natural insects that might be on the water at the time.

Goofus Bug, #12-18

We often used to use the Goofus Bug on the Madison in size #6. We sold them by the ton. For many years there was a group of high school coaches that spent their summers in a camp on the Madison, about fifty of them. These men had apparently never heard of small dry flies, or selective trout, and they pretty much made up their own tradition, without much outside influence. They were a fun group and worth paying attention to because they worked out all their problems for themselves. One of their most effective patterns was nothing but a #8 hook covered with clipped deer hair; it looked like a cigarette butt floating along, and it worked great. This was 30 or so years ago, and I think the trout are now more demanding, but there are still people who swear by very simple hair patterns, such as the Hank-O-Hair, which is nothing more than a few strands of deer hair tied along the hook body so they splay out and apparently have a buggy silhouette. No fisherman can ever claim that anybody promised him this sport would necessarily make sense.

Hairwing Variant, #16-18

It was Don Martinez who, back in the 1940s, seems to have started an approach to tying western dry flies that, though they have the names of traditional patterns, would more accurately be called Variants. The Hairwing Variant is only one of many, though it's the easiest to find in the tackle shops. The Whitcraft, the Multi-colored Variant, and others were promoted by him, and they set a sort of standard for western dry flies for many years. Some commercial tier should revive some of Martinez' flies, not as historical curiosities but because they work so well.

The point is that a variety of Variant ties, whether of regional patterns like those of Martinez or of nationally known patterns like the Adams and Art Flick's Grey Fox Variant, are really successful out here. If you look around, especially among the veteran fishermen, you'll see that many tiers over the years have found that there was a value in overhackling western dry flies. That school of practice has lost preeminence, but it still has a lot to teach us about what flies work here. Fly preferences change, but they don't change totally in only thirty or forty years.

A typical scene for many years in the Yellowstone country—Charlie Brooks seining a favorite stretch of stream for local insect life. Charlie's flies, developed specifically for Yellowstone-area waters, have joined the permanent arsenal of western anglers.

Royal Trude, #8-14

The Royal Trude is another fabulously successful western fly. Merton Parks, one of the best-known guides before 1970, used practically nothing else. He would start in the spring with about a #4, and by fall would be using a #16. On fast water, it will often do a better job even than an Elk Hair Caddis, and I even use it during the salmonfly hatch.

The Royal Trude is one of those flies that makes some serious angler-entomologists nervous, but it shouldn't, if only because some of the country's most knowledgeable hatchmatchers and fly-fishing empiricists praise it so highly. In his 1990 book, *The Dry Fly,* Gary LaFontaine, discussing which fly patterns he considers essential in a basic selection, asked, "How could I leave off a Royal Trude, which has caught more trout for me than any other dry fly?"

Renegade, #10-14

Here's another odd-looking pattern, with fore-and-aft hackling, that defies convention and fly-tying fashions. But don't be without a few.

I've listed the Renegade as a dry fly because that is how it's tied, but I think that even today it's probably fished more often wet in this region, especially on Idaho streams. I also think that it's an effective wet fly in good part because of the pulsing action of those fore-and-aft hackles as they're pulled along through the water.

Elk Hair Caddis, #14-18

When it comes to an all-around caddis imitation, the Elk Hair

Caddis is beating the Goofus Bug out of a lot of sales in the tackle shops. The Elk Hair Caddis, the creation of Al Troth, is proving to be just that much more effective. But the Goofus is still a standard, and still a great fly.

Another wonderful caddis pattern that I often use is the Goddard Caddis, with a clipped body that imitates both the body and wing of the caddis.

Henryville Caddis, #14-18

I include this one on the list to give you a finer, lighter caddis dry fly than the Elk Hair, but I could have included Leonard Wright's Fluttering Caddis, or a number of others. Just as there are a variety of hairwing caddises, such as the Antron and Fluttering Caddises (recommended and illustrated by Craig Mathews and John Juracek in *Fly Patterns of Yellowstone*), there are a variety of more sparsely tied patterns. I see the Henryville as more of a spring-creek pattern. It doesn't float as well or as long as the Elk Hair caddis, but it does the job on quiet water.

Green Drake, #12

There are some beautiful extended body patterns available now, but you can do fine with less fancy patterns. I've done well during the green drake hatch with a green-bodied Goofus Bug. The Grizzly Wulff is likewise an effective imitation of the green drake hatches.

Brown Drake, #12

The brown drake mayfly seems to require very high-quality water. Most locals recall better brown drake hatches years ago, though some streams in the West still have them and they appear to be increasing in number on some waters. I don't have any good idea why they would have declined, especially on well-protected waters, but now and then I hear of a fine brown drake hatch on some stream, and if you meet one without a few good imitations in your vest, you'll regret it.

Sofa Pillow, #4-8

Sig and Pat Barnes created and popularized this pattern, and though there are now a number of more contemporary designs incorporating synthetic fibres like Gantron, bullet heads, and other innovations, the Sofa Pillow is still a favorite of mine.

Stimulator, #8-#14

This relatively young pattern is a great bridge between flies that were clearly intended to imitate a salmonfly and those that were designed to look like hoppers. It does both very well, and is also a good all-around attractor pattern. I suspect it also imitates some large caddis that we don't see very often (perhaps because it hatches at night), but that the trout know.

It's hard to sort out which element of a fly is really the one that's making it effective. Like the Woolly Worm, the Stimulator is made in a lot of colors. On a given day, it could be the color, size, or just the general silhouette of the fly that's making it so effective.

There are many excellent fly-fishing catalogs out there these days, but I especially admire what Dan Bailey's achieves each year with their fly selection. They offer you a really thorough selection of patterns, and though they have a national clientele, they provide as comprehensive an assortment of western fly patterns as anyone could ever need. But I also enjoy looking at their catalog for the changes each year as flies come and go. So many patterns are being experimented with all the time that it's fun to see what's new and what has already failed the test of public popularity. In that regard, I suspect that the Stimulator is one of the new patterns that is here to stay, at least in the West.

Joe's Hopper, #8-12

For fast or broken water, I usually prefer a high-silhouette, heavily winged hopper that will be as easy for the fish to see as for me. Another terrific heavy-water hopper is John's Elk Hair Hopper, which is also an excellent fly during the salmonfly hatch.

I'm not sure it's entirely fair to even list the Joe's Hopper here, because it's just about impossible to get a good-quality one any more; they only really work well with the best, largest-size furnace hackles, which means that they can't be mass-produced. If you're a fly tier, you can make what you need, and I encourage you to.

Gartside Hopper, #8-12

And for quieter water, I want a pattern that will stand up under the closer scrutiny of a trout who's not in a hurry.

Madam X Rubber Legs, #8-12

Maybe the trout think it's a grasshopper, maybe they don't. But they like it, and it's a great attractor.

Turck's Tarantula Rubber Legs, #6-10

Another recently developed attractor that shows good signs of lasting for a long time. Montana isn't known for its tarantula hatches, but I've seen this work well everywhere from the roughest pocket water to the quietest spring creeks.

Beetle, #12-18

Beetles come in all shapes and sizes, and there are as many imitations. There are good deer-hair and herl patterns. Realism is especially important with both beetles and ants, partly because they come into their own as trout foods late in the year when the water is low and clear and partly because they are mostly of importance to fishermen on meadow streams where the water is smooth anyway. These terrestrials often demand the finest tippets you will use all year.

Datus Proper, in his thought-provoking book *What the Trout Said,* introduces a simple peacock-body, brown-hackled beetle that should be a lot better known than it is. It floats right in or below the surface film, and works great on spring creeks.

Ant, #12-18

There are many good ant patterns. We use both fur-bodied ants and hard-bodied ones, winged and wingless. Have them in black and red or ginger.

Nymphs and Wet Flies

Bitch Creek Nymph, #4-8

A thousand barroom debates have been held over the attractiveness of patterns like this one and the next. Is it the ragged silhouette that makes them so great, or those wiggly rubber antennae and legs? I think it's both.

Rubber Legs, #4-8

I don't fish a Rubber Legs the same way I would fish a more traditional large nymph like the Montana Nymph. I will let it dead-drift downstream until it starts to swing, but then I'll treat it more like a streamer, to get as much action and enticement out of those legs as possible. I think that the rubber legs tend to "work" in the current even when it's dead-drifted, but you can add a lot to that motion through line handling, moving the fly at different speeds as you retrieve it, and doing anything else to provoke a strike.

I've often fished a hole with a streamer first and caught nothing, then immediately gone back through the same water with a Rubber Legs or a Bitch Creek Nymph and caught good fish. It may seem improbable to the dedicated hatch-matcher that these big ugly things could have some individual qualities that make them different from each other, but it's true. Fish are selective to different kinds of big flies just as they are to small flies.

Montana Nymph, #4-8

Lots of variant ties of this pattern out there. Charlie Brooks' version has been adapted and adjusted in a hundred ways, with rubber thorax, hackle legs, tails, antennae, nylon ribbing, and other things. The key elements seem to be large size, fuzzy silhouette, and perhaps a slightly curved body.

Woolly Worm (black), #4-8

Who knows what trout think the Woolly Worm is? I do know that it has always been used especially as an imitation of the large stonefly nymphs. There are many other excellent patterns that serve the same purpose, and it seems that every year new variations appear. These flies are usually at least slightly weighted. My favorite Woolly Worm is black with grizzly hackle and a red tag, that being the pattern developed by Don Martinez in the West Yellowstone area fifty or more years ago. Yellow and brown are also popular, and Dave Whitlock fancied them up beautifully with multiple colors and a back of peacock herl, which probably helped revive interest in a fly that people were neglecting just because they thought it was too old.

Henry's Lake, with its amazing assortment of insects and other fish foods, was always a great puzzle to fishermen when I ran the Trout Shop. With so many different possible choices, the fish were impossible to predict from day to day. At one point I had a fly tier produce a huge number of Woolly Worms in every imaginable color. I put them in a big fish bowl and when people would come in and ask what was working on Henry's Lake, I'd say, "Take one of each."

One of the great modern innovators of fly-tying, Dave Whitlock has had an enormous effect on western fly patterns.

Gold Ribbed Hare's Ear, #8-14

This is still about the most popular smaller nymph in this country, and has countless uses. Once you have an exceptionally good material, whether it's chenille, deer's hair, hare's ear, peacock herl, or pheasant tail, you can use it all over the place. You probably can't have too many flies with hare's ear in them, including the wet fly and the nymph. There are now some great Hare's Ear Nymphs available with fine rubber legs.

Zug Bug, #8-14

Anything with peacock herl on it seems to be better than anything without peacock herl. The Zug Bug may imitate countless life forms, from smaller stoneflies to beetles to caddis larvae. It, like the Prince Nymph, is a great searching fly when there's no action and you're just covering the water.

Cowdung, #12

Don't forget the old standards, the traditional wet flies from 100 years ago. The Alexandria, the Silver Doctor, and a number of other old-timers like them are still very good flies, and I've had experiences where they were all that would work, even on trout that were famous for being choosy. Fishermen will never stop debating what they imitate—emergers, little fish, nymphs, or just something buggy—but they work.

One of the most interesting parts of Howard Back's book *The Waters of Yellowstone with Rod and Fly* (1938), which is regarded as one of the few classics of Yellowstone fishing writing, is his discussion of fly patterns. He used a strange assortment of flies very successfully, including Jim Pray's Optic Bucktails, traditional brook trout flies, and even full-dress Atlantic salmon flies. If you're open-minded enough for the experiment, you might give the old wet flies a good try some time. I think you'll catch a lot of fish.

There is no question that fish somehow become familiar with artificials and the flies lose their effectiveness. I don't know how this works, but I've seen it happen again and again. The Muddler Minnow is still a great fly to have, but it does not work nearly as well as it did 50 years ago here. This is why fly-tying innovation is important, and is more than a good marketing ploy. On the other hand, now that some of the older patterns haven't been used much for a long time, they may be effective all over again.

Serendipity, #16-#20

In the San Juan River in New Mexico, we see changes in the style of nymph fishing that have occurred around the West. When the fishing there became really popular, most people used the large, heavy flies, and gradually they've shifted over to smaller and smaller flies. Little flies are not new to the West, especially on the quiet spring creek-type waters, but more and more small flies are being used on other waters as well. I still don't think you'll ever see the kind of attention to precise hatch-matching detail you do with dry flies, but you need to have an assortment of these smaller flies, wherever you go.

I personally had a hard time adjusting to this, and you might too. It's hard to accept that you can throw a #16 nymph into a big, brawling river like the Madison and expect the fish to see it, or to move very far to get it if they do notice it. But they will, so don't let that skepticism stop you from experimenting. The way I made the adjustment was to use two-fly rigs, perhaps with a #16 Serendipity and a #10 Royal Wulff. It was amazing how often the fish preferred the smaller fly.

It appears to me that the Serendipity is past its peak in popularity. It's still a very good fly, but I think it may fade away over the next several years, into a minor position as a popular western fly. Like the San Juan Worm, it seems to me that it's getting less effective.

Brassy, #16-18

Gone are the days when people made fun of western flies for having so much wire and lead in them. Here's a small fly that's made of little else but metal, and the most demanding entomological purists are happy to have a few.

Pheasant Tail Nymph, #12-16

One of the few things almost everybody seems to agree on is that the Pheasant Tail Nymph is an essential fly. Like the Hare's Ear, there are many variations, and all of them seem to be good.

Otter Nymph, #12-16

Another all-purpose pattern, not offered in many catalogs anymore, but if you can get some, or tie your own, you will be glad you had them with you.

Potts Lady Mite, #10-12
Potts Sandy Mite, #10-12

These are two great old Montana patterns, tied by a company that has gone through several hands over half a century; I talked about them in part one of this book. They are woven-hair patterns, the progenitors of George Grant's elegant flies, and they are flies I grew up with. They still have their place, and I have used them successfully even on the Firehole River's famous post-graduate trout.

Woolly Bugger (black and olive), #6-10

Woolly Buggers are fished dead drift, dragged across the current like some bizarre swimming critter, pitched against rip rap and jerked out into the current by passing floaters, and used in any way that will make the most of that great flowing tail. Some people think they imitate leeches, but they catch a lot of fish in places where leeches would never live.

With big attractors like the Woolly Bugger, there are several factors that will affect your success. One is depth; you have to figure out just how weighted it needs to be. Most Woolly Buggers are sold with some weight built into them, but you may have to add more, and the only way to know if you're deep enough is to experiment.

Line control is just as important. Whether you're chucking the fly against the bank from a boat or working it into a quiet pocket behind a rock while wading, you absolutely have to have the fly under control at all times. That may mean mending line or holding line off the water while you swim the fly through the best spot, or it may mean, in the case of bank fishing from a boat, that the instant the fly hits the water you get it moving right away. If there's a bunch of slack between you and the fly, you're not fishing it, and you're wasting your shot.

Color seems to matter a lot with Woolly Buggers. The most popular colors are black, brown, and green, and you just switch them around until you get the right one. I sometimes wonder if the success of one color over another is related to leeches. In Henry's Lake or other water with a lot of leeches, it may be that the prevailing color of the local leeches is the key to which Woolly Bugger to use. But as I mentioned a moment ago, leeches aren't common in fast-moving water, so something else must be in effect there.

Another thing to experiment with is the speed with which you work the fly through the feeding zone of the trout. This is true with many big flies, and it's especially important with Woolly Buggers. If you think there may be some fish holding in some relatively fast water, you may need to slow the fly down, by mending line. If you're fishing a slow tail of the pool, you may need to speed the fly up. I'll talk more about techniques in the chapter on presentation, but I can't overemphasize the importance of experimenting. Knowing the "right fly" is only the beginning, and the best advice you can get on how to fish it will usually be advice that encourages you to experiment and to adjust to local conditions, even if that means fishing it ten different ways on ten stretches of the same stream.

Shrimp, #8-14

There are several excellent shrimp patterns, and they are a case where imitation can be of great importance, especially on waters with lots of different aquatic life forms, like Henry's Lake. There, it is often the case that just any old shrimp pattern doesn't have a chance. You are best advised, if you plan to concentrate on one lake known for shrimp, to seek local guidance on the best pattern. Otherwise, Dave Whitlock's shrimp pattern will serve you as well as any.

Streamers

Light Spruce, # 1/0-6

I like really big streamers, and I'll say more about this later. You'd be amazed at how large a fish other fish are accustomed to eating, and the only limitation on a streamer's size should be how large it can be and still look lifelike.

Earlier I said that some flies become less effective over time. When they're first introduced, they're great, then gradually they seem to lose their effectiveness. The Spruce Flies are an exception to that. They've been great for me for many years, and are still as good as ever. Maybe it has to do with that collar puffing in and out like something alive, which may be why the Renegade has also stayed effective so long.

The same general guidelines to success apply to fishing a Spruce Fly and other streamers as I've already described for the Woolly Bugger. You have to experiment, and the more you experiment the better the feel you'll have for the current and what you need to do to get the trout's attention. Many good fishermen who've done a lot of streamer fishing develop a kind of intuition about this, and they know almost reflexively, from some combination of feel and experience, when the fly is in the best places and when it's left them.

Dark Spruce, #1/0-6

If you ever get a chance to watch a sculpin swimming from place to place along the bottom, you'll know one good way to fish this dark pattern. Make it hop along in little surges, letting it settle to the bottom like a sculpin looking for cover, and don't neglect the still water off to the side of the main current.

Muddler Minnow, #1/0-6

Don Gapen got it right more than half a century ago when he created one of the most original of American fly patterns. In a pinch you can treat it with flotant and have an excellent low-profile hopper imitation, or a tolerable salmonfly pattern.

I don't want to do any harm to anyone's fly-tying business, but I doubt that I could find a Muddler anywhere in my vest now. I think it falls into that category of patterns that has lost much of its effectiveness because it was so incredibly popular for so long. At the same time, I still recommend having a couple, partly out of a sense of tradition and partly because you never can tell.

Marabou Muddler (black and white, weighted), #1/0-10

Dave Whitlock's good work in developing new color combinations of marabou Muddlers has opened a whole new field for western streamer tiers, and I think there's still a lot to be done in experimenting with different color combinations.

Zonker, (black and white weighted) #4-8

The strip of fur seems almost as lively and attractive as marabou, and it can't get tangled in the hook shank the way feather wings do.

Chapter 13

Finding the Fish

Calendar Fishing

Until recently, most of the articles about where fish are in western streams seemed to be written by people who didn't live here. The author had been here say, in July or August, or some other time, and he'd talk about where the fish were right then, that year. He may or may not have believed that the fish were always in those same spots, but he almost always gave that impression. Now that we have so many fly-fishing writers of our own—Craig Mathews, George Anderson, George Kelly, Richard Parks, and others—they're helping to straighten out that misconception.

Throughout the fishing season, many fish move as the water level and the food opportunities change. The best example is probably the famous Barns Pools on the Madison just inside Yellowstone Park. That short stretch of water used

Many stretches of western freestone streams, such as the Gros Ventre in Wyoming, are continuous pocket water with fish holding in the calm spots around large rocks and in deeper runs.

PAUL SCHULLERY

This private spring creek is only a few feet wide and six inches deep, but the day this photograph was taken in 1997, trout of 12 to 18 inches were holding under the cover of the banks. See the thin line of dark water under the bank in the right foreground? Drift a hopper an inch from the grass and brace yourself.

to get more ink devoted to it than some entire rivers, and every story told of giant browns and rainbows falling to the flies of various experts. Visitors will come here in August and spend a few days dredging flies through those pools and catch nothing, or at least nothing that looks like the pictures in the magazines. The writers did not tell them that the Barns Pools are only really at their best for a short time in the late fall when spawning fish are coming up from Hebgen Lake. This is true for every stream—the Missouri, the Henry's Fork, the Madison, the Yellowstone, and all the rest. The fish just aren't tethered to a certain spot.

Water temperature will move fish to better spots in only a few days. Spawning will move fish many miles in certain seasons. Water level changes will dictate not only cover but food availability.

It's most useful to think of these changes on a seasonal basis. In the spring, in high water, there is substantial erosion, sometimes too much because of poor land management, but always some even under natural conditions. That time of year many of the big fish move to certain shoreline areas where they gorge on what we call angleworms and

anything else that is washed loose in the high water. A few weeks later the same fish may move to other shoreline areas to eat the emerging salmonfly nymphs or to catch the adults as they fall from streamside vegetation. At that time you can't beat a bank lined with willows; the trout will be hugging the roots, just waiting for the flies to fall. Later in that same hatch, many of the larger fish will relocate, especially if the water is lower, in midstream. You have to be watching the middle of the river, around rocks; the fish feel safer out there, which has taught us that angler pressure also can determine where the fish will be. A big trout won't get as much food during the salmonfly hatch if he's out in the middle of the river, but he'll still get a lot and will feel much safer. Whether or not he is safe is up to you.

Angler pressure will really reduce the amount of bank feeding done by trout on a heavily fished stream. On the Henry's Fork, for example, so many people walk the banks and the shallows that the fish often can't get in there.

In August, when hopper season starts, fish have additional incentive to move to the banks to get those hoppers that fall in. Some of the big varieties of hoppers can fly

Bud Lilly's Guide to Fly Fishing the New West

practically as far as a salmonfly, and may end up anywhere in the stream, even out in the middle, and so trout also watch for those. A critical factor with the hoppers is wind. We spend a lot of time cussing the wind that seems to blow all the time out here, but it blows a lot of trout food into the river. The best time of the day for hopper fishing may be mid-afternoon when a wind comes up and gets the hoppers moving.

But even at that, it's a good rule for the newcomer to start a search for fish by checking the banks. We have hundreds of miles of meadow streams with undercut banks that are often the best cover available for big trout. You may drive for miles along a stream in Montana without seeing a tree or even a substantial collection of bushes along the stream. Under those circumstances the trout have to adapt to different kinds of cover than they may have found if they had hatched out somewhere in Pennsylvania. (That also is why you should never just stomp up to the bank of a meadow stream and hope the fish won't know you're there.)

Fishing by the Clock, and by the Thermometer

The western climate has effects on fishing that a lot of people welcome. Most of all, you probably won't have to get up as early. Even on our hottest days, our nights are cool, and we don't have very many warm ones. In the higher elevations it may freeze any night of the year. The rivers are correspondingly cool, and fish feeding periods (except in spring creeks, of course) come on later. Couple that with water that is very cold anyway, and a lot of the time the best feeding periods will be in the afternoon after the river has had a chance to warm up. Once the sun has gone off the water, the fishing may slow down. There are plenty of times when there is good evening fishing on high western streams, but such occasions are not as predictable as they are on lower-elevation waters on either coast.

This can be a big adjustment for a fisherman who has spent 20 years waiting for the evening hatch on the Au Sable. Over the years, lots of my clients said "We really want to get the best fishing of the day, and so we'll meet you here at the shop at 6:00 tomorrow morning." And I'd say, "Well fine, I'll put the coffee on tonight, and I'll be over about 8:00." It's just too cold at that hour for much to be happening. Only in the hottest dog days of August do you have an advantage in fishing really early and late.

Another effect of weather is what rain can do to a stream during a day. If the weather has been hot, and you're fishing a stream that is a little too warm for the fish to be as active as you like, a good cold rainstorm or snowstorm (either can happen) can be a real blessing. Many times a nice rain in the middle of the day has brought a stream to life for me or my clients. It can drop the water temperature just enough to

cool the water and trigger a hatch or get the fish into a more active mood. A hard enough cloudburst can loosen bank materials, including worms and insects, also getting fish out on the prowl. Weather changes fast here, and we don't always fear the appearance of thunderheads. Sometimes we hope for them.

Of course be careful during the storm. No hatch is good enough for you to risk waving a nine-foot graphite rod around during a lightning storm.

Trout Rhythms

We've all heard the stories about a fisherman—it may have been you—who said "There I was, standing by old Joe, and Joe and I are using exactly the same fly, covering exactly the same water, and Joe was catching them and I wasn't." There is an almost indefinable quality in presentation of a fly, whether you're working a nymph, or retrieving a streamer, or drifting a dry fly over rising fish. The best word I know for that quality is "rhythm."

Nature has rhythms. Some of them are as simple as the steady feeding pattern of a rising trout, some so complicated we don't begin to understand them yet. I don't want to sound mystical about this, but there is no question that one of the reasons that old Joe was catching all the fish was that he was in some way more tuned in to the stream and its rhythms. You might only acquire a sense of these natural rhythms through fishing experience.

I'm not sure how to teach you to do this, but I think it helps to try to imagine where the fly is at all times, and what it's doing. Is it passing right under a sheltered place now? Is it sideways to the current, or is it moving along headfirst, or is it rolling this way and that with every little eddy? Can you feel anything about its movements in the line you're holding?

Many fishermen have commented that they could almost "feel" when the fish was about to strike, or when a fish turned at a fly or lure but did not take. If you've never had that experience, you can take my word for it that it's real. It's happened to me many times. I'll make a cast and I will know just about when and where the fish will hit; I sense it. It's some combination of experience and intuition that sharpens your awareness of what's going on in the water. It may not be possible to teach, but the best way I know to learn it is to work to keep in touch with the stream's rhythms.

For example, the Bud-man Pump mentioned in the next chapter, has seemed to me one of the best ways I've found for working a fly in some kind of cooperation with the stream's own directions. The fly is moved rhythmically, it works with the current, and it has a great attractiveness to the fish, whose entire life is bound up with the stream's rhythms. The mechanical part of fishing—casting, working the fly, and so on—is only the start. If you concentrate, and think about what you're doing, you will discover that eventually you develop these other skills, more like intuitions, that enable

Chapter 14

Presentation

FOR A LONG TIME, PRESENTATION WAS WRITTEN about too little, compared with fly-pattern theory. Does the fly have any action, or does it accidentally work across the current? Is the tippet small enough to avoid influencing the fly's motion? Is the size of the fly right? There are lots of things that are important besides fly pattern, and even having a proven pattern isn't always good enough if your particular samples of that pattern are poorly tied.

For example, it's very hard to get a good Joe's Hopper now, and bad ones are almost worse than worthless. There's no shortage of things to worry about when you're trying to take a fish on a fly. We shouldn't concentrate on just one of them, especially when it's the one that is the most susceptible of all to changing fashions. New flies come and go like the weather, but if the fisherman knows how to read the stream and handle the fly rod, he can do well with relatively few patterns, most of which have been around a long time. After all, this is the West, you know; our fishing may be getting harder, but it hasn't been that many years ago that Dave Bascom was catching trout on Yellowstone Lake with a lure made from a beer-can opener.

The late Lee Wulff was a good example of a fisherman who knew the basics so well that he could do well under difficult circumstances. Lee was, of course, one of the best-known anglers of this century, and I was able to fish with him, and Joan, a few times. Lee was a marvelous fisherman in that he knew where the fish were likely to be in the stream; he was superb at reading water. He also knew that if he gave the fish the right impression in a fly, he didn't have to worry about exact imitation; the superior fish-catching qualities of his Wulff series of dry flies, my favorite being the Royal Wulff, prove his point.

"Henry's Fork Midge Sipper" by Dave Whitlock

Lee was always known as a very athletic fisherman, catching an Atlantic salmon by casting for it by hand and playing the fish with only a reel and no rod, and other equally impressive tricks. What was surprising to me, and I think it should be instructive to all of us, is that his casting looked pretty rough. It made mine look deluxe. But he caught fish.

I fished with him on the Firehole one August, a stream and a time that will test anyone's skill. As usual Lee was trying out some new patterns, this time some plastic-bodied grasshoppers he was getting ready to market. He was very lackadaisical about his presentation. Like me, he didn't go in for the modern fly fisherman's fashionable crouch (the famous Henry's Fork Hunch-back), but he didn't make much effort to cast nicely, either. He just sort of slapped it out there, which often is the best way to fish grasshoppers anyway, and he was picking up fish regularly.

It's interesting to contrast these great fishermen sometimes. For example, we had Ed Shenk out one summer doing a clinic for us. Ed is almost a legend in Pennsylvania for his ability to take large trout on flies, and he is of course best known nationally for developing some excellent fly patterns, especially terrestrials. We took him into the Park one hot August day, the hardest time of the season to get Firehole trout to take, and he put on a show of precise, careful casting that his clinic group will probably never forget.

Ed was using one of his little six-foot bamboo rods, and he worked up the river, popping a little Letort Hopper right against the bank, taking fish after fish with those precise, almost delicate casts. His approach was different from Lee's, or mine, or other good fishermen I know, but it worked beautifully. There are lots of ways to catch a trout. Maybe that's why there are so many experts.

Wind Casting

If you are new to the West and your first day out it seems too windy, don't assume that later it will get better. You could wait for years. Wind is just a fact of life out here, and once you adjust to it you're likely to have as many good days as bad days when it's windy. If it's howling so much that it's dangerous, say from blowing a weighted streamer off course so it hits you in the head, then go home. But most of the time, just try to work with it.

The new rods of the past 25 years, and the great advances in fly lines, have made wind casting a lot easier. With a good strong rod you can throw into a stiffer breeze, especially if you've got a line built for such casting, say a weight-forward

especially if it's got a big, wind-resistant fly on the end of it. Cut back your tippet, even if you have to go to a larger diameter than you usually would. Shorten the whole leader if you must.

Some people try to use the wind, looking for fishing situations along the river that allow them to cast with the wind. That works sometimes, and it sounds really good in the books, but it means that you'll have to pass up a lot of good water. It's better to learn how to punch the fly out there.

Don't forget that wind is often gusty. Many days, you can actually wait a few minutes and cast when it's quiet. I don't have the patience to wait too long, but if the wind is really bad it may be your only choice short of quitting.

Casting directly across big, fast-moving streams requires great line control, quick reflexes, and realistic expectations. Trout rising 70 or 80 feet away may be reachable but not really fishable.

line made to turn over heavy flies. You lose a lot of delicacy with this gear, but you don't have to swear as much, either.

If it's windy, adjust your expectations. Don't try to cast to every far-off corner of the stream that you would normally be able to reach. Make shorter casts. Wade closer to the good spots so you don't give the wind so much line to work with.

Western fishermen learn to throw very tight loops at high speeds to punch that fly out there. Another important consideration that gets overlooked is leader size and length. If you're fishing a windy day on a big open river, and you want to pitch a hopper way out there, you have to be prepared to sacrifice some leader length. That monofilament leader is the least willing part of the cast when it comes to turning over,

Most of the time I'm grateful for the wind. It gets the hoppers out on the water, it moves the salmonflies around, and it ruffles the surface of the water and makes the trout a little less cautious.

Roll Casting

Roll casting is neglected these days. There are several good books and videos that will tell you how to do it, so I will concentrate on why you should.

Learn it, and get really good at it, and your fishing will be better for several reasons. First, there are so many situations where you have trees or a bank right behind you, and there is no other way to get your fly even 25 or 30 feet out there.

Second, use it to lift your dry fly off the water at the end of a cast. If you rip the line off the water with a normal back-cast, you're likely to spook more fish than if you smoothly lift the line in a nice, quiet roll cast.

Comments on Streamers

I have a fairly simple approach to streamers. I use as large a streamer as the law will allow, practically all of the time. In the winter I often use flies that were really developed for saltwater, like Joe Brooks' Blondes, as well as freshwater streamer patterns, in 3/0 and 2/0. In the fall, when I'm fishing for spawning brown trout, I will use flies almost as large. Most streamers that are available commercially for trout fishing are not very large, really, and there seems to be an unspoken assumption that trout won't take streamers that are larger. They will. A study a few years ago in Yellowstone Park showed that large cutthroat trout tended to prey most heavily on fish that were 25-30 percent of their size. Twenty-

"Madison Sculpin Grabber" by Dave Whitlock

inch trout commonly ate chubs of five or six inches. If you still have doubts about big streamers, let me tell you about a huge brown trout that someone caught in the Bear Trap Canyon on the lower Madison in the 1950s. I don't remember hearing how big it was, I do remember that when they cleaned it, it had a 16-inch whitefish in it.

Streamers aren't just for certain seasons. A lot of people associate them with certain events, such as the spawning runs of various fish. I use them any time of the year, and just about anywhere, except under low water conditions when they just don't seem to be effective, and under extremely cold conditions, when the fish just aren't as interested in chasing food.

I always have loved streamer fishing, but I think it was Joe Brooks who really popularized the big western streamers. Joe was a good friend of Dan Bailey's and he didn't spend much time in the West Yellowstone area. He used to stay in a cabin right on Nelson Spring Creek south of Livingston, back before anybody had heard much about the tremendous fishing in the spring creeks. He and Dan started using really large streamers, larger than those to which trout fishermen were accustomed. Joe often used his famous series of "Blondes" (saltwater flies

five or six inches long) on a shooting head, and he took some enormous trout from the Yellowstone with them. It didn't take long for me to get interested in that, and since then I've always been a believer in very large streamers. Now, what with some excellent new books and videos, there's no shortage of information on streamers, and there are a huge number of good patterns. But for the really large trout, especially the big browns on their fall spawning runs, you can still do very well with the big Blondes.

Getting the Lead Out

Keith Fulsher developed a series of flies a few years ago that were absolutely gorgeous, called the Thunder Creek series. The first time I met Keith he came into my store and gave me some samples and told me he was testing them out. After he'd spent some time fishing the flies in our area, he came back in to the shop with a perplexed look on his face. "You know something, Bud," he said, "I've tested these flies on the eastern streams with a great deal of success. But these western trout, all they want is lead and rubber."

That does typify a lot of our fly patterns, in that they are heavily weighted. In the streams here in the headwaters area of Montana, Wyoming, and Idaho, where I have done most of my fishing, the streams are fast, and they drop quickly. If you don't have a fly that gets down fast, you don't get results.

Paul and I got a vivid demonstration of that some years ago on the Firehole. We were fishing with our friend Larry Aiuppy, an outstanding photographer from Livingston, Montana. I fished through an excellent wet-fly run using a small nymph, and I caught nothing. Larry and Paul followed me through the run only moments later using streamers and sinking lines and took six fish in half the time. The weight factor is critical, but it isn't simply a matter of making the fly as heavy as possible. Like all other kinds of fishing, you don't dare stop thinking. Weighted flies follow a set of rules. It isn't just a matter of knowing when to use weight; you have to know how much to use.

This is where we've found that fishermen from other parts of the country run into trouble when we guide them. We tell them to put on a weighted Zonker, and maybe we'll add a few split shot on the leader, too. They cast that awkward rig for about half an hour and say to hell with it. It's very discouraging to the newcomer, but it's also very effective. For a lot of western fishing (and I know this goes against a modern fashion), the first factor is to get the fly down. Don't worry so much about what color it is, or even what you think it's supposed to look like, as long as it wiggles and gets deep.

There is a seasonal trend to weighting flies. In the early spring when the water is high and cold, those fish are lying on the bottom and you'd swear they only feed about once a week. If you don't hit them on the nose with it, you might as well not be fishing. They're too lethargic, or cautious, to rise through several feet of fast water, or to chase a fly that goes racing by. You've got to put it right into their little mouths.

Of course when the water level goes down and the water temperature starts to rise, it is less necessary to fish so accurately; they'll come for it, sometimes a long way (understand that these are general rules, not absolute ones). You certainly need less weight then. In late summer, when the water gets warm and even lower, you face new dilemmas because the fish are again slowing down, especially on some of the streams that get dangerously warm or low because of irrigation diversion, or due to hot springs on unusual waters like the Firehole. They feed less energetically, and are easily overstressed when caught. To hook them you've got to get the fly close again, like in spring. And then in fall it cools off again and there is a little less need for perfect presentation of the fly at a certain depth.

The only absolute rule is that you have to experiment. Don't think that if you've fished a run thoroughly with one fly you've proven that the fish aren't taking. If you went back through the same run right away with the same fly, only a little heavier or lighter, you might have fast action.

Again I know this is a form of sacrilege, but you don't have to carry a full assortment of nymphs in half a dozen different weights. You don't even have to use split shot, which I must say makes for even more awkward casting than a weighted fly because you've got weight positioned along the line rather than in just one spot. What my guides and I often did, and what many of my friends do, is carry a spool of some weighting material (use the new no-lead substitutes) and take a few turns around the body of the fly with it. Obviously I'm talking mostly about the larger flies here, though you can do the same thing with smaller flies down to #14 or so using fine wire. The first time you see this done you might be offended, because there is a fly that someone worked hard to produce, getting the proportions right and all the details in place; how could it still work with all that metal wound around it? Welcome to the West—it works. You can change the behavior of a streamer or nymph in only a few seconds, and you can add as much or as little weight as you want. If the esthetics of it give you the willies, pretend that the wire heightens the segmentation of the nymph's body, or that the wire sparkles like trapped air bubbles. What at first glance appears to be a violation of all the good taste of the fly tier's craft is in fact a very revealing piece of information about flies and about fish. You take a two-dollar nymph that someone spent half an hour tying and smother it in wire, you're getting to the opposite extreme of fly-tying theory from the people who collect pee-stained fox hair and that sort of thing. But you're still catching fish.

You can overweight a fly, either by applying the weight in such a way that it kills the fly's action or by somehow ruining the fly's silhouette. Orvis offers tungsten beads that can be slipped over the tippet right above the eye of the hook, giving you a sort of disjointed bead head instantly. Don't weight any fly to the point where it looks like a golf ball when you lob it into the river. There is always a point that's just right.

Weighting the Leader

Weighting has become a little more complicated lately as we've learned of the harm that lead, the greatest of all weights for fishing, can do in a stream ecosystem. There are a growing number of pretty good substitutes out there, and we'd better get used to using them; more and more streams are going to no-lead regulations.

The general rule in faster western streams is to weight the fly itself. Several writers have suggested systems for designating how much weight a fly has by using different colors of thread to mark the head, and if you are new to a water you simply have to experiment to see which amount of weight will work best.

On meadow streams, on the other hand, it is often better to weight the leader.

Wet-Fly Casts

Fly fishing, especially in the past twenty years, has gone through a revolution, with many new fly patterns, and rod materials, and books of theory, and all kinds of other fun developments. That's all good, but I think we can easily lose sight of older techniques that were abandoned more because they were old than because they didn't work. Sixty years ago, when my Dad was teaching me to fish on the streams in the Gallatin Valley here in Montana, our fly fishing was limited mostly to the old wet-fly approach of cast it across and let it swing around. We caught lots of trout, and we hadn't even heard of dry flies, and had only a vague notion of what the fish might be taking those flies for. There's no question that a fished-over trout population gets harder and harder, but there are still lots of times out here when that same simple method is deadly.

Even on a stream as famous for hatch-matching as the Firehole River, there are runs I've fished for more than forty years using all kinds of flies and techniques, and even today nothing else is as consistently successful as tying on a Zug Bug or some other nymph or wet fly and pitching it straight across and letting the current swing it around. There is something about the current, or the flies in it, or the fish's perceptions, in those spots that brings them up every time. Maybe they take it for a swimming nymph, or maybe there are just a lot of things drifting along in the current and the fish don't especially care whether it's drifting straight downstream or swinging across.

Bead heads might seem a little tricky to fish because they're weighted like a jig, and tend to nose down as they sink. I almost always fish them dead drift. My speculation is that when it's dead-drifting, the uneven weight of the fly as it's worked on by the currents gives it some extra little jiggle that produces the action.

Two-Fly Rigs

The traditional methods for fishing more than one fly were quite a nuisance. Whether you tied in a separate section of leader for the dropper, or simply left a long end on your blood knot when you tied the first fly on and then tied the dropper on that long end, the whole thing tended to twist like crazy, and in no time you were busy trying to untangle the mess. A much simpler approach, that works whether your using a combination of two dry flies, a dry fly and a wet fly, or two wet flies, is to tie your first fly on the normal way, then tie another section of leader directly to the bend of the fly's hook, and then tie the second fly to that leader. I've never seen any evidence that the leader on the bend of the hook impairs the fly's hooking qualities, and the whole thing is symmetrical, in a straight, balanced line, so it doesn't twist nearly as much.

Fishing Big Wet Flies—An Unorthodox Approach

How you should fish a large fly—and by large I mean something more than #8, all the way up to 3/0—is often more a matter of the water than the fly. The character of the water—depth, speed, clarity, obstructions in the current—will often dictate what you can and can't do. There are of course many recommended techniques for fishing these flies, and there is no point in my repeating them all here. Streamers are most often fished by casting them across the stream and letting them swing back over to your side; a variety of actions are imparted to the fly by pulling on the line, working the rod, or some combination of the two. Weighted nymphs, especially the big stonefly imitations and related large flies that I am concerned with here, are most often fished "dead drift," that is by finding a way to get them as deep as you can and enabling them to drift straight downstream the way a large clumsy nymph might drift if it suddenly was loose in the current. I want to offer my own variation on those techniques, one that I have found to be very successful. I have many times used it when following right behind a good fisherman who used some other approach, and I've repeatedly taken fish that ignored his presentation. It's not a difficult technique, and it's not one whose success is always easily explained. But it is the most important part of my wet-fly strategies, and has accounted for more large fish than I could ever tell you about.

One of the unorthodox things about this technique is that I fish streamers and big nymphs exactly the same. I know that minnows and stonefly nymphs don't typically behave the same, but I've learned that their imitations can be fished the same. Some of my guides at the Trout Shop, who watched me fish this way, used to refer sarcastically to my technique as the "Bud-man Pump," which is just about as formal a name as it should have.

Fish often do not show much interest in flies that are zipping straight across the current. That is why I prefer the Bud-man Pump, and here is how I do it. I usually get off a fairly long cast, either across the stream or upstream, depending upon how deep the water is and how far I think the fly needs to sink. The most important thing is trying to control the fly's speed. The active fishing begins when the fly begins it swing. Up until then, though I try to be prepared for the occasional strike, I am busy controlling the line, mostly by mending, so that the fly has sunk to the depth I want by the time it starts its swing.

Once it starts its swing, I start a pumping motion with the rod. This is another advantage of using a long rod; I can control that fly so much better at a distance. I vary the length of the pull, and the pace of the rhythm, experimenting until I find what works best. The effect is that the fly, rather than swinging straight over in the current, makes a series of surges upstream, moving the fly three or four feet up. Each surge is followed by an equally long downstream drift of the fly as I drop the rod and let the current take the fly again. Once the fly has swung across and is hanging in the current below me, I then retrieve it with a hand-strip retrieve. That is usually the first point at which I retrieve any line in the cast.

I can't overemphasize that I use this for both nymphs and streamers. It may not match the actual behavior of every large insect or small fish, but the repetitive pumping of the fly over the fish's hold unquestionably triggers a rise by the fish. When I know there is a good holding lie under the surface, say a rock or a log, I make a special effort to get in as many pumps as possible right near it.

The fly-fishing theorists could probably cook up several explanations of why this technique works so well. Perhaps the pumped nymph looks enough like a small fish. Perhaps it does remind the trout of small fish lurking among the rocks, or of stonefly nymphs clambering along on the bottom. Perhaps it even reminds them of some of the stronger mayfly nymphs that are very active swimmers. But I suspect that it isn't a simple matter of the fly imitating anything in particular. The fish sees this big wiggly thing moving through the water and decides to eat it. That may be too simple for the hard-core hatch-matcher, but it gets great results.

One reason that this technique has done so well for me when I'm fishing with dead-drift fishermen is simply that I rarely have any slack line between me and the fish. The dead drift is a terrific nymph-fishing technique, whether you're fishing an emerger in the surface film or a big nymph on the bottom, but the deeper the fly is, and the farther away from you it is, the harder it is to keep contact. Even the best nymph fishermen acknowledge that they miss a lot of strikes.

What all this comes down to, whichever technique you are using to fish your wet flies, is fly control. If you don't have contact with your fly—if you don't know pretty much where it is and what it is doing all the time, if you have to make half a dozen poor casts that alert the fish to your approach before you make an effective fishing cast, if you aren't in charge of the fly—you aren't going to catch many fish, and you aren't likely to catch any good ones.

Fishing the Salmonfly

Out here one of the things a guide simply has to know about is the salmonfly hatch. salmonflies are the large stoneflies, some as much as two inches long, which appear on various western rivers in June and drive trout into the greatest surface-feeding binge of the year. It's a breathtaking event, and it's also the best time of the year to find really large trout—four pounds and up—willing to take a big dry fly. In the 1950s the few other guides were pretty secretive about it, and I was on my own. I had a couple from Texas who wanted to fish the salmonfly hatch, and I had little else going for me except that I knew a few stretches I liked to fish. So I took them down to an area I happened to enjoy, not knowing anything about the hatch.

We had an incredible day. I led them around just like I knew what I was doing, and we caught large browns until we were tired, including several that weighed over four pounds. When we quit for the day, we kept two, as was the custom then, and headed back to the car. As we crossed the road, some passing fishermen saw us dragging a couple of these big trout along. They swerved to a stop and ogled the fish while they asked us where we'd caught them.

"Oh, we just got them over there, in some good water."

"What on?"

"Salmonflies."

"My God, we just spent the entire day twenty-five miles down the river where the salmonflies are supposed to be, and we haven't gotten a thing."

What made that day stick in my mind wasn't the dumb luck of being in the right place at the right time. What was so memorable was that we caught only large fish. We caught lots of browns in the sixteen- to eighteen-inch range, plus the really big fish. We were probably ten miles upstream of the hatch, so apparently the fish had been feeding on the nymphs as they moved to shore and were really ready for the adults. Our big dry flies were just what they were waiting for, and there wasn't another fisherman for miles.

Everybody dreams of finding the large western stonefly hatches under ideal conditions. The most experienced fishermen in the world can't tell you what day, or where, or anything else precise, about the salmonfly hatch. The salmonfly is one of the hardest hatches to plan a trip around.

The salmonfly is one of the real bruisers of the insect world. You would think that if any fly could hatch regardless of environmental conditions it would surely be the one. But it doesn't work that way. Salmonflies are as sensitive to changing conditions as any other flies. If there is a sudden spring rain or snow, or if there are high winds, or some other change in conditions, the hatches in a stretch of river can be scrambled instantly and never make sense again that year. If there is a sudden air temperature change while the adults are exposed, they may die (like flies!), and a sudden dramatic change in water temperature when the nymphs are about to emerge may also kill a lot of them.

From my observations it appears to me that the big stonefly nymphs begin to show pre-emergence activity as much as several weeks before they actually emerge from the water. In that period they begin crawling toward shore, so there is a general migration toward shore. It goes on for weeks, and offers a real service to guides, who can more or less track the nymphs by turning over a few rocks and seeing where the biggest concentrations of nymphs are.

There is a well-known western recreation called "following the hatch," which involves careening up and down the river in your car with your head hanging out the window as you look for the bugs in the air. A lot of the time, however, there is no clearly defined "front" of the hatch. At times, depending on the various environmental conditions mentioned earlier, the flies may actually be emerging or laying their eggs along 25 miles of river at once. There may be no one "magic" section of river, and the fish may be on the lookout for the flies for weeks after the heaviest part of the hatch has passed by. Paul tells me he used to use salmonfly imitations most of the summer on smaller freestone streams in Yellowstone Park, and the fish didn't seem to lose interest in them.

One little-known element of the salmonfly hatch is that the fish will sometimes migrate to follow the hatch. Most resident trout in a stream may live their lives in a fairly short stretch of river, at least through a summer season. They'll move as water temperature, depth, and other factors dictate, but usually they won't move too far. But I'm sure that some fish will travel long distances to follow the heaviest part of the salmonfly hatch. A friend of mine hooked and lost a trout once on the Madison, using a Sofa Pillow he'd tied himself. The next day he caught that same fish, with his fly still in its mouth, about a mile upstream. There was no mistaking the fly, so we knew that at least this one trout was willing to move a long way to keep up with the food. I've seen similar movements on the Henry's Fork, when the salmonfly nymphs are moving and get washed out of the mouth of the Box Canyon area in great numbers. Trout will move up to the mouth of the canyon from the meadow stretches downstream to take advantage of the food.

The fish can get sated. They will first gorge themselves on the nymphs, and then they may start taking the adults on the surface. We have had the surface feeding seem to go by species, with the browns switching to the adults first, then maybe the next day browns and rainbows, and then there may be a day when all you catch is whitefish. It may be that the browns are the quickest to switch to the surface flies because of some trait we don't fully understand, but I've seen this sequence often enough to know it isn't occurring by chance. Eventually, if the hatch is heavy enough, all the fish may stop feeding, having become lethargic from being so stuffed. Interestingly, the largest fish are often the last ones to stop feeding, so if you're fishing a stretch of water after the hatch has gone through you may have an unusually good chance at the big fish who had enough appetite to keep feeding longer.

The salmonfly is at its best from about the last week of May until the first ten days of August. Some of the rivers, such as the Yellowstone, may still be in high water during the hatch. The Yellowstone north of the Park is out of condition for dry-fly fishing during the salmonfly hatch four years out of five.

Most of the time you fish the adult of the salmonfly as you would any other dry fly, but there are times when it's useful to work the fly. If you find a small back-eddy you can give the fly a twitch now and then; the adults struggle and flutter a lot on the surface.

There are several sizes of the naturals, and when the hatch is really heavy I use a large fly, probably a #4. I have used #2's, but they won't all take a #2. When they're feeding less heavily I'll use a smaller fly, a #6 or maybe even a #8. There is a good bit more to this than just pitching it out there. There are times when they seem to prefer a fly that is partly drowned, and I've taken many fish on a dry fly that has sunk completely. The advantage of the Sofa Pillow, or the Bird's Stonefly, under some circumstances is that they have such a low profile that they simulate the naturals in the last stage of their lives when they're just barely floating along. It's like fishing with grasshoppers; sometimes you have to be open-minded enough to fish your dry fly wet.

You may not think of trout feeding on these big flies as being selectivity, but there are lots of kinds of selectivity. I've noticed that the fish can be selective to the size of the salmonflies. There is a period when they seem to prefer the larger flies, and there may be a period when they want something as small as a #8. Keep in mind that everything else on the river doesn't go away just because the salmonflies are hatching. One reason the fish may prefer smaller flies is that the golden stonefly hatches about the same time, and they may switch over to this smaller fly. I think that one of the reasons the Stimulator works, especially in smaller sizes, may be that the fish have abandoned the salmonfly and taken up some local caddis hatch.

I remember a day on the Madison during the salmonfly hatch, years ago. I was fishing with a good friend, Sam Radan, and we'd already caught some big trout, when just downstream from Varney Bridge I saw a fish rising to the naturals in midstream. I worked my way out to him, right up to the top of my chest waders, and confidently put a fly over him. No take. I moved closer and tried again. I tried different flies, different tippets. I moved closer. I could see that he weighed four or five pounds; he was throwing spray like another fish weighing more than five pounds which I'd caught earlier that day. I got so close he was actually throwing spray on my glasses when he rose. Sam was watching from the bank. I'd cast, the fish would rise and take a natural, Sam would cuss, and I'd cast again. Nothing worked.

I didn't catch him. He never stopped rising, and I never spooked him, but he just wouldn't take. It may be something you didn't think you needed to learn to do, but it's a humbling part of your education as a fly fisherman to have to walk away from an eagerly rising trophy trout just because you can't catch him.

Hopper Fishing

I love hopper fishing. There is nothing more exciting than slapping a big hopper down along a grassy bank and waiting for a big trout to come out from under the bank and attack it.

Size is very important with hoppers. We used to just use a size 4 Joe's Hopper a lot of the time, which is a very large fly. But now we find that it is necessary to experiment with size and even with type of hopper. The Joe's Hopper, John's Elk Hair Hopper, the Gartside Hopper, the Letort Hopper, the Parachute Hopper, and Dave's Hopper, all have different profiles and different qualities of color and flotation. The fish will sometimes key in on some characteristic that you had better be prepared to match.

Once there are lots of hoppers in the meadows, and the fish are accustomed to them, they seem to get a little less selective and you may be able to get away with a larger-than-average size fly. But be prepared to experiment.

As a general rule, you should think of hopper types as corresponding with water types. The dainty and more realistically made hoppers, such as the Letort Hopper and the Gartside Hopper, with their narrow profiles, are your best bet on the meadow streams. The big hoppers that are tied more like ordinary dry flies, such as the Deer Hair Hopper or the Joe's Hopper, are usually best on bigger rivers with rougher surfaces. On the big rivers, you can use huge, crude hoppers and do very well.

Speaking of big rivers, watch the whole river. Just as with salmonflies, the biggest fish might be out there getting the big fliers who can reach the middle. Hopper fishing isn't just bank fishing.

Don't forget the sunk hopper. If your fly sinks, don't immediately yank it out of the water; hoppers drown, and fish take them just as avidly then. The fish are often looking for the drowned ones.

Finally, be sure to have some hoppers if you're fishing lakes. Hoppers fall all along the shoreline of a lake, and the fish love them. Look for shorelines bordered by meadows, and prospect both near the bank and farther out.

Chapter 15

Guidance and Guides

AS I'VE WATCHED THE guiding business over the past 50 years, I've seen a steady improvement in the qualities of the guides. A lot of them learned to fish in the last 15 or 20 years and have been introduced to all the new ideas and methods that have appeared in that time. They keep up on new tackle, many are expert or professional fly tiers, many are college educated, and most are fun, interesting people to be with. Your chances of having a good experience with a western guide get better all the time.

In trying to find a good guide, it is always wise to talk to people who have fished the area before, and rely on a well-respected tackle shop. If they've got a good reputation, their guides probably do too.

The guide is instructor, naturalist, historian, emergency medical specialist, and many other things, but it's up to the client how much those skills help with the day's fishing.

do you the most good in the fishing you choose to do. The outfitter knows his guides best (I'm going to speak of guides and outfitters as "he" here because almost all of them still are, but keep in mind that some of the best are now women, too).

What to Expect

Your outfitter will certainly be able to give you some solid information on your fishing well in advance. He will be able to tell you what kind of tackle is appropriate, and what special conditions you may encounter. But don't ask him for more than that. If you've booked a trip months in advance, which is the best way, he's not going to know what the weather or water conditions or hatches are going to be like then. A few days before you arrive he will

Even if you have talked to someone, be careful about assuming too much based on what they tell you. Their experience may not be the experience you want. For example, if your friend tells you that he fished out of such-and-such a tackle shop, with a guide named Dale, he may insist that you try to get Dale when you go there. That shop may have six or seven guides, and they all are probably specialized to some extent. Your friend may have fished with Dale on the Fryingpan, and you may want to fish Colorado's alpine lakes. Dale may never have hiked a day in his life. By insisting on Dale you put him, the outfitter, and yourself in a bad spot. It's better to rely on the outfitter to assign you to a guide who can

have a better idea, but even then, with those things being so susceptible to sudden change, he can't tell you for sure. That is just a reality of fishing, wherever you go, and an outfitter and guide can't change those unpredictable elements of fishing, though they may be able to react creatively with alternative plans if need be. The smartest thing you can do is relax and put yourself in the hands of the outfitter and guide. Let them use their best judgment. Once you start trying to second-guess the guide, proposing places to fish or trying to overrule his plan, you're increasing the chance that your trip won't work out. If he's a good guide he'll consult you about any decisions and plans, either the night before or as the day

Montana guide Don Kast and Michigan angler Leon Martuch concentrating on a riser on a small Montana stream they insist remain unnamed.

goes along, but don't forget that he's in charge. Order him to go where you think you ought to go and he'll start to lose interest; you are not respecting his professional position, and he'll be inclined to think, "Well, this guy thinks he's so hot, he doesn't need me." You're paying for him to make the decisions. Let him. If you're not satisfied at the end of the day, the best thing to do is not hire that guide again.

Fishing is exciting partly because it's so uncertain. No guide can or should guarantee you that you'll catch a lot of fish, or even any fish. But a good one will work his tail off for you trying.

Well in advance, you can get a lot of basic information from the outfitter: what size rods you'll need, leaders to bring, fly patterns you ought to tie or buy, and so on. These things are not absolute either, though, and you may need to buy something when you get there. You're starting off on the wrong foot if you are instantly suspicious that your outfitter and guide are trying to bilk you by encouraging you to buy a few flies. The sale of a few flies is not a life-or-death matter for them. You've already spent several hundred dollars getting there and hiring the guide, to say nothing of what you've

already spent on tackle. If you are told at the last minute that there's been a surprise hatch of #14 Lavender Wulffs the last few days and you only have #14 Chartreuse Wulffs, you ought to trust your outfitter that you need a few flies. Their success is your success.

If you are out on the stream and you find that you don't have the right fly, the guide may provide one. The guide often will try to anticipate possible hatches, and he may recommend that you buy some at the shop, or he may choose instead to bring some along and provide them only if you need them. It is customary, if he does provide you with flies, for him to put them on your bill. Unless he tells you otherwise, assume you will be billed for them. Guides often bring flies along because some clients are suspicious and are unwilling to buy enough of the flies they are told they will need. They'll say, "Oh well, I guess I'll take one of these and one of these, just in case," and of course having one of some pattern is almost worse than having none at all; that single fly will last fifteen minutes, then it's up to the guide to be ready with some flies or the client's fishing may be over for the day. It's not good manners for the client to ask to "borrow" a few for the day that he can return if he doesn't need them. Few flies that have been shaken around all day in someone's vest are still new, even if they haven't been tied on a leader.

You can help the outfitter and the guide, and increase the chance you'll have a good trip, if you make clear in advance any unusual problems or circumstances they should know about. There is nothing wrong, and a lot right, about telling them if you have a bad knee and can't wade fast water, or that you have never mastered distance casting. You don't need to say too much about it; once the guide has been alerted to it, it's his job to watch and see just what you can and can't do. He'll ask you before undertaking any adventurous wading, or he'll check your casting the first place you stop to fish, and judge his options from there. He may well coach you on improvements. The best guides are good teachers, partly because they have seen every imaginable fishing problem.

It's also very useful to let them know what kind of fishing you favor. Do you favor dry flies, or hate streamers? Do you prefer quiet waters where hatch-matching is important, or fast pocket water where a big nymph is best? This gets even more important if you're bringing your family, and your nine-year-old son wants to fish (or you want him to fish, which is an entirely different thing from the guide's point of view). If you want the guide to concentrate on the son, make it clear and mean it. Of course the outfitter must be forewarned of how many people will be along, and how the guide should divide his time.

Any kind of problem—diet restrictions, sun problems, anything—should be brought to the guide's attention before you go out.

You also should consider any special interests that may require the guide's expertise, such as photography. Many guides are enthusiastic photographers, and will happily take some pictures of you and your fish, but they are not expected to. If you want to have good pictures, and are not equipped to take them yourself (or to bring a camera for the guide to use), let the outfitter know what you want.

Transportation

Customarily transportation is the guide's responsibility. If you want to use your car for some reason, that's fine, but you're paying for transportation either way. On float trips, the outfitter is usually responsible for picking up the trailer and arranging the dropping off of the car at the end of the trip.

Going Fishing
with a Guide

First, don't be afraid of the guide. If you lack experience, or confidence, or skill, don't worry about it. The guide has seen it all before, and has fished with people ten times worse than you. All he needs from you is that you pay attention and do the best you can. He is used to accommodating his fishing trip to the needs, strengths, and limitations of the people he's guiding on any given day.

On the other hand, don't treat the guide like a lackey. He isn't just a servant you hired. If he's good, he's a professional in the fullest sense of the word. He's devoted a major part of his life to learning the craft of guiding, and he almost certainly does it because he loves rivers and fly fishing.

On this same subject, it isn't his job to try to impress you with his fishing ability. If he's a good guide he can catch a lot of fish, and he has no need to prove that to you. He wants you to catch them. If things are going well, you should feel free to encourage him to go ahead and fish too. If you're new to the area and feel that you're getting the hang of it, maybe you'll want to send him off up the river for a while to let you alone for a while; it does make some people nervous to have someone constantly hanging on their shoulder, no matter how helpful they may be. Feel free to ask for some solitude if you get in that mood. If a guide fishes too much and doesn't give you enough help, you've got a lemon and may have to remind him that he's the guide. But he should do enough fishing to help locate the fish, see what they're feeding on and get you into the right spot with the right fly and coach you as needed.

Every now and then you may get a poor guide, who is either unable to communicate with you, or simply doesn't know what he is doing, but people like that don't stay in business long, and usually can't find outfitters to associate with them.

You don't hire a guide necessarily just to find the good places so you can return to them later. A good guide has much more than that to offer, in hints on reading the water, fly choice, and a hundred other things. What you want to learn from him is not so much where all the good spots are but how to fish the water. It's a mistake to think that if you hire a guide for a few days you will learn what you need to know about fishing the area and will never need to use a guide again. Perhaps a few days is all you can afford, and you have learned enough to get in a lot of good fishing. But remember that the guide has been fishing the area every day for years, and knows which spots become good at which water levels, which spots are affected by a sudden storm that muddies the water, and all kinds of other things that only can be learned from that depth of experience. If you were fortunate enough to be able to afford a guide every day of the season, then you would get some idea of just how much he has to know to do his job right.

The length of the fishing day is also a matter that you'll almost certainly have reason to wonder about. It isn't a clearcut thing, but there are some general rules. There are clients who, about 5:00 in the afternoon, announce that "I'll bet it will be good this evening." The guide has already put in an eleven or twelve-hour day, starting very early to get the boat ready, get the lunches together, and so on, and he's getting cross-eyed from wrestling the oars. What happens next is up for grabs.

Let's say that you fished all day and caught nothing. The mosquitoes were bad, you got soaked in three storms, and you dropped your sandwiches in the river. All of a sudden, about the time you're thinking of quitting, the sun comes out and there's great hatch and the fish are feeding everywhere. If at that point the guide wants to walk away from it, he's a jerk. He is obligated to stay in there and see to it that you get some good fishing.

But let's say you've been fishing all day, and have caught some good fish and had a lot of fun, and it's getting late. You are getting tired, and you can see that the guide is too. If at that point you don't quit, you're the jerk. Be reasonable.

It's easier to judge what is a complete day of fishing when you float a river, because the guide can judge how long it will take to fish from the put-in to the take-out. But if the guide meets you at the river at 10:00 and you're home by 4:00, you really haven't had much of a day. A reasonable day is from about 8:00 in the morning, when you leave the place you meet, until about 5:00 or 6:00 in the evening. Then you'll be back at the meeting place by 7:00 or so, and nobody will be exhausted.

A river is sometimes a dangerous place. Most outfitters have some firm rules about anything that endangers either the client or the guide, and perhaps the most frequent risks are because of drinking. Hard liquor is a bad idea on a fishing trip, especially on a float trip. If you want beer in the cooler, you should not expect the guide to pay for it, though you can arrange with the outfitter for it to be provided. A beer or two is a welcome refreshment on a hot day, and some wine with lunch is also popular. Excessive drinking is not only dangerous, it is probably a violation of the guide's insurance.

If you want something out of the ordinary in the way of food, let the outfitter know. The normal lunch is some sandwiches, fruit, potato chips, cookies, cheese and crackers, chocolate, and other picnic-type items. If you want more, you usually will pay for it. Some outfitters specialize in cooking lunch, which takes time from fishing but can be a wonderful break in the middle of the day. A cooked lunch may use up an hour and a half or two hours.

Off-Stream Guide—Client Etiquette

If you're going to fish with a guide for several days, try not to eat up all his time by having breakfast with him every day or inviting him out to close the bars with you. If you do it thinking that you might wheedle a few extra secrets out of him, he'll see through it right away. If the two of you really do hit it off and want to spend more time together, that's fine too. But respect his privacy. The best thing to do, as a rule, is meet him for fishing every day and maybe buy him a dinner at the end of the trip. If you overimpose yourself on him, or get too chummy, you can get tired of each other or lose that barrier of professionalism that protects both of you. As long as the relationship is a professional one, the guide feels an obligation to do the very best job he can. Once you're buddies, some of those responsibilities lose their clarity.

Keep in mind also that the guide is doing this every day all summer. He isn't just doing this for a week and then falling into a hospital somewhere, and may not like a series of 18-hour days.

Tips on Tips

If you've had a good day and are satisfied with the trip, it's customary and expected that you will give the guide a tip. The tip money is what keeps the guide's car running. The regular fee is pretty much taken up in his expenses involved with the boat, licenses and insurance, and his labor.

Some fishermen will give the guide some flies, or a book, or some gift of that sort, which can be nice, but the guide can't eat those things. He needs cash. I've been given some gifts that I treasure, and that have lasted a lot longer than the cash I've been given, so I don't want to understate the importance of such gifts. But it's no secret that fly-fishing guides, especially the full-time ones, just barely scrape by most of the time. And buying him dinner is not a replacement for the tip. Most of the restaurants near western trout streams don't have anything on their menus that costs as much as a fair tip. Nowadays the average guide fee is $230 to $250 a day, and the average tip is 10 to 15 percent. If you take the guy out to dinner, then you still probably ought to give him $15 or $20 besides. Of course if you've had a great day, and he's done some spectacular work, then you shouldn't hesitate to give him more if you can afford it. The more people who do that, the more guides who will be aware of the likelihood of that extra incentive. He's obligated to do the very best he can, but it's just human nature to work harder when you know it's worth more.

Outfitters and Guides

These days more and more guides work independent of any shop. Some started out by working with a shop, then after they developed a clientele they went on their own, probably for the greater independence and to save themselves the outfitter's commission. If they're good, pretty soon they will be busy just from referrals, and many of these guides are excellent. I've spoken mostly about guides here as associated with shops, and I've done that because that is my experience and because that is the way most guides work. If you find an independent guide through referral, that's great too. For a lot of people, especially those who don't have access to many referrals, the shop is just the easiest way to go. An outfitter with several guides also has an advantage because some of them will be specialists and may be best able to give you the trip you want. But don't rule out the possibility that you may find a superb independent guide. You may even be referred to one by an outfitter who is all booked up; guides can often shift from outfitter to outfitter as needed.

One of the biggest advantages of the outfitter who has a number of guides is that at the end of the day that outfitter will talk to all of those guides—where did you go, what

Guides are happy to help with special interests you may have; many anglers and guides are serious photographers, and a good photograph is usually all the trophy you need.

did you catch, what flies did you use, and all the rest. The outfitter who has all that information coming in has the best chance of putting his clients in the right spots the next day. A guide who works for more than one outfitter may actually know very little about fishing an area because no outfitter is going to trust him with information that may be passed along to a competitor a few days later. The key here is loyalty; the guides who stick to one outfitter, or the guides who have their own independent operations, are the ones who have the best chance to stay informed. The drifter who moves from outfitter to outfitter, guiding here and there, may be so independent because no one really wants him too badly.

Most guides today are hired by outfitters as independent contractors. They are responsible for their own insurance and related business expenses. What they get from the outfitter is the connections with clients, access to the outfitter's network of information sources, and all the amenities of the shop, which are important to many clients.

Coming Back

Once you're acquainted with an outfitter and his guides, you may well want to return and use the same guide or guides again. That's just fine, and often the outfitter can arrange the schedules so that you can fish with the same man year after year. Sometimes clients and guides maintain a professional and yet very friendly relationship for many years, corresponding in the off season.

Fishing with a professional guide can be a rewarding and memorable experience, an important part of a western fishing trip. For a resident westerner, even for one who thinks he knows western fishing well, it can be a revelation. The professional fishing guide fishes more water, and sees more of an area's fishing possibilities, than even the most energetic "expert" outdoor writer. I'm convinced that everyone who is serious about fly fishing ought to try a guide at least once, and I'm sure there is no better way that the newcomer to an area or the person with limited time can get the most out of his fishing.

Chapter 16

Floating

ONE OF THE MOST EXCITING EXPERIENCES A WESTERN fly fisherman can have is to drift a good stretch of trout stream in a boat or raft. Whether you're dead-drifting big nymphs in the middle of the current, dropping a grasshopper imitation over still pools, or slamming big streamers into slick pocket water at the edge of the main current, drift fishing provides you with opportunities much different from those available to the wading or landbound fishermen.

I'm not saying that drifting is always better, though on many occasions it has great advantages as far as the number of fish you might see. Drifting is another, unusually exciting, way to enjoy western fly fishing.

Its big advantage is that it allows you to cover so much water. The wading fisherman who drives to a place on the river and starts to fish can make many casts to each good pocket. The drifting fishermen will make one cast to each of many good pockets. The drifting fisherman not only sees and fishes a lot more water, he exposes his fly to hundreds of times as many fish. That holds true whatever type of fly fishing he is doing that day. He won't get the fish that needs some coaxing, because he will only make a cast to each spot. But he will get a chance at a huge number of fish in the course of the day.

The other big advantage of drifting, and one that too few people appreciate, is that it lets you pick the best spots you see all day, in several miles of river, to stop and wade. Drift fishing shouldn't just be a long boat ride. It gives you the opportunity to stop now and then and fish areas that may be inaccessible from land. There are many miles of outstanding wade fishing on the most famous western rivers that can only be reached by floating to them, and stopping for some wading in a promising side-channel or along some isolated gravel bar is a great break from floating.

Drifting allows you to fish the river from a new perspective. You may drift through water you've often wade fished, and notice many pockets that you could reach, along the bank, where the brush was too thick for fishing from shore. You will fish water that only gets fished from boats, and you will get a whole new outlook on the river, no matter how well you know it. You're suddenly fishing the river from the middle rather than from the edges, and you'll be surprised at how the experience changes your understanding of a trout stream.

Rivercraft

Many people float western rivers in rafts, canoes, johnboats, and all manner of craft, but most serious fly-fishing guides use McKenzie driftboats. Each type of boat has its advantages, though, so I might mention a few of them here.

The four- to eight-man raft is light enough to load on and off the top of a big car or truck. It has an incredibly shallow draft so that you can get it into places you could not normally get a driftboat. It's comfortable and easy to get in and out of, and if it has a good rowing platform mounted on it, it is fairly maneuverable. It doesn't approach a driftboat in maneuverability, though; the entire underside of the raft is in contact with the water surface, and that's a lot of friction and resistance to overcome when you want to turn or hold in the current. You can't stand up in it, at least not long enough to fish safely.

The johnboat shares the raft's weight advantage; it's not that hard to load one on the top of a car or truck. It's a little more maneuverable than the raft, and perhaps a little easier to stand in, but again it does not approach the driftboat in those ways. Like the raft, it costs less than the driftboat.

Canoes are not used much for fly fishing western rivers. People occasionally use them on the rivers, and they can be very handy on small, relatively quiet streams, but most people who use them on big western rivers are either not fishing or are using the canoe to get to a good spot where they will get out and wade.

The driftboat, because of its unusual shape, has very little surface area in contact with the water compared to most boats. It is much easier for the guide to hold the boat in place in a good current, and also much easier for him to maneuver it here and there as needed, back and forth across the river to good fishing spots. It is stable, and has braces for the fishermen's legs so that they can stand and fish. Being able to stand in the boat is a great advantage, partly because you can cast better and see better, and partly because many people find it awkward and uncomfortable to cast sitting down all day.

A McKenzie driftboat provides two anglers with a stable platform for hours of comfortable casting.

This is not a chapter about how to handle a boat or a raft; it is about how to fish from such craft while the craft is being handled by someone else. There are some good books on boating and rafting for those who want to obtain their own boat. Because most guides use driftboats, I'm going to talk about float fishing in terms of fishing from a driftboat. You can easily enough adjust what I say here to suit the other watercraft.

Getting Set

Just getting into a driftboat is a challenge for some people, it doesn't need to be. Just because you see the guide performing various acrobatics climbing around the boat, don't feel you have to mimic him. He does it all the time.

The safest way to get in and out of the boat is with both legs at once. If you put one foot in, as soon as it hits the floorboards it's almost sure to start pushing the boat away from you, and there you stand doing a very poor imitation of a cheerleader doing the splits. Turn your back to the boat at the spot where you want to get in, sit down on the cross-braces that hold the seat, and scoot yourself into your seat, then swing your legs in. The same is true for getting out. Swing both your legs over the edge, drop them down, and ease into a standing position in the water or on the bank. Get in fanny first, get out feet first. Driftboats are remarkably stable, and though the boat may dip when you sit on it, it isn't going to go over. You could sit right there all day and it wouldn't go over.

Once in, get your gear organized, and get anything you don't really need stowed out of the way. The guide may have a waterproof container for things that should not get wet, such as clothing or cameras, though it's wise to bring your own camera container. If you are not familiar with boating, you will be surprised how anything in a boat can get wet even though there is no water to speak of in the boat. You track in water when you get in and out, your fly line will drag in water that in a few hours of rubbing against a coat can get it quite wet, and in other ways water seems to find its way to whatever you want to keep dry.

Two Fishermen or One?

If you are floating alone with the guide, you'll be in the bow, because that's the position in which the guide can most easily

manage your fishing. If there are two of you with the guide, one will be in either end. It's possible, but not really comfortable, for more than two to go with the guide in one boat, but one or two are normal, and only two can fly fish at once from the boat.

It always bothers people to be put in the back of the boat. There is no real disadvantage to being in the stern seat, though of course the two anglers can trade off during the day. The guide will handle the boat differently depending upon whether he has one or two clients that day. If he has one, for example, he will often drift with the bow angled in toward the bank; if he has two, he will just keep the boat parallel to the bank so both fishermen have as easy a time casting to shore. Where you sit isn't all that important as far as your fishing goes, though you may prefer to sit up front because you like the view better.

It isn't all that important where you sit because there is so much good water that each of you will often be hitting spots with your casts that the other didn't hit. If you're fishing a bank, you're moving along and pocket-shooting with the flies, and nobody is fast enough that they hit every pocket. The fisherman in the stern might occasionally watch to see where the fisherman in the bow has put his casts, so he can hit alternate spots. But it also pays to hit the same spot again; sometimes the first fly that goes into a little pocket only alerts the fish and is gone before it reacts. The second one gets the strike. The fisherman in the front should alert the other fisherman to any such spots where he thought he saw a fish turn at his fly; the second cast could be the one.

Line Management

There are two important rules to line management. The first is keep your line free of entanglements. Driftboats usually have a little shelf in front of the bow fisherman's legs, and that's a handy place to keep extra line, coiled loosely, to be shot if needed. Watch your line, and don't let it get tangled around things in the boat; the guide should be careful to keep his boat as clean as possible for that reason. The more oars, rods, thermoses, vests, and seat cushions near you, the more likely you are to tangle your line.

One advantage of floating is that you don't need to keep your vest on all day; you can lay it down somewhere, out of the way but handy, and just get flies and leaders as you need

DAVID KUMLIEN

Working the bank from a driftboat requires quick casts and accuracy, as well as an ability to lengthen or shorten casts almost reflexively.

them. For some of us, who like to carry a lot of gear in our vests, it's a real relief for the shoulders not to have that vest hanging on us for eight hours. But that means that the vest, with all its little zingers and clippers, is one more thing to catch a stray loop of fly line just when you wish it wouldn't, so stow it out of the way (and don't forget to put it back on when you get out of the boat to wade fish for a while).

The second important rule of line management involves casting. Always cast across the boat. Don't cast lengthwise of the boat or you'll risk hooking your companions. Greg, who has floated far more clients than I have, tells me that he has yet to be hooked by a client, but that clients do now and then hook each other, because the two fishermen are higher, on the ends of the boat, and he is low in the middle. The flies go over him and nail the other fisherman.

The guide will do all he can to keep the boat parallel to the shoreline or to whatever area is being fished, so that the fishermen can cast without risking harm to each other. If the boat is temporarily out of position, don't take a chance on a cast. Wait until it's safe.

Crossed lines are almost inevitable when two fishermen are casting at the same time. The one in the bow may see a spot he missed and cast back to it just as the one in the stern sees a spot he doesn't want to wait for and casts up to it. The one in the bow may see a spot way ahead and cast to it just as the one in stern sees a spot behind him and casts back to it, and their backcasts then may cross. Only vigilance and courtesy can keep these problems to a reasonable number.

Distances

One of the real surprises for the first-time drift fisherman is how close to the fish he can be. When fishing banks and ledges along shore, you may be only fifteen or twenty feet away, towering over the fish, and you'll see fish seem to abandon all caution to rush the fly. Only on rare occasions does drift fishing require real distance casting. Don't worry too much about the boat's shadow or shape spooking the trout. It probably isn't coming into their field of vision until after they've taken off after the fly, and even if it is, it doesn't seem to matter to them much. You will even see fish chase the fly right to the boat, or appear from the bottom of the river when the fly is right alongside the boat. There is nothing more exciting than the long follow, when a trout appears and hangs right on the tail of the fly as it swings out away from the bank, and you often have to suppress the urge to yank the fly away. Wait until you think the fish has it, then wait a little more.

Long-Drifting Flies

Driftboat fishing gives you the chance to do something most wade fishermen never get to do: fish a practically endless drift with no drag. If, for example, you're floating a river with many long productive riffles, like the Madison, you can cast your hopper or your nymph over the most likely part of the river and let it go for hundreds of feet, twitching it or working it now and then if you like. There is often no need for repeated casting; the goal is to keep the fly on or in the water as much as possible.

This works especially well, by the way, with large nymphs such as the stonefly imitations. With the help of a strike detector you can fish a lot of water with very few casts. It's an odd feeling for many people, because we're so conditioned to believing we have to cast a lot to keep the fly in the good water. Don't worry about that; if you can keep it in good water without casting, that's fine.

Fishing a Hatch

Fishing a hatch from a boat is different from fishing it while wading, of course, because you only get one or two shots at each rising fish you see. There's nothing to keep the guide from stopping to wade fish if you find a big stretch of river with many rising trout, but you can do just as well by moving along.

Dry flies can be fished very well as "prospectors," putting the fly into likely pockets using the same techniques I'll outline in the next section for big wet flies and streamers. But they can also be fished well from a boat over risers. This is a matter of looking ahead for the likely spots, finding the risers, and making the good cast when within range. You won't get to work any individual fish, of course, but you'll put the fly over many, and in situations where fish are rising throughout a long run, one cast will cover many fish until one takes it. This fishing requires no more casting accuracy than does dry-fly fishing while wading, but it often requires more speed;

Floating is a big experience that depends upon small details. As the bank hurries by, you'll see many spots like this—quiet, shaded little shelters where the overhanging willows and concentrations of insects attract good fish. You must get your fly back in there, and keep it there as long as you can.

you have to be ready to make the cast, and you have to make it quickly when the fish rises.

Big Flies Against the Bank

This is some of the most exciting and exacting drift fishing you can have. It is most often done early and late in the year, with large streamers, nymphs, and combination flies that defy traditional categorization (the Woolly Bugger, for example). Most rivers have miles and miles of good holding water right up against the bank or only a few feet out over a gravel bar. If you've never fished this kind of water, you may be amazed at how many fish there are so close to shore.

The guide will be your biggest help here, by showing you the kinds of spots where the fish hold. You're usually looking for small, quieter stretches of water right against the bank; there may be raging current only six inches out, and the fish are holding flat against the bank. When they see food, or something that excites them, they have to act fast and make their decision based on very little information— "Aha! It's big, it's wiggly, and I gotta get it before it's gone!" Quite often your fly will only be in the good water for a second or two before the faster current and the motion of the boat drag it away.

That makes fly control (and line control) very important. My son Greg describes this kind of fishing as a form of target shooting, and that's true; it's where the fisherman who is both quick and accurate has a real edge. If you think the spot behind that rock is a good one, stretch the rod out so that the fly holds in there just a little longer. Try to give the fly as much action as possible while it's in the good water; twitch it, jerk it, make it pause. Much of the time it will be all you can do to get it into the good spot in the first place, never mind making it act in a certain way, but there are lots of times when how you maneuver the fly will make the difference. Experiment. The guide should tell you what has been working best.

I will repeat one point I made earlier, though. I don't know why it's the case, though I assume it has to do with water clarity and sunlight, but you will often find that the fish prefer one type of big fly to another. One day White Zonkers may be best and they may ignore Yuk Bugs. Another day they may prefer Woolly Buggers. Again, you must experiment.

When you're fishing to these pockets, whether from the front or the back of the boat, try to hit the pocket before the boat drifts even with it. The fish are reluctant to take these big flies when they are dragging directly downstream. Occasionally you'll see a good fish turn and chase the fly, but you'll do better if you can keep from fishing on a downstream drag.

The pace of this fishing is sometimes very demanding, especially if you're fishing a stretch of river with lots of good holding water along the bank. You're fishing a heavier rod and a heavier fly, usually in the #6 to #2 range, and heavily weighted, and you're making an astonishing number of casts very fast, firing the fly into one pocket after another. At the same time, you're trying to check the good spots that are coming up (the guide will help here), and you're adjusting the length of the line as the bank moves closer and farther away (the guide will keep you within a reasonable distance, but cannot be expected to hold you constantly at the same distance from the shore all the time). The result is a nearly frenetic pace: fire the fly into that quiet pocket behind the willow, work it out, backcast, adjust the rod to put the fly in the hole behind that rock, shooting a little line because the boat has moved out a couple feet, watch for the snag, yank the fly back (was that a fish flashing under it? Can I put it in there again without interfering with the other caster?), making the forward cast before the line falls behind you. . . .

Some people don't like it, some do. I think it's great fun, and when the fish are hitting, or at least rolling after the fly a lot, two fishermen and a guide can make a lot of noise, yelling and whooping and cussing as they see the fish coming out after these fast big flies. It's a kind of fly fishing with more action than almost any other kind.

Of course nobody is requiring you to hit every spot, or even half of them. If you find it tiring, slow down, and just pick a good pocket now and then. If you need more time to get your distance right, or to spot the good water, take it. This is supposed to be fun, so fish as you like.

A special treat on a float trip: lunch along the stream.

Landing Fish

Driftboats are high, and a wildly flopping fish can often not be lifted by the leader. The guide will have a long-handled net, and in any situation where the fish or the leader is at risk the net should be used. As always, get the fish in as quickly as possible, not just for the fish's sake but for the fishing's sake; remember that as long as the guide is waiting for your fish so he can net it, he is unable to keep the boat in a good fishing position for the other fisherman. Obviously if it's a trophy fish, don't rush it too much, but the common tendency is to play the fish too long. The longer you play it the greater the risk that it won't survive when you release it, and in the boat you are not in a good position to revive it. You pretty much have to let it go as it is and hope for the best. If you've played it fast it will be fine. Just slip it back into the water (don't toss it over the side) .

The Well-Behaved Floater

Floating has increased in popularity in recent years maybe even more than fly fishing in general. Some rivers are getting pretty full, and people are rubbing up against each other more than ever before. As with all other fishing situations, the more of us there are, the more we must watch our manners.

Floating manners are just an extension of the manners discussed in Chapter 17. Give others as much room as you can. The guide has the biggest share of responsibility for this. He must see that his boat waits its turn in line to be launched, or to get out. He must keep the boat a proper distance from other boats and from waders, so that he and you do as little as possible to interfere with other fishermen.

For example, if you're passing some wading fishermen, pass them as far to one side as you can, to avoid crossing over their rising fish or in any way interfering with their casting. If you're about to start floating after beaching the boat, and you see another boat coming down the river, don't rush to jump out in front of it. Let it go by and start out leisurely after it.

There is only so much fishing a boat can do, and even if you follow right behind another boat, or several other boats, you're still likely to fish water they've missed. If you approach other fishermen, either wading or fishing from a boat, and it's at all narrow in the stream, stop fishing and get your lines out of the water. It never hurts to overdo courtesy a bit, and it may pay off in the fishing later, if they approach you in the same situation.

Remember, this is fishing. It's not competition, and it's not a test of your manhood. If you want to look for fights along the river, bad manners are a good way to find them. You and your companions will have a lot more fun if you just exercise a little common courtesy.

Conclusion

A few years ago, my son Greg took Paul and me for a day's float. He chose the lower Madison, the last fifteen or so miles above Three Forks, where the river joins the Gallatin and Jefferson to become the Missouri.

The day was a great object lesson in why everyone should try floating, especially with a good guide. Using big weighted flies and casting them directly against the bank, we turned more than 100 fish, hooking at least forty or fifty of them. The excitement of that kind of fishing is increased by having a great guide maneuvering you into position; it's the closest that fly fishing comes to true teamwork. Greg was constantly aware of who was about to be in position for a good cast to a likely spot, just as he was looking ahead to see if he should quickly take us to the other shore for some good water. As busy as that, he was still often the first to see a fish following one of our flies even though we were concentrating only on the flies! The opportunity to share that kind of knowledge of the river, to enjoy and benefit from a person who has floated, as Greg has, ten thousand or more miles just like this, is certainly as good a reason to try floating as is the fishing itself.

Chapter 17

Fishing Manners

USUALLY AT THE END OF A FISHING BOOK THERE WILL be a chapter or two on nontechnical parts of fishing. There are some such chapters at the end of this book. But here, while I'm talking about the tackle and the techniques, is where I should also introduce a subject that is as integral a part of your daily fishing as knowing how to cast. You may be an avid trout conservationist without having to be always conscious of conservation. But if you're going to be a good fisherman in the complete sense of the word, you can never stop thinking about how you deal with other fishermen.

There is a lot more to being a good fisherman than obeying the laws of the land and practicing conservation. There is something that used to be called "stream etiquette" but that could more practically just be called fishing manners.

As I've mentioned before, in the past thirty years we've seen a big growth in interest in fly fishing, especially among people with hefty incomes. They get enthusiastic, and they go out and buy all the right gear (and speaking as a successful tackle shop owner, I'm glad they do), and they take the sport very seriously. They would be horrified if someone told them that their manners stink, because a lot of them were raised in upperclass homes where you learned which fork to use as soon as you learned to sit at the table. They know they have good manners. But they forget that they had to learn them, and fishing is a whole new world to them. You don't buy manners when you buy your fly rod. You just have to learn them.

If you come from a more crowded part of the country, you may think nothing of standing a few feet apart, dozens of fishermen, all fishing the same little pool. The scale of things is different in the West, and you must be very conscious of the distances you keep between you and other fishermen. On some western waters, like the spring creeks, people can fish fairly close together because there are so many fish rising steadily that no one will have to move much anyway. But on most waters, you must give other fishermen lots of room. That is probably the most important general guideline: don't crowd. If someone else has the pool you want, and you think

maybe you can just squeeze in ahead of him, think again. How would you feel if you were in the pool and he did that? Always put yourself in the other guy's waders, and be honest with yourself—are you about to do something that will disturb his fishing?

It is extremely important to be on your best behavior on any private waters. Always ask permission, always leave gates as you find them, always avoid littering or making a fire. If you have to go too badly to wait until you get to a bathroom, don't make a mess in the trail or leave toilet paper spread all around. Don't try to "bribe" the landowner with a fifth of whiskey or any other gift. These landowners are more sophisticated than that, and you're going to offend them. Don't offer to catch a "mess of trout" for him! If he's letting you fish his property for free, there is probably nothing you can do to return the favor that will be as appreciated as plain good manners.

Specifically, never cut in front of someone who is fishing in an obvious direction, whether upstream or down. If a fisherman is working his way up a bank, for example, casting dry flies to a series of rising fish that are spread out along 30 feet of the bank, only a jerk will come in the water above him and start working a wet fly down to those same fish. Let him alone and find another place. The fish aren't that important.

Don't walk along the banks, or walk up to the bank, when a fisherman is obviously working fish in that area; you may put them down, and on many streams fish can be spooked from 100 feet away. Many of us have had the experience of carefully stalking to within casting distance of a rising fish only to have a carload of people pull up, send the kids out to "look at the river," and put down the fish. Fishermen do that to each other much too often. On many streams, especially those with undercut banks, your footsteps may be telegraphed to the fish as you walk along the bank. It's hard to overdo keeping a good distance between you and other fishermen.

Don't walk along the banks even if you don't see any other fishermen. Just because you aren't going to fish a pool

doesn't mean someone else won't come along in ten minutes and want to fish it.

Always give other fishermen more room than you think they need. There is nothing wrong with a little exaggerated courtesy, and remember that if you come to a possible conflict, or a situation where you really aren't sure how to handle some other fisherman's possible "rights," the best thing to do is ask him. "Where do you plan to fish, upstream or down?" "Will I be in your way if I go up there?"

The same thing is true even in congested waters, like the rush-hour conditions on the Henry's Fork. If you hook a big trout in close quarters, don't try to wade around among all the other fishermen, putting down their fish, just trying to land it. There is a type of angler who seems to be a sort of athlete, who likes to run up and down the river, kicking water all over, fighting a trout like it's a boxing match. Most of that is unnecessary if you handle the fish firmly, and unless it's a truly exceptional trout, it's more sporting to risk losing it than ruin everyone else's fishing.

There is the complicated matter of rotating pools. In some waters, local custom has established that when you have a pool and are fishing it, you stay until you want to leave or have to follow a trout downstream. In other waters, rotating is practiced. This is simply a matter of several anglers working their way through a pool, casting as they go, in a series, and as they finish casting at the lower end they can either leave or get back in line at the top of the pool. This is usually the case with very busy steelhead pools and some trout pools, where wet flies are being used. It rarely seems to be the case in pools usually fished with dry flies, where trout are visibly rising. The difference seems to be that an angler, once he starts to work on a rising fish, has certain sporting rights to try his best to take that fish however long he needs. In the rotation situations, the fish are often either sea-run or spawning-run fish, with no clear indication of any individual fish feeding, so the anglers are making their casts in a less specific manner.

Rotation or non-rotation are usually matters of local custom, and the best policy for the visitor is a "when in Rome" philosophy. If you see a line of fishermen, watch to see if they are fishing cooperatively before you just slosh in between them. And if you have any doubts, ask.

Though it still happens, most of the time you won't have the West's beautiful trout streams to yourself. How generously you share the water says a lot about you as a sportsman, and will make all the difference in the kind of day you have.

Bud Lilly's Guide to Fly Fishing the New West

Chapter 18

Releasing Fish

THIS SUBJECT ALSO TENDS TO GET BURIED IN THE BACK of most fishing books, but it's too important to put there. This the way to keep the total experience total, and I am continually surprised at how many people still don't understand the sense of releasing fish. Some believe the fish will all die, others just refuse to stop thinking of wild trout as something they have some "right" to eat. We know from a huge number of studies that the fish aren't going to die, at least not very many of them. And we know from history that a lot of things we once thought of as rights turned out to be wrongs.

With barbless hooks it is often possible to release the fish with very little handling; just make sure the fish has revived enough to swim under its own power before setting it free.

PAUL SCHULLERY

A sixteen-inch brown being released. Handle them gently and as little as possible, and make sure they can navigate and orient themselves before you let them go.

One of the unfortunate side effects of the movement to increase catch-and-release regulations is that many baitfishermen feel that they are being discriminated against by other kinds of fishermen who seem to think they're better somehow. I don't deny that too many fly fishermen think they're something special, but the fundamental objection to baitfishing, at least among managers who are trying to maintain wild-trout populations, is that you simply can't release enough baitfish-caught fish that will live. There have been many studies done that demonstrate beyond any doubt what fly fishermen have known for a long time: the majority of fish caught on bait will swallow it so deeply that you will kill them just getting the hook out. You can't maintain a strong wild-trout population when you kill half the fish just releasing them. Flies and lures with only one hook or group of hooks typically kill less than ten percent, often less than five percent, in the many studies done.

In Yellowstone Park, in the famous catch-and-release water between Canyon and Fishing Bridge (many writers call this whole area Buffalo Ford, which is actually only one spe-

cific part of the river), a healthy wild-trout population, cutthroats, is maintained in a river so heavily fished that each trout in the river is typically caught several times a season.

How to Do It

Releasing your fish in good condition is something you start working on even before you hook it. Many fishermen use barbless hooks, and though there is no scientific evidence yet that barbless hooks reduce the average hooking mortality of trout, they are easier to get out of a fish. You aren't doing the fish any favors if you use extremely light tackle, and you aren't really increasing your sport. If you can't handle the fish, and if you have to play it for such a long time that it is nearly dead before your tackle will bring it in, you're not helping the fish or the fishing.

Once a fish is hooked, play it as fast as you can. Tire it as quickly as you can, and get it to the net. Don't think that it's good sport to coax "one more jump" out of a trout. Get it in fast, even at the risk of losing it. Better that it gets away than that you exhaust it just to release a dying trout.

Bud Lilly's Guide to Fly Fishing the New West

Once in, handle it as little as possible. Much of the time, it is possible to release a trout without even touching it, certainly without even taking it from the water. Many lip-hooked fish can be freed simply by sliding your hand down the leader, grasping the hook shank, and twisting it out. If you must take the fish from the water, don't squeeze it. Many fish will become immobile if you hold them upside down. Often they are easily handled if you hold them, still in the water, against your waders.

Studies have also shown that trout that are heat stressed, that is trout who are just getting by in a midsummer stream that is at its warmest, are far easier to kill by accident. They don't have the same reserves of energy as they would in cooler water, and must be handled with extreme care.

Once free of the hook, the fish may need reviving. Hold it in a gentle current until its gills are working slowly and regularly and it is able to slip from your grasp. We've all seen fishermen loft their trout back into the water with a grand gesture, tossing it 20 feet out into the river. That may make the fisherman feel good, but it kills a lot of trout. Be gentle, and be quick.

The New Ethic of Trout Fishing

I hope to see more and more waters in the West regulated in a way that will allow the fish population to remain robust while providing a lot of sport. That may mean catch-and-release, or it may mean some other form of special regulations, but as I already pointed out, it will usually mean the elimination of bait fishing, which simply kills too many fish to be permitted in a wild-trout fishery.

The big thrill for the modern angler is catching, not eating. It's like golf: you don't have to eat the balls to have fun. I know that many people still enjoy killing and eating trout, and there is nothing wrong with that in moderation. Many of our streams will probably always be able to sustain a certain harvest. I also know that bait fishing is one of the longest established sporting traditions in this country, and that there are some people for whom it is the only way to fish. We will always have to have some bait fishing. But times must change. I'm proud of my education as a Montana sportsman, which started out with bait fishing as much as it did with fly fishing. But I learned that it is no longer possible to fish the way I did fifty or even thirty years ago. I used to kill as many fish as any other fisherman, probably more because I was pretty good at catching

them. I hardly ever kill one any more, because I know that the fishing experience is in greater demand now, and we have to share this resource among a growing number of people.

It looks to me as if here in Montana more and more people are switching to fly fishing. The ranks of the bait fishermen are being thinned. There are still plenty of places where bait fishing is popular, and there is comparatively little water even now where bait fishing is prohibited. Bait fishermen do not yet have much to complain about.

But I'm not sure I believe that bait fishing is essential in modern sport fishing. I've heard all the traditional arguments like, "Here's old Joe, he's eighty, and he can't get around," or, "Here's little Johnny, he's only four," and these people have to fish with bait. If the fishing is well managed so that there are plenty of fish, those same people can take fish on artificial lures. Spinning rods and fly rods don't cost any more than casting rods, and anyone with even a little coordination, such as almost all eighty-year-olds and four-year-olds certainly have, can learn to cast those outfits. "Well," they say, "old Joe just wants to sit there with his line in the water. You can't do that with flies or spoons or spinners." And that's true, but I don't think that old Joe has to worry for a long time about not finding a place to do that. If I were pushed to the wire, I guess I'd say let's keep some places where old Joe can bait fish. Even Yellowstone Park has reserved some streams for kids to bait fish. But if we manage the water correctly, we can greatly reduce the need for that kind of fishing by making good fishing so common that fewer and fewer people will even want to use bait.

But let's be honest about this. Those very old and very young fishermen are always trotted out to defend bait fishing, but the people doing the justifying are healthy, adult fishermen who are really just using those small, special groups to defend their own preference for bait fishing. Even if we have to take care of the needs of some special groups, that doesn't justify bait fishing by the rest of the people. We can find good fishing places for old Joe, and we can teach little Johnny how to spin fish or fly fish by the time he's six or seven. We shouldn't confuse our desire to protect the needs of these special cases with our greater need to maintain good sport fisheries, and we shouldn't sacrifice the opportunities to develop those good sport fisheries out of some misplaced sense of loyalty to a tiny minority of the fishermen who may need special attention.

Western Waters, Western Seasons

Chapter 19

Big Rivers

SOME OF OUR BEST RIVERS ARE GETTING BETTER THESE days, and that's great news, because many of the big rivers, whether the Kootenai or the Missouri, have fantastic potential. If they're cleaned up and better managed, they just get better, and they can support not only great numbers of fish but huge fish. But they need more help from fishermen, because in some states fishermen aren't even aware of how great those big rivers once were. The fishing deteriorated before any living fishermen were born.

If most of your fishing is done in smaller streams, your first sight of a big western stream may be pretty discouraging. Where do you start? Even if you are used to fishing the bigger

Even on big rivers, think twice before wading out toward what seem to be the good spots.
The Madison, often described as an "endless riffle," will hold good fish in surprisingly small places even close to shore.

ROY BISSELL

Here's a stretch of the Madison with a completely different character: slow, smooth currents over thick weeds and open sandy bottom. Before approaching it closely or casting, study the possibilities. Is the water deep or undercut along the banks? Which of those breaks and other disturbances in the surface indicate submerged weed beds or rocks? Can you see how deep the channels are between the weeds?

"Madison River Stonefly Freak" by Dave Whitlock

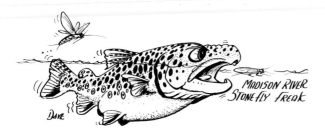

rivers in the East, such as the Delaware, the geography of western trout waters is going to throw you some curves. A lot of the trout savvy that you've learned elsewhere can be just as helpful here, but some of what you've come to think of as surefire just won't apply.

As you stand and look at a big river, especially a big deep one like the Yellowstone or the Missouri, keep in mind that you will not be fishing most of that water. A river 200 feet wide and eight feet deep only has fish in certain places because only certain places have fish food. A lot of this chapter will be devoted to suggesting where to find the fish.

Big powerful rivers are intimidating to many visiting anglers. The trick is to take them apart in your mind and only fish the parts that need fishing.

water within 50 feet. It's easy to find water farther away that looks good, and go ahead and fish it, but you usually will have plenty of good water within reach, and the far-off water only looks good because it's far-off, like the greener grass that's on the other side of the hill.

There's a common opinion out there that long casting is just showboating because it's difficult to actually hook a fish with most of your line on the water. That opinion has been disproved countless times. Lefty Kreh has said that the really good caster can hook a fish no matter how long his cast, but I do think that on a big, fast river, with lots of current variation between you and the fish, it is harder to control the line and thus manage the fly on really long casts. As you get out toward the edge of your ability to cast, you also get close to the limitations of your ability to handle the line or even set the hook (Lefty, on the other hand, is famous for his ability to hook fish so far away that they spoil by the time he gets them in).

The best way to approach a big river for fishing is to break it into small parts. Often the places that I like to fish are side channels, which have the feel of small streams or even spring creeks. Stream ecologists say that trout often will be found in the shallow water and along the edges, where the sun has its effects on insect activity and there is shelter from predators and the faster currents. When you walk up to a really big river, don't even think about all that water that is over your head in depth and that you can't reach anyway. Think of the narrow band along the shore as a small stream; you'll be surprised how it will change your outlook when you suddenly stop worrying about what might be out there beyond your reach. The "little stream" along the shore is all you're concerned about at that point.

Think of it this way. Big rivers don't necessarily demand long casts. When you see all that water, something inside just aches to cast clear to the other side. Most of the places you'll fish on a big river like the Yellowstone or the Missouri, you're probably going to be working good

Fishing over this five-foot vertical cutbank put the angler so high above the water that silhouette is a problem; keep low and out of sight, especially on bright days.

PAUL SCHULLERY

Chapter 20

Small Streams

EXCEPT FOR SPRING creeks, which are famous for reasons of their own no matter what part of the country they're in, you don't hear all that much about small western streams. All the fame and good press goes to the medium and large waters. But the West is criss-crossed with little rivers. Many of them are along or near back roads, and many of them are less accessible. They're on private land, where you have to get permission or even pay a fee to fish them.

If you've fished all your life, you probably remember fishing some local trout stream that supported some trout no matter how abused it was. Small stream experience may be the most transferrable from other regions to the West. Little creeks and brooks from three to thirty feet across are pretty much the same in how they hold trout and how you fish them, whether you're in the Blue Ridge or the Rockies. These freestone waters have an abundance of pocket water, with fast little fish holding behind the bigger rocks and under the logs. They're great fun, and they're perfect classrooms for beginners.

Approach is everything in these boulder-strewn streams, and my first advice is to stay out of the water whenever possible. Not long ago I was in a fly shop here in Bozeman when two visiting fishermen were talking about wading. One of them said, "We've been coming out here from New Jersey, and the first few years we busted our asses trying to wade out

Narrow, brushy streams often provide the fisherman with concealment for approaching closely, at the same time that they make backcasts and line control a miserable job.

PAUL SCHULLERY

in the middle of the river, then we hire a guide to take us fishing in a boat and he drifts fifteen feet out from the bank the whole day, telling us to cast into the bank."

The heroic image of the western angler has him standing on his tiptoes in five feet of rushing stream. As I suggested earlier, I am more and more inclined to just wear hip waders whenever possible, and that isn't just because I'm not as anxious to wade deep as I was 30 years ago. It's also because I've learned that very often you can wade right through the best water, right near shore, getting into what feels like a comfortable spot to fish. Do a minimum of wading at all times, and in small streams try not to get into the water at all.

Try first to see if you can handle each fishing situation from shore. Being in the water, besides getting you closer to some fish, will lower your silhouette and decrease the chance of spooking the fish, but a lot of the time you don't need to get in the water at all. You don't have to be up to your eyeballs to be in the right place, and the fish aren't impressed just because you can stand up in a torrent.

You aren't doing other fishermen any favors, either, by wading through the middle of a pool and putting down the fish. If you must wade, do so, but do it discreetly, and in still water, or in situations like those that prevail on most spring creeks, wade very quietly.

Never assume you have to be in the water to be fishing properly. Most stretches of small stream can be fished well from the bank, with a lot less disturbance to the trout and the stream bed.

MARSHA KARLE

right behind it, but kind of tucked up against its downstream side, because that's where the surface of the current gathers into the tightest channel and concentrates the most food, and the fish will hold right beside that fast water, in the slower water against the rock, and come out to feed. You'll not have to think all that out when you see it; you'll just recognize it as a good spot and cast to it.

Fishing small freestone streams is pretty much exploratory like that. If you don't learn to pick the good spots, you'll waste a lot of time and fish a lot of dead water. At the same time, you may spend the rest of your life trying to figure out the finer details. For example, you'll come to recognize long "slicks" of quiet water behind rocks. Sometimes the water is quieter behind the rock for ten feet or more, even in a fairly small, shallow stream. You may cast to a thousand of these spots, mending line so the fly rests in that quiet water as long as possible, and never learn to predict whether the fish will be at the head of the slick, in the middle, or at the tail. There is too much else going on, especially with the contours of the bottom of the stream but also with the current along the edges of the slick, for you to be able to figure it all out for sure. But then, who would want to know everything for sure?

You have to learn that in these rough little streams the fish don't feed in the textbook manner. You might hike miles of a little stream and never see a rise. These fish are opportunists; ten bugs might go by in an hour, each one different (there are stretches of big rivers, like the Madison, that are like this, too; they may be rising but you can't even see them, and most of the time they're not coming up regularly). I've seen a number of smaller western streams where the native cutthroats don't display any devotion to Old World ideas of how trout rise. This isn't some liesurely business for them, with dainty, slow-motion rises to a smooth surface. This is a wild burst of action, followed by no evidence at all.

So most of your fishing is being done blind, which means you have to recognize the good water. You can't see the fish, and you can't see the insects, so you have to read the water. Whole books have been written about reading the water, and I'm not sure even a whole book could get the full idea across. You start by looking for depth and cover where there's a moderate flow, but beyond that it's almost impossible to predict where the fish will be. Like so many other elements of fishing, you'll develop a sense of it through experience. You'll look at a stretch of water and somehow you'll know that the fish is most likely to be near that big rock; probably not

Large stream or small, stay back from the bank whenever you can; biologist John Varley, director of the Yellowstone Center for Resources, fishing a tributary of the Gibbon in Yellowstone Park.

PAUL SCHULLERY

Chapter 21

Spring Creeks

THERE ARE A LOT OF SMALL, PRIVATELY OWNED spring creeks within an hour of my home in Bozeman. A few have some kind of public access, either through a tackle shop or by asking permission of the owner. One day in late June, Paul and I fished one of the latter, a creek that I'd known about for sixty years or so. Unless you lived here as long as I have, chances are you haven't heard of this one. It's never been written about, though it's as good as the famous ones.

It was a perfect day for a difficult spring creek. Late June is a good time for hatches, the sky was cloudy and threatening rain, and a friend had fished it only a few days earlier and done very well.

But the fishing was literally impossible. The trout, which we could see from distant slopes, were so jumpy that we couldn't even approach the bank, much less enter the water,

without sending wakes of spooked trout in all directions. Neither of us is new to spring-creek fishing; we usually manage to catch some. But this day there was no amount of crawling and sneaking and sidearm casting that would let either of us get within casting distance of a trout. The fish were unreachable. The next day, who knows? Maybe they were catchable again.

Spring creeks are referred to as the Ph.D. fishing of the West. They should be equally famous, but are not, as priceless little aquatic ecosystems that bring a startling variety of life to otherwise sparsely occupied landscapes. The spring creek experience is not as easy or inexpensive to have as the public fishing experience in the West, but it is something that every serious fly fisherman should try now and then, if only to broaden his perspective and keep him humble.

*This angler faces one of spring-creek fishing's
most challenging situations: the slow tricky currents have woven themselves through
a complex tangle of brush, roots, and snags along the left bank, and the trout are rising eagerly in the middle of the mess.*

Montana angler Jan Aiuppy setting the hook in a good spring-creek trout.

Flies and Hatches: A Practical Approach

Spring creeks have gotten a great deal of attention in the fishing magazines and books in the past 25 years. Relatively little was said about them before that, though a few people had known and enjoyed them for many years. I suspect that even yet they get a disproportionate amount of attention in print when you consider how few people ever actually fish them.

One important reason for this imbalance is that they have inspired so much in the way of fly-pattern theory. They are the western equivalent to a few famous eastern streams, like the Letort in Pennsylvania, that very few people fish, really, but that offer such special and unusual challenges that fly fishing makes some of its most interesting advances on them. The spring creeks are the special pets of the hatch-matchers, and they have slowly yielded many of their secrets over the years, though even yet nobody strings up a rod at one with absolute certainty that he will catch fish that day.

There are many beautiful new patterns of flies now available for these creeks, and each tackle shop near one, whether near my home here in Bozeman, or down in Idaho or Wyoming, or anywhere else, will have the latest fashions in spring-creek flies for you to try, or will have interesting ideas for how you might develop your own patterns. The Swisher-Richards no-hackles are quite popular for the quietest waters, as are small Comparadun-type flies. Someone is always cooking up a new poly-wing spinner or super-realistic beetle.

But as with other western trout fishing, the staple fly patterns, the long established ones, will still do well much of the time. The Adams is still one of the best all-around small fly imitations in sizes #18-22. The Light Cahill still does good work imitating a variety of little mayfly duns commonly called "sulfurs." The other established fly patterns listed in Chapter 12 all have their place. They may not always work, but nothing always works, and these patterns are a good start for a spring-creek selection, and most of the time they will be good enough.

Some of my favorite fishing on spring creeks has been during the hopper season. Not only are most of the spring creeks bordered by meadows full of hoppers, but there is also something almost breathtaking in the way a big trout will take a hopper in these quiet little streams.

But these creeks are specialized little ecosystems, and have their own unique little insect assortment. You can't beat local advice, usually from a guide or shop, about unusual local patterns.

Other Tackle

These streams often demand the lightest line you can throw. But they also demand at least some distance casting, and they often have shoulder-high banks along them. Use a long rod, a nine-footer or longer, and a four- or five-weight line. If you can handle the lighter outfits, the threes, two, and even ones, give them a try. The long rod is important; not only will it help keep your fly out of the weeds when you're standing in the

Chasing a good trout upstream in a winding spring creek makes up in excitement for what it lacks in dignity. Michigan angler Steve Schullery on a Gallatin Valley spring creek.

stream, you will also find it easier to cast while on your knees in the grass. Also, don't be afraid to wade, or at least approach a rising fish, on your knees.

If you know your casts are going to be short, and that there aren't many obstructions behind you on a certain creek, go ahead and use a shorter rod. The light, small tackle makes a 15-inch rainbow feel like a five-pounder.

You hear a lot of talk about long leaders being required on spring creeks, unusually long ones up to 24 feet. First, such absurdly long leaders really aren't necessary, and second, with the high winds in this part of the country, they can make life miserable. I use a 12-foot leader when I can, under ideal conditions, but frequently use 7 1/2- to 9-foot ones even on spring creeks. Being able to put the fly over the fish at all is better than being able to brag that you used an 18-foot leader but the wind was just too bad for you to make good casts.

The Long Season

Though the spring creeks, especially the famous ones, get booked up through the busy summer months, they often provide excellent fishing earlier and later in the year. I'll say more about this in a later chapter, but don't forget the spring creeks if you're here in the so-called "off season." The fishing may not be "off" at all, and they usually charge less on the creeks.

Access

The most challenging aspect of fishing spring creeks is not flies, or leaders, or any other technique problem. It's getting on the creek in the first place. The few that are famous are the exceptions. Armstrong and Nelson's, in the Yellowstone Valley, or Silver Creek, in Idaho, are busy places because they are among the few that anyone with the time and money can fish. There are dozens of others. There are more than sixty in Montana, there are some good ones on Indian lands in Idaho, there are some superb cutthroat trout streams in Jackson

Hole, but most of them are at best questionable of access.

The state of Montana has done some important work in improving public access. Poindexter Slough, in western Montana, and Darlington Ditch (unlikely name for a great stream, isn't it?—the ditch isn't a true spring creek, but for fishing purposes it acts like one), near Manhattan, Montana, are both public streams with excellent fishing.

But most are still private, many are tragically degraded, and many have landowners who for one reason or another dislike fishermen. If you live near them, you can gradually get to know these people and their streams, and through local knowledge can discover some wonderful fishing. If you are visiting from some other part of the country, you will be best off if you work through some outfitter who can help you get on the creeks.

Access is a growing issue in the West, one I'll discuss at greater length in a later chapter. In Montana, legislative debates have stirred up rage and resentment among many landowners. As of now, the law gives anglers the right to fish almost any stream as long as they stay in the stream bed, and that may seem like a real victory for the fishermen, but it has hardened the hearts of many landowners who, if they had been treated with a little respect, might have actually been willing to open their gates and work with the sportsmen so that everyone benefitted.

The Future of the Creeks

It's not my intention to mix conservation sermons with fishing instructions throughout this book, but the spring creeks are too important, and too much in need of help, for me to pass up any opportunity to alert people to their needs.

In January of 1986 the American Fisheries Society, in cooperation with the Montana Department of Fish, Wildlife and Parks, published "An Inventory of the Spring Creeks in Montana," a summary of conditions and characteristics of 68 different creeks in the state. It was written by Janet Decker-

Hess, a researcher from Helena, and it is both exciting and disheartening.

It is exciting because it shows the amazing number of creeks in just this one western state; Wyoming, Idaho, and Colorado all have their own.

It is disheartening because of the sad condition of so many of these wonderful little streams. The author summarized the long list of problems in her "abstract":

> Major land use activities along the creeks were generally agriculturally related, including cattle grazing and hay production. Waters from the creeks have been diverted for irrigation and augmented by river flows. In general, Montana's spring creeks are being severely abused and their fishery potential is currently not being met.

Anyone who has ever seen one of these creeks when it is in good condition and providing the finest trout fishing to be had in the world will know how shameful it is that we have let dozens of them get into such bad shape.

The spring creeks are one of the last and most important undeveloped fishery resources in the West, and in the future there is going to be more and more attention paid to them by management agencies and private landowners. Their economic value is becoming recognized and is increasing steadily. A lot of ranchers still don't have much idea of just what the economic potential of that old creek on their property (the one their cows are this minute sloshing around in) might be. It would be most helpful if the state had a program much like a soil conservation service, where some agent could go to the owners of the waters and give them a little help and direction. With very little investment, a lot of the creek owners could make $20,000 to $30,000 a year. If they worked out a cooperative arrangement with some local outfitters or tackle shops, they could avoid practically all the nuisance of having fishermen come to the door; just put up a sign telling who to call for access.

Another possibility for improving the creeks would be the establishment of a state-wide use fee that provided money to the state to undertake research and restoration work and that in some form compensated landowners for sharing the creek, as well as rewarding them when they improved the creek's condition.

Whatever we do, and I think we will end up going several directions at once, with some creeks becoming public and some being managed privately for fee-fishing, we must do more to protect and enhance these creeks. They are a national treasure.

The past few years, Paul and I have been fortunate to watch the restoration of a fabulous small spring creek in the Gallatin River drainage. The new owner has taken a beaten-down watershed and through wise planning and the construction of dozens of log-enforced pools has created one of the best fisheries in this part of the West. I've seen fish as large as 26 inches come from it, thanks to this intelligent management. As we've fished that water over the past few years, each time it seems more exciting and more healed up. It's exciting to think of all the additional stream mileage all over Montana and other western states just waiting to be brought back to life, so it can fill with wild trout and support all the other wildlife that flock to such a wonderful setting.

Maine angler David Ledlie showing that the smallest spring creeks can hold good trout.

PAUL SCHULLERY

Chapter 22

Still Waters

IT SEEMED TO ME IN THOSE EARLY YEARS AS AN OUT-fitter that some of my best triumphs as a guide were the ones I didn't deserve. When I was still new to guiding, a client insisted that I take him fishing on Hebgen Lake. Now, the routine ways to find fish in a lake are well known; springholes, inlets and outlets of creeks, weed beds, and so on are all things a guide should look for. But this trip taught me about another one of nature's subtle signposts, the shoreline tire track.

We were trolling, not my idea of exciting fishing, but this man was a good friend and his mind was made up; Bud was going to take him fishing on the lake. When I finally got the motor started and we headed out, we worked along the shoreline until finally we started to catch fish. It seemed like a real hot spot, so I circled around back through the area a few times, and we caught fish each time. My client was really impressed, and I'm sure that part of my early reputation rested on just this sort of luck. What I noticed as we circled in the second time was that the bank was covered with tire tracks. The hatchery truck must have just left, and those poor rainbows were still bunched up trying to figure out where they were. My client didn't seem to notice that the fish were all exactly the same size.

Some years ago I had a customer who spent his summers here in southwestern Montana on the shore of Hebgen Lake. At that time most of the fish being caught were taken by people using huge Flatfish, Rappalas, and other fish-imitating lures. My friend was the studious type, and he couldn't help noticing (as I'm sure other people did) that the fish spent most of their time feeding not on smaller fish but on insects. So he spent some of his time for years collecting insects and having them identified, with the result that eventually he had found over 80 kinds of insects that fish ate in that lake.

It will be no surprise to the modern fly fisherman that a lake is a rich ecosystem, but this story has two points. One is that the variety of food in lakes can be very large. The other is that fly fishermen, in America at least, have devoted relatively little of their attention in recent years to the study of still waters. There are many dozens of articles, and dozens of books, written about trout fishing in streams for every one article or book on trout fishing in lakes.

I share the average fly fisherman's enthusiasm for moving water. I've fished a lot of lakes and ponds over the years, but they don't yet attract me the way a stream does. This is a personal preference, and we all have those and should be honest about them. But I would like to interest you in the western trout lakes. There are many reasons, most having to do with the pleasure of the experience of fishing these waters whether you catch many fish or not, but the reason that will probably be most persuasive is that it is here, in these lakes, that you have your best chance of catching a really large trout. Lakes grow them big.

In the West, where we have so many miles of good trout streams, lakes have often been the poor sisters in fisheries management. Many here in Montana were for many years just big holes full of water where any sort of trout might be dumped for the public to come and pull out. There wasn't much long-range thought in the process, and it did satisfy a lot of people, or at least allow them to catch some fish. Unfortunately, it also led to the introduction of some inappropriate non-native species, whose presence pretty much assures that they'll never become good trout fisheries again.

More recently, as sportsmen and managers have had to reconsider traditional approaches to managing streams, lakes have begun to benefit from that process. Now a lake may get some study before the tank trucks pull up. But we have a long way to go before lakes become first-class citizens in our public fishing domain. A whole new world of experimentation with special regulations, with getting the right fish into the right lakes, and with appreciating the non-fishing recreational values of lakes, lies before us. I'm confident that in Montana, at least, things are going to get better and better for the fly fisherman who wants to fish still waters.

The West has an amazing variety of still waters, from small glacial lakes at over 10,000 feet elevation to huge, canyon-filling reservoirs with bass as well as trout. But what has always struck me about lakes isn't so much their geographical variety as the variety of approaches they have inspired in fly fishermen.

Hebgen Lake, for example, is famous for its "gulper fishing," usually done from a float tube with small dry flies. Not far south, Henry's Lake is hardly fished with dry flies at all. For years, locals believed that it was actually impossible to catch fish there on a dry fly. Even yet the process of fly selection on Henry's Lake is an almost mystical business. People used to come in to the shop and ask what they should use on Henry's Lake, and I'd say, "Well, bring in your fly box and we'll go through it, and whatever pattern that you only have one of, that's the one that will work."

I've mentioned this mystery of the Henry's Lake fly patterns before. There was a period years ago when many of the Henry's Lake fly fishermen had a pretty stiff competition going to come up with a fly pattern that would work. I know this sounds almost silly now, but these people caught a lot of fish by this method, which was really nothing more than random experimentation. The flies were nearly bizarre. Someone would come up with a brown Woolly Worm with green and yellow hackles, or a yellow eye, or something else. That would be red hot for two or three days, really successful. Then someone would come up with something equally strange.

The point of all this is that lake-fishing requires more attention to specific types of flies. The general patterns that you can take out and slap down on the Madison with some hope of catching fish just won't be much good on lakes. The fish are feeding on something they are searching out, perhaps a hatch of damselflies, or some abundant mayfly. It has been my experience that hatch-matching is often more important on lakes than on streams.

This means more than finding a fly that looks right. In still water you have a lot of responsibility to duplicate the fly's action in ways you don't often have in a stream. Henry's Lake in Idaho was a great classroom for me in the importance of the right action. You had to experiment with retrieval speed, fly depth, and motion of the fly (jerky, smooth, irregular?) on the retrieve.

High Country

One of the most distinctive types of fishing in the Rockies is that provided by the high-mountain lakes. By high, I'm referring mostly to the small pocket lakes above about 8,000 feet, the lakes in country that doesn't see snowmelt until late June at the earliest.

These lakes, which are scattered over the western mountains by the thousands, are rarely large enough to be known individually outside their immediate area. They are usually fished only by a few hardy souls willing not only to hike several miles but to climb a few thousand feet in elevation. Because they are so small, and because you'll rarely see one specific one written up in a book or magazine, they aren't as easy for the newcomer to learn about as are the bigger, more popular waters. But they're worth the effort, and in recent years the alpine lake fishing in some parts of the West has

been the subject of locally-produced books and guides. The state of Montana, for example, has produced a nice guide and map to the many small lakes in the Beartooth region northeast of Yellowstone Park. The Beartooth has one of the premier concentrations of small high lakes anywhere in the west. One of my guides one summer, Dick Hatfield, was a real enthusiast of that area, and he catalogued those lakes for the Forest Service, who then produced the published guide.

The stereotype of the small mountain lake is only a few acres in size, and its fish are small. The growing season is short, and insect life is often sparse. Many of them have no natural reproduction; they have been stocked by pack-train or plane, and the fish grow as large as they can, live their lives, and die.

But the stereotype is not always accurate. Some of them hold very large fish, perhaps only a few, but fish that would be considered trophies by any standard. They do not keep these big fish by being well known, and even one careless person can ruin a good fishery of this type by spreading the word to people who don't release their fish. I know of a number of small lakes with very big trout in them, and I wouldn't dream of writing about them.

There is another stereotype that is not accurate, and that is the belief that wilderness fishing is always easy fishing. The fish in these small high lakes can seem impossible to catch. Whether it is because they can see the angler so easily, or because their feeding is often limited to just a few species of insects, or for some combination of reasons, they can be so choosy that you'd swear they'd just been flown in from the Henry's Fork. This is true of the golden trout and the grayling, though maybe less true of brook trout.

I know I've said it before, but it must be reinforced: get local information. These high-country lakes are especially vulnerable to environmental changes, and one that your buddy visited two years ago and had a great time may be without fish today. Nowhere is advance homework more essential than in planning a trip to some high-country lakes (try not to make your whole trip depend upon one; try to visit two or three so that your odds of finding at least one good one are increased). Contact the relevant state fish and game department about stocking records, check with local shops, and read up on anything else you can find. Or, turn yourself over to a guide who knows the high country and can be sure of giving you a good chance at some decent fishing.

Many of the small high-country ponds are suprisingly deep; they're in little pockets carved by glacial action or some cleft in volcanic rocks, and the fish are swimming around at the bottom, well out of reach. One of the most innovative high-lake fisherman I know, Ernie Strumm has developed a technique that is sort of like baitfishing with a fly and fly rod. Using a 10-foot level leader of four-pound test, he'll cast well out into such a pond with a sinking line, and just put the rod down and wait. He may stand there ten or fifteen minutes before he gets a strike, while that fly on the light leader very slowly swims down into the deep water. But he catches a lot of fish that way.

One of the important lessons here may not be that you have to fish deep, but that you should experiment with a fly that is sitting still or slowly sinking. I know it may feel a little too much like bait fishing, but remember that not all insects in a pond are constantly moving. They spend a lot of time just hanging around in one spot, and fish don't necessarily require a fly to be going somewhere to be attracted to it.

When you fish these little ponds, you will do well to always keep in mind that life is hard at high elevation. That reality shapes everything to do with the fishing. Often there isn't much aquatic life in the pond itself, so fish rely more on terrestrial insects that are blown into the water by the incessant winds. Be grateful for those winds, and watch their direction. On lakes of all sizes, fishing is often more productive along the shore toward which the wind is blowing because it pushes all kinds of floating debris, including insects, that way and concentrates them there. On the other hand, in a small high-mountain pond, it may be that the food concentration is best right along the windward shore, because that may be where the most terrestrial insects land when they are blown into the water. And just to make it more complicated, Gary LaFontaine has recently pointed out that the sheer topography of some mountain ranges creates vertical winds of great force that may carry insects thousands of feet straight up before releasing them to rain back down on land and water.

Even the aquatic insects reflect this harsh environment. There isn't enough food in the little lakes to grow the larger mayflies and other juicy bugs you will find in most lower-elevation waters. Expect small insects, though don't be surprised if they emerge in amazing numbers. Don't get your hopes up for large creatures like leeches, either, because there isn't that much for them to live on.

In most lower-elevation waters, it is often quite easy to figure out what flies will work because the insects are so obvious. In high-elevation ponds you often have to look a lot harder just to figure out what's out there. You may look out across the pond and see no activity, and assume that there's no activity, but you wouldn't make such an assumption if you were fishing a river; you'd start trying to figure out what's going on under the surface. Do the same here.

And look in certain places first. As with most still waters, there are parts of these high-country ponds that are most promising. Inlets and outlets, because of their greater motion, tend to gather food in nice, moving channels where fish can get it more efficiently. The first time you are able to stand on a high ridge a few hundred feet above one of these little ponds, you'll be amazed at how far out into the water of the pond the current of the inlet stream extends. It's almost as if there is a small stream running across the middle of the pond. So you're not just fishing the first few yards of water where the stream empties into the pond; you're trying to fish that same current well out into the pond. Often the stream will

When you approach a pond like this, study its character from high above if you can. Look for the inlet and outlet streams, and shallower places that might hold vegetation and fish. Use your binoculars to check for fish moving or feeding; once you're at water level, it will be much harder to spot such things.

have built up a "delta" of sediment so that there's a long, shallow bar that reaches out into the pond. Treat it like the bottom of any other stream, where insect productivity and behavior may be more familiar to a stream fisherman.

Likewise, the water leaving the pond creates a larger current than you might expect. When water moves out of a little pond like this, it doesn't just come along in a straight line from the middle of the pond. The motion of the water coming out of the pond into a stream is spread across the whole 180-degree half-circle of the pond. That is, the water is moving along both shores just as it is moving from the middle of the pond. You can test this by casting a fly progressively further from the outlet stream, to see where the strongest currents are.

The harsh environment dictates other places you should look for fish, too. The most productive parts of the pond will be those where the sunlight can reach. If you do approach the pond from above, while you're up there make

Bud Lilly's Guide to Fly Fishing the New West

sure you locate which parts of it look shallower. Some ponds drop straight off on all sides, but most will have some shallower shelves extending well out into the water. Those places with the most sun are almost always the most productive biologically.

Dry-fly fishing on ponds offers some special challenges to an angler's patience, probably because we're so accustomed to letting a stream give the fly all the motion it needs. The first time you cast a dry fly onto a pond you may discover that you're getting bored after only a few seconds. Resist the temptation to rip the fly off the surface right away. You may want to experiment some with a very slow retrieve; that's an excellent way to cover the whole pond, or however much of it you can reach, with a series of concentric casts, each one retrieved very slowly. But if the real flies you see on the water are just sitting there, then yours should just sit there too. The fish are probably cruising around looking for them, and you may just have to wait your turn unless you can track a riser as it moves along. Then, if you've seen a few rises in a row, you can estimate where it will come up next and try to put your fly there. On smaller ponds, however, it often works just as well to put your fly right on top of the last rise, as quick as you can. During a heavy hatch, the fish may not be cruising

High-country wildlife,
like this Glacier Park mountain goat,
are an added attraction of fishing wilderness ponds.

PAUL SCHULLERY

quite so intentionally; they may just be looking for the next convenient bug to eat.

When these ponds first become ice-free, usually in early to mid-summer, there can be some very exciting fishing right along the edge of the ice. See my comments on fishing ice-out in Chapter 24.

Big Lakes and Reservoirs

These are the well known ones, the ones everyone sees and tries. In my experience, they are all different. On Yellowstone Lake you may try some kind of bright Gantron-bodied Woolly Worm with great success, while that day on Henry's Lake the only thing that will work is a heavily weighted leech imitation dragged along the bottom.

Though it is still true that most fishermen on big lakes are using lures and bait, the lakes can be approached and fished successfully by fly fishermen if they learn how to concentrate their attention. Look at a big lake the same way I suggested you look at a big river. Break it down into manageable parts. It's surprising how many people will spend their day randomly casting out in deep water while fish are working under the trees along the shore, or off the mouth of feeder streams, or in some other localized situation. Several excellent books, including ones by Rex Gerlach and John Merwin, have been written about fly fishing in lakes, and I can't begin to duplicate that kind of detail here. But I can say that if you treat the lake the way I suggested that you treat a big river—if you rethink it as a series of manageably small bodies of water, like the shoreline areas, the places where tributary currents or wind will concentrate food, and the areas of aquatic vegetation that are within a few feet of the surface—you're going to have a good chance.

Farm Ponds

These are the hardest to find, but if you can locate some, you may find some huge fish. I know of small farm ponds in western Montana that I wouldn't dare name or locate for you, ponds that annually yield fish of 8 to 12 pounds. They are fished by a few fly fishermen who have specialized in them for years, experimenting with tackle and techniques, collecting insects, developing fly patterns, and getting out to fish at just the right times of year, which can often be learned only by experience.

The farm-pond fishing in the West is one of the least accessible types for the visiting angler, but if you live here, and can spend the time looking, it's worth the effort.

Farm ponds are often not even on county maps, much less government topographic maps. If you really want to know what might be in your area, either get up high on a nearby mountain range, or hire a plane and do a proper survey from a few thousand feet up. A big ranch may have so much land that most of its terrain is invisible from the nearest public road.

Float tubes are the biggest change to come to stillwater fly fishing in many years.

One of the most extraordinary pond fishing situations in the West has developed on the Blackfoot Reservation east of Glacier National Park. The tribe has done a great job of managing these ponds, and local guides have emerged with the special skills needed to catch the big fish in these ponds (some are big enough to be called lakes). Like many other topics in this book, entire books have been written on this one fishing area, with special emphasis on float-tube fishing. Try Robert Fairchild's book, *Fly Fishing the Blackfeet Country.*

Float Tubes

Float tubes have changed stillwater fly fishing in many ways. Their advantages over small boats are chiefly their portability out of the water and their maneuverability in it. The new lightweight models are finding their ways to many tiny backcountry lakes never before fished from a watercraft; in this way they are allowing fly fishermen to put flies where they've never been seen before.

Float tubes put you fairly low in the water, and most skilled tube fishermen insist on rods at least nine feet long in order to keep their backcasts up.

Float tubing has been taken to almost incredible lengths.

The tubers who fish giant western reservoirs have even developed tube systems that allow them to stay on the water overnight and go miles from shore.

I don't harp about safety in this book because we're all supposed to be grownups and know how to be careful, but I have to tell you that float tubing, like backpacking, adds new risks to your fishing. They aren't risks that you should fear so much that you don't fish, but they are risks that you must not take lightly. There are lakes within 100 miles of my home that even in midsummer can kill you in 20 minutes if you must stay in the water without adequate warm gear. Float tubing brings you in constant contact with heat-sapping water, so it's essential that you thoroughly investigate local conditions before you fish anywhere.

There are float tubers who like rivers, too. Except in a few very specialized circumstances, in streams that are more like sloughs or still waters, I think this is a pretty bad idea. Float tubes just aren't good watercraft in a current. The fact that you see very few float tubers on rivers suggests that either there are only a few people willing to try such a thing or that those who do try it don't last long. If you want to float a river, buy a boat.

Chapter 23

The Backcountry

THOUGH IT'S TRUE THAT THE GOOD FISHING DOESN'T have to hide far from the road any more, it's also true that the backcountry is often where the easiest fishing is. A roadside stream, no matter how well managed, gets hammered pretty hard, and the fish get wary. Many fishermen have noticed that as they followed a stream away from the road, the fishing gets easier not long after the road is out of sight.

If you enjoy backpacking, but find that just walking along carrying all that fun gear isn't enough any more, then fly fishing may be just the thing for you. On the other hand, if you really love fly fishing, but have never backpacked in your life, then you might want to give it a try; it will open a whole different world of sport to you.

The backcountry need be no more rugged an experience than the roadside streams. If you choose, and can afford it, you can hire an outfitter with a pack string and go anywhere you want, fish incredibly beautiful, remote lakes and streams, and enjoy steak and fresh bread every day. Or, if you prefer (or can only afford to), you can carry all your own gear and food, and have just as wonderful a time.

If you're going to fish the backcountry with an outfitter and a pack string, you have the luxury of carrying pretty much everything you would carry to fish a roadside stream. You're putting yourself in the hands of your guide even more completely than you would in the frontcountry, and there's relatively little that I can add to the advice I've given elsewhere in this book about how to fish different kinds of waters, what tackle to use, and so on. I will add only two thoughts here. First, pay absolute attention to your outfitter's advice on what you need to bring and what you should do while you're on the trip; this is even more important in the backcountry than it is on roadside waters. Second, never forget that there is something embedded deeply in the genetics of horses that makes them want to step on fly rods.

There is more to be said about backpacking on your own. If you're going to backpack and haul everything you need on your back, you will quickly discover just how basic fly fishing can be. It's a great exercise in economy to take all that stuff in your vest, spread it out on the kitchen table, and figure out what you really have to have and what you can get along without. You'll find that you can get along without most of it.

Unless you just love carrying an extra few pounds along, your first goal is to reduce the weight. In the West, backpacking fly fishing is mostly going to be small-stream or small-lake fishing, so you don't need a big reel with lots of backing. Use a small light one, well ventilated so it has even less metal in it. If you know you're going to fish ponds, you'll probably want a spare spool with a sinking line.

Flies weigh practically nothing, so take plenty. You'd be surprised how many flies you can put in one of those light cheap, clear plastic fly boxes with a dozen or so compartments. Usually, most of us have several fly boxes in our vest, and enjoy just opening them up and admiring the nice rows of nymphs or dry flies displayed roomily in them. But you don't need to have that spacious an arrangement; a single compartment in your average trout fly box will hold several dozen small nymphs. Take a good variety of flies in different sizes. You may not need your big-river nymphs, but you'll almost certainly want some large nymphs to imitate dragonflies and damselflies, which are common pond residents.

Don't forget an assortment of tippet sizes, and, if your trip is more than a couple days, a spare leader. Some serious backpackers, the obsessed people who drill holes in the handles of their fork and spoon to save weight, might want to take the tippet material off the spools and wrap all the different diameters on some very light piece of cardboard or something. If you enjoy that sort of thing, go ahead.

Some backcountry fishermen like to take their favorite two-piece fly rod along in its aluminum case, which they use as a walking stick. Paul, who goes through several walking sticks a year (he says that the fires of 1988 made Yellowstone the world's foremost source of natural walking sticks) because he inadvertently leaves them behind when he stops for lunch, recommends against this unless you are sure you won't walk off and leave the rod lying by the trail. The alternative is a three- or four-piece rod that you strap to your backpack. These come in a great range of sizes and prices, and have

High-country ponds offer the rewards of incredible scenery as well as exciting fishing.

completely lost the stigma of four-piece rods from forty or fifty years ago, which had "stiff spots" all along their length where the ferrules joined. Modern packrods are just about as good as two-piece rods. You might be tempted to leave the rod case behind to save more weight, thinking you can just carry the rod in its cloth sack; yield not to this temptation, because fly rods stick out from your pack at odd angles, and it will be at precisely that angle that you run into a tree, or drop the pack in exhaustion at the end of a long day's hike.

And speaking of carrying things, you will probably be taking your backpack off while you fish, so you should think about a good way to carry this small assortment of fishing gear. You can put it all in a stuffsack and then hang the stuffsack off your belt while you fish, but that's a little clumsy, especially if you want to wade. Consider buying a small fanny pack, with perhaps two compartments. Put all your fishing gear in it, and strap it to the outside of your backpack wherever it fits well. Then, when you want to fish, take off the backpack, put on the fanny pack (or hang it around your shoulder).

The peskiest addition to the backpacking angler's load is waders. What you take depends upon how much you're willing to carry. Boot-foot chest or even hip waders add an awful lot of weight, even if you're only hiking in to a backcountry stream for the day. Stocking-foot waders are compact and very light (pack them in a plastic bag, in a separate stuffsack, so they don't get everything else wet), and you can carry some light tennis shoes or even rubber sandals (the kind that you can tighten securely on your feet); this additional footware might come in handy anyway, if you have to ford any streams during your hike. For short trips, you might even forgo wading socks, if you don't want to have to worry about soggy socks on the way home; lightweight waders, like the Royal Redballs, will stand the additional abrasion of shoes or sandals okay occasionally.

Remember that once your waders, shoes, or sandals are wet, they're going to have to be kept from soaking everything else you're carrying. Keep a couple large plastic bags handy to store them in. You can hang the shoes or sandals from the pack on a sunny day as you hike, to dry them out.

If you're struggling with the question of whether or not to even take waders, thinking, "well, I'll just wade wet," think again. People do it, but remember you're going to be fishing the highest, coldest parts of the river system. Some of the water you'll wade in might have been snow just the day before. It can be shriekingly difficult to wade up to your crotch in water like that in order to reach the risers out in the middle of the pond just at dark. Don't put yourself through that, or the deep chill you'll get the minute you step out of the water into the frosty air.

Early Spring
(The Season Before The Season)

IN MARCH THE YELLOWSTONE VALLEY ABOVE Livingston is alive with waterfowl. The bald eagles are still hanging around, doing some last-minute fishing before heading north for the summer, there are tame swans on the spring creeks and ponds, and wild ones on the river. Ducks and geese are everywhere, and lucky floaters might see the residents of a great blue heron rookery hovering above their cottonwood grove in alarm at the approach of some threat.

This is the season that doesn't exist in many parts of the country. Many western waters are open all year long, and are worth fishing at the most unexpected times. This is not just streamer and nymph fishing either; there may be a rise to hatching flies any day of the year on the Yellowstone River, and some of the heaviest hatches occur in the early spring, before the snowmelt has commenced and muddied the river with runoff.

The heaviest emergence of caddisflies I have ever seen occurred on May 1, 1986, when Paul and I were fishing the Yellowstone a few miles south of Livingston. The flies were so thick on the water that it looked as if someone had backed a grain truck up to Carter's Bridge and dumped the whole load in the water. We did well that day, mostly in the periods between the heaviest emergence periods. As usual, when the hatch is that heavy an artificial fly has little chance of being noticed among the millions of naturals. My largest fish was a 19-inch rainbow still lanky from spawning. It won't always be that good, but it is consistently good enough that outfitters are finding more and more of their clients calling up to plan an early spring trip. Most big western rivers have this early spring fishing. It used to be sort of the secret season, but that is changing fast now.

Early spring is your first opportunity of the year to fish a spawning run. I will also talk about spawning runs in the fall chapter, but a few basics are in order here.

Many of the biggest western fish pictured in outdoor magazines were taken during spawning runs; they are fish that are normally out of reach of fly fishermen, living deep in some big river or lake. In the spring, rainbows and cutthroat spawn, as do grayling. In the fall, the browns and

brooks come up to spawn. All offer some fabulous fishing opportunities, and some require you to learn a few new rules about how to fish.

First, spawners are nervous fish. Until they get into the height of their spawning activity, when they don't seem to care much about anything, they are spooky. They've just moved up out of some deep, secure river or lake, into a narrow, shallow side channel or tributary stream, and they are insecure at being so exposed. That is probably why they love shadow. They seem terribly light-sensitive, and though they may feed any time of the day, I've had my best fishing to spawners early in the day and after sundown.

Best Times

I usually start fishing in February. I don't go out of my way looking for bad weather, but I will go out on what we think of as a tolerably miserable day. But I go out knowing the limitations of the season and being realistic about what I can expect from the river and the fish.

This water is cold in the late winter and early spring, and often the temperature of a given river won't get into the 50s all day. The most insect and fish activity will be in the early to mid-afternoon. The hatches usually don't last a long time, but they are sometimes incredibly heavy.

The most important exception to this rule is one I mentioned a moment ago: spawners seem most active when they aren't directly exposed to light, though this is more true, I think, with fall-spawning browns than with spring-spawning fish whose activity is more controlled by low springtime water temperatures.

High Country

In the Rockies? In May? Don't even think about it.

Small Streams

Most small streams are going to be very cold even before spring runoff. There are a few here and there that will be good. The obvious examples are those influenced by springs or geothermal activity, such as the Firehole River in

If you're prepared for the occasional late snow storm and other surprises, early spring fishing can be exceptional, and you'll often have the water to yourself.

Yellowstone Park, or the spring creeks. But for the most part, small streams do not provide reliable fly fishing before runoff.

Big Rivers

The best chance for good fishing in the early spring is on the major rivers. They are at their lowest level then, except possibly for late summer.

From February on, and actually throughout the winter, there is no day of the year when a hatch of insects is impossible on many of the big rivers. These are the flies that are known locally as "snowflies," though actually they are a mix of species, including especially mayflies with some stoneflies and midges. In my experience there aren't many caddisflies this early, though later in the spring they become about the most important hatch.

The snowflies seem to hatch on warmer, sunny days, and on the streams in my part of the West provide excellent dry-fly fishing to a mixture of trout and whitefish. I don't look down on whitefish, especially in the middle of February if I haven't fished for two months and suddenly I see a long pool with dozens of rise forms all over it. At that point I'm just pleased as can be to cast a #16 Adams to a whitefish.

In late April and early May the hatches improve. Around Bozeman we have some fabulous fishing to caddisflies, especially the emergence I mentioned at the beginning of this chapter. We see these caddisflies on the Yellowstone first, and then they appear on the lower Madison around Mother's Day.

You can often find hatches in April and May, and though they aren't well known enough to have been written about

much in the hatch guidebooks some of them are very intense and provide excellent fishing. Only local knowledge will be able to provide the information you need, partly because the hatches seem to vary from year to year and partly because so many of them are just local hatches. For example, down around Chester and St. Anthony on the Henry's Fork, there are some marvelous early-season mayfly hatches in April and May, just as there are some productive hatches in midges on the Yellowstone. My experience is less extensive in Colorado, but I know that some of the best streams down there also have these early-season hatches.

There is no overstating the variations from water to water, even in streams in major drainages. I've just told you about some of the exciting winter and spring hatches on the Yellowstone, and yet, one valley to the west, the Gallatin River is completely different. For geological reasons, it is not as rich a stream as the Yellowstone, and when cold weather comes in September it becomes almost impossible to get Gallatin River trout to rise to a dry fly. There are so few insects hatching, and the water is so cold, that the fish simply won't move up to the surface to feed except under the most unusually bright warm conditions. The studies done on the Gallatin indicate that the river just isn't that full of insect life. It flows for many miles through a long, narrow canyon, and the resultant reduction in sunlight probably has substantial effects on a river already low in nutrients.

On the other hand, the Missouri River downstream from Helena, Montana towards Great Falls is a huge trout stream that can be clear most of the year because of the moderating

Bud Lilly's Guide to Fly Fishing the New West

influences of various dams. There can be marvelous dry-fly fishing there all year.

But often you will not encounter a hatch, so much of this early-season fishing will be with larger wet flies. In early spring the nymphs of the large stoneflies are nearing their maximum size, and some may even be increasing their activity and movement in preparation for their migration to shore for emergence. Early spring is a good season for large nymphs, fished either in the traditional dead-drift styles or with the technique I recommended in Chapter 14.

In any off-season fishing, except in the dead of winter when the rivers are just too cold for the fish to chase anything, streamers are absolutely essential. In recent years Woolly Buggers and Zonkers, which might be thought of as streamer/nymph hybrids, have become extremely popular in the West, and are often deadly in this early season.

In those very coldest seasons your wet fly will have to be a nymph, and you have to put the fly right on the bottom except for some very brief periods on unusually warm days. The fish are very lethargic and will just not move far for a fly, and if you wait for those few moments when the fish are more active, you may wait all day. This is the time when you must be extremely watchful or you will miss most of the strikes. A strike detector can make a big difference for you in the coldest weather because when the fish are this lethargic their strikes are often nothing more than a brief pause in the drift of the fly.

In those first days when winter appears to be breaking, I begin to use streamers. Sculpin begin their spawning movements in late winter; bait fishermen on the Yellowstone have long known about this activity, when the sculpin move into shallow areas to spawn. Many of the river's largest trout have been removed then.

Cal Dunbar and I fished the Yellowstone River one February using sculpin imitations. We were fishing Yankee Jim Canyon north of the park when the ice had piled up along the river ten or twelve feet, and fishing was a matter of standing on the edge of the ice and dropping a big streamer down to where we could jig it right along the edge of the ice. Fish would roar out from under the ice to grab the fly, and then it was just a matter of hoping your rod could stand the strain. One morning a huge brown grabbed my streamer and I got a good look at it before it got free, so I told Cal about it, and that afternoon we returned to the same spot and Cal took it on a Muddler Minnow. It was 24-1/2 inches long.

I know this isn't a lot of people's idea of graceful fly fishing, and it does seem a lot like bait fishing with a fly, but it's deadly when the timing is right. The effectiveness of sculpin in late winter was demonstrated much too well by bait fishermen on the Madison, who for years cleaned out many of the bigger fish that time of year.

Lakes and Ponds

One of the most exciting events, both in terms of the fishing and of natural attractions, in spring lake fishing is what we call ice-out, when the winter ice breaks up and floats off the lake and down the outlet stream. In some western lakes, including some of the big ones, it may not occur until early June, and it is part of the process of spring runoff that I consider the end of this early season. Ice-out can provide some very good fishing.

Apparently a lot of food is loosed, either from the melting ice or from areas the ice erodes, so that the fish seem to go on a feeding binge as the ice is moving out. If you can get to a lake just then, and safely get yourself into a position to fish along the edges of the broken ice as it moves out, you will sometimes find some wild fishing. It could also have to do with the fish getting back into heavy feeding, or the movement of the ice stirring up the lake bottom or churning more oxygen into the water and making the fish more active. Perhaps the increased sunlight reaching the lake bottom triggers some insect activity. The lake water in the Clark's Canyon near Dillon is a good example. There are some huge fish in that water, and the fishing is open all year long, so you can fish whenever ice-out occurs. I've seen fast fishing at ice-out on both the big lakes and the small farm ponds.

Spring Creeks

As I mentioned earlier, the spring creeks of early spring look radically different from how they look in mid-summer. They also are different in the tactics they demand from the angler.

This is a surprisingly good season for spring creeks. The fish are sometimes not as tough to catch, particularly in April and May when spawning rainbows and cutthroats come into the creeks on spawning runs from the bigger rivers. You can fish with big streamers and nymphs, flies uncharacteristic of most spring-creek fishing but very effective.

I know it's almost irreverent to talk about using big ugly fly patterns on these delicate little creeks, but early spring seems to be a time of relatively limited food choices on some of the creeks and the fish are either feeding more indiscriminately or are recognizing the big flies as similar to something they are eating, and the flies work very well.

Recently, commercially tied Woolly Buggers have become available in a wider range of sizes, and the smaller ones are useful in the spring creeks all summer. George Anderson, who in recent years has developed a reputation as a real master of the spring creeks, offers some very small Woolly Buggers at his shop in Livingston. The fish may be reminded of the motion of leeches when they see one of these little Woolly Buggers go by.

An added attraction of the spring creeks in the early season is that the public ones, like Poindexter Slough over near Dillon and Darlington Ditch near Manhattan, are usually uncrowded, sometimes almost unfished, this time of year, and the private ones, including the famous Yellowstone Valley creeks and several in other parts of the West, are less expensive for a day's fishing in the off season.

Chapter 25

Spring

WINTER USUALLY BRINGS A LOT OF SNOW TO WEST Yellowstone, six feet or more. Of course up in the headwaters of the streams of our areas, up around 8,000 or 9,000 feet, the snow is really serious, piling up much higher than that. Besides the snow, many of the rivers have been stacking up icejams along their shores, huge cakes of ice sometimes ten feet thick or more. Millions of tons of ice and snow cover our mountains, and when warm winds come through and it all starts to thaw and go down the same little river channels at once, it's quite a show. Rivers move their beds, farmers find themselves an acre or two short, trout hug the best cover they can find, and fishermen might as well stay home.

Late May can be a discouraging time for the western fly fisherman. Many of the rivers, and practically all of the small freestone streams, are torrents of mud. Rivers the size of the Bighorn and bigger swell and darken, with tree trunks and all manner of garbage floating along over places where only a few weeks earlier we were drifting small dry flies.

For the fisherman's purposes, I define spring as that period from about the middle of May until late June when our weather seems to break and you get so you don't really expect a blizzard any time. I know that temperatures rise long before the middle of May, and that many of the signs of spring appear sooner, but the fisherman's spring as I see it is when the temperatures have risen enough to affect the flow of the streams.

High water, of course, doesn't hit everywhere at once. As the hatches seem to work their way upstream, so does the snowmelt. There may be good fishing on streams at 7,000 feet for a while after the lower valley rivers are muddy and high. For the determined stream fishermen, finding fishing in this season is a matter of keeping up to date on daily developments around a region, and is also a matter of being willing to settle for the best of the worst.

Times

This is the one season where your fishing isn't so much at the mercy of the time of day. The waters are mostly muddied, which means that the overriding temperature effect on them

is being had by the snowmelt that is flooding them. With the water so cloudy, the sunlight has less effect on life in the stream. Fish aren't feeding much on the surface, and whatever fly fishing you do will be very much like bait fishing.

High Country

The high country will still be snowbound, and the lakes, though their ice may be thinner and rotten, are still unfishable even if you can reach them. Spring snow, with its crusts and instability, makes travel difficult and unpleasant.

Small Streams

These will be at their worst, though the persistent fly fisherman may find pockets of quiet water where the current doesn't reach. A weighted nymph or streamer, run through a back eddy or under the shelter of a logjam, may produce a great fish. But the main current will be unfishable.

The salvation for fly fishermen in my area during the runoff is Yellowstone Park. The Firehole will be fishable except in extreme runoff conditions, throughout this period, from Opening Day in late May. Even when it is out of its banks, its waters are still usually clear enough for streamer or nymph fishing, and even though this is the coldest time of the year for water in the Firehole, the tremendous geothermal influences keep the fish active enough to feed.

Silver Creek and Wood River, in the Sun Valley area, are also good during this period, as is the Lost River, near Twin Falls, Idaho. There are a few of these public streams scattered around the West that may provide good fishing during runoff.

We normally have to contend with high water from early May to late June, but there have been a couple years in the 1990s when many of our streams were still running very high in mid-July. They were clear enough to fish, but I wouldn't try to wade them where I would in a normal July.

Big Rivers

As the small streams fill the big rivers, they too become brown and unfishable. Spring is generally the worst time of year to try to fish western rivers. Some, like the Henry's Fork, don't get as bad or stay high as long, but on the average this is the worst season for fly fishing the major rivers.

But it isn't impossible. The fish have to put up with the mud and silt too, and they respond to it by moving to shelter. Many of them find that shelter along the banks, where they don't have to fight that heavy current and they don't have to face the worst of the crud that is in the water.

The fish may still feed now and then under these conditions, if the food is easy to get. Remember that the runoff was snow only a few days ago, so the fish are going to be lethargic with the cold. But if you can find a river safe to float, and a guide willing to float you, or if you can make your way along the bank with a long rod and a short line, you can work a large streamer or Woolly Bugger through those likely fish holds and have some startling fishing. The effective fishing zone is hardly a foot wide in many places, and the fish may only be able to sense the fly a few inches away, so it's essential that if you try this kind of fishing, you put your fly right up against the shore. There are times in the early spring when an amazing proportion of the good fish in a stream will be sheltered within your reach, and you will never find them less leader-shy than in these dark waters.

Fishing in muddy water can be rewarding, though the esthetics may leave a lot to be desired. But there is fly fishing to be had, as in the small streams, in the big rivers during high water.

The best time seems to be as soon as the muddiness has peaked and the flow has just begun to decline. There is enough visibility for the fish to see food, and there is a world of food being carried in the current right then. When the fish can manage even the least visibility, streamers and big nymphs become effective. You may feel like you're bait fishing, but you can catch fish.

Look for backwaters and quiet spots, especially side channels. Use enough weight to get the fly down, use fast-sinking lines, and stick to large flies. Among the nymphs, my favorites for high water are Bitch Creek Nymphs and Rubber Legs. Dark colors are best, the colors of the big stonefly nymphs working fine. A yellow or tan fly isn't especially visible in muddy water.

Be flexible. Be willing to use a very heavy tippet, or to switch to a light leader if you find a side channel where the silt has settled out and you can see fish taking smaller nymphs. You may not find the conditions pleasing, especially if you like clear water, but you have a good chance of catching a really big fish that by mid-summer will be all but out of reach to the fly fisherman.

Lakes

With the rivers out of shape, many fly fishermen move to still waters, ranging from the smallest farm ponds to the giant reservoirs. I mentioned the fishing at ice-out in Chapter 10, but good fishing can be found from ice-out on. As the summer progresses you will share the fishing with more and more people, of course.

Spring Creeks

For the fisherman that can get on them, the spring creeks are aptly named, because they provide some of the best fly fishing available in spring. The first couple of weeks in June seem to be when they really hit their stride with hatches and actively feeding fish, and the fish aren't yet as selective as they will be in a month or two.

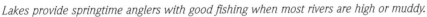

Lakes provide springtime anglers with good fishing when most rivers are high or muddy.

PAUL SCHULLERY

Chapter 26

Summer

IN THE SUMMER I AM ALWAYS IMPRESSED BY THE clarity of the air. It seems as if I can hear for miles. I may be fishing alone on the Madison, in apparent solitude, when a voice will drift in from some riffle upstream, "What'ja gettin'em on, Joe?" There is a quality to the air, something I'm not sure I could prove but am sure I experience. And what makes it so valuable on a trout stream is that all you hear is what you want to hear. At midday there are birds, and all sorts of insects. Sometimes, if there are a lot of wildflowers, the noise of the bees will drown out the water. But as the day advances it gradually gets quieter until at dark it may be almost silent except for the crickets. If there are no crickets, by nightfall there may be no sound but the river.

This is when it gets good just about everywhere. Summer in the West, which by my reckoning starts for fishermen sometime in mid to late June, is when you have the most choices and the best choices. The peak is from about mid-July to early September. The weather is least likely (though that's not necessarily saying much) to surprise you, the winds are a little less terrifying, and practically all of the water is fishable.

This is the season of the well-known insect hatches that are so widely reported in the magazines and in many books: the green drake, the salmonfly, and others. The serious angler-entomologist for whom finding, identifying, and fishing certain hatches is important, will want to come in late June and July, and anyone who prefers dry flies will want to fish this season over any of the others.

As the song says, in the summertime "the livin' is easy." The rhythms of the trout are different than in the spring. There is plenty of food, and the hatches are longer and more reliable. The fish don't as often work themselves into a frenzy, except during the salmonfly hatches or during an exceptional fall of grasshoppers. What that means for you is that you should take your time; the fish is not going to feed for five minutes and quit, and you should study its feeding rhythm for a moment before splashing out there and covering it with a fly. Learn the pace of its rises, and time your cast to fit that pattern. Watch the fish, and get tuned with its feeding rhythm.

Be aware of the possibilities of terrestrials. There are some spectacular flights of ants on many western streams that have not been written up to speak of, and a small beetle, either floating or just under the surface, is often a great fly to try on a finicky riser.

By the end of August, and certainly by early September, the major hatches are past, and the popular attractor patterns, such as the Royal Wulff and the Humpy, come into wider use. The fish see fewer insects, and they're still hungry, so a big bushy dry fly looks very good to a fish that isn't locked in to feeding on any specific hatch.

But eventually, as fall approaches, the fish will be less and less willing to rise to a big attractor. Then if you want to fish dry flies you will have to wait for the rare hatch, while most of us switch to nymphs and streamers.

Best Times

In June it is still often fairly cool in the West, and though the duration of the best fishing period is lengthening, it is still mostly in the middle of the day, when the air temperature and sunlight can have their best effects on the water.

By July and into August, depending upon how fast it warms up in a given year, and upon how good the snowpack is, a split occurs so that in most cases the warmest, brightest time of the day is no longer the best. Gradually heat becomes not an advantage but a disadvantage, so that by the dog days of August the best fishing is when you can avoid the heat. This is the only time of year in the West when it can be an advantage to get up early in the morning to fish for trout. Their activity patterns, dictated by water temperature and light, will be early and late in the day.

In September the process begins to reverse itself. The evenings get cooler, the days begin to shorten noticeably, and the fishing times start to move back to the middle of the day.

You can play tricks on the usual rules of time of day by watching for shade. If you're fishing a river on a bright hot day, and it's early afternoon and nothing is moving, look for shade. The fish will almost certainly be more active in shady water. The shaded spot may not be big enough to actually cool off the water, but shade seems to increase the fish's sense of security, and it may have an effect on insect activity as well. If the shaded area is 100 yards of bank sheltered by a cottonwood grove, then the water may actually be a lot cooler. But even a small spot, under a single snag or along a low bank, should get special attention. There often will be a "mini-hatch" occurring just in that little stretch of shaded water.

So watch for banks that shade the water, or for willows or other plants that create a narrow band of shade. Even if it's only a few inches wide, it can signal good fishing, and even a concentration of rising fish. It happens all the time on hot, bright days. Cover any shade with your fly.

Conversely, watch for rock when the sun has gone off the water. In the evening, after a hot day, the water may cool so much that the fishing is slow. Look for rock walls along or above the river. They'll hold the heat of the day for hours and slowly radiate heat to the water, so that in those areas the fish may still be active. I've seen this situation on the Madison and the Henry's Fork, along stretches of canyon or palisades.

High Country

These lakes are starting to thaw now, and by late summer will begin to get fishable.

Summer arrives, more or less, in the high country in August. Of course, so does fall. But there is a short period in this month, and with luck into September, when you can get in to the thousands of small, high-country lakes in the West. The Beartooth region of southern Montana, for example, has over 300 lakes with fish, and most of these small waters must be hiked to. It is a magnificent resource for the backpacking or horsepacking fisherman, and in most areas the lakes have been mapped or even written up in local informational brochures. This fishing is the closest you will probably get in modern western fishing to a real exploration experience, and it will take you into another world, where the ecological and scenic character of the land

is as foreign as you can find without leaving the lower 48.

As I suggested in Chapter 22, it is a matter of fishing through research. Find an area you are interested in, then find out which government agencies administer it. Order the appropriate topographic maps either from the agency or from some outfitter in the area, and begin your exploration by studying the map. There are books available on how to orient and use such maps, if you are unfamiliar with them. Take a close look at almost any map of the high-mountain West and you will see many tiny blue dots here and there, many without names. There is a lifetime of trout-fishing adventures in those little dots.

Luckily for the fisherman, more and more such areas are being written up by management agencies or by individuals, so that you may also find a published guide to the area in which you are interested. That's not all good, of course, because it takes some of the excitement out of exploring them yourself, but published guides to almost any kind of wild-trout fishing are out of date very quickly, and if the publication is only three or four years old you may find the lakes in very different condition than the publication claims. You still will be doing a lot of exploring.

More than any other kind of western fishing, high-country lake fishing does mean overnight trips, either on foot or by horseback. This is where solid, up-to-date advice from professionals in the area, whether they be forest rangers or outfitters or friends, is absolutely essential. Weather is always a prime concern, because at 10,000 feet there is no time of the year when it is impossible for you to get trapped for a few days by snow.

Small Streams

I most often recommend summertime small-stream fishing for the newcomer to fly fishing. Beginners, and those planning to teach them, should be aware of the advantages of using a small freestone stream as a classroom.

Most of the time, the deepest stretches of a stream like this might be best, but on a hot, bright summer day the fish may leave it. Look along the far bank, behind West Yellowstone angler Cal Dunbar. See the narrow band of shaded water under the overhanging grass? Not only are fish more likely to be active there, but also they may be watching for terrestrials falling from the grass. It's more than worth the risk of hanging up your fly in the grass to get your fly right up against that bank.

The beginner has relatively little concern about how big the fish is, or what species it is, or what type of rise it makes, or what it is feeding on. The beginner wants to catch fish. A small stream, with lots of broken currents and smaller, less-choosy fish, is much more forgiving than a big smooth glide on a major river. It gives you the chance to hone your skills, and for a beginner that is priceless experience.

Many of the smaller tributary streams are perfect fly-fishing classrooms. I think of Pebble Creek and Soda Butte Creek in Yellowstone Park, or the Taylor's Fork of the Gallatin, but there are hundreds of others, all over the West. They give you the opportunity to make a real fly-fishing cast and to fish many types of water in only a hundred yards of stream. But they rarely have any holes more than three or four feet deep, and they move so quickly that their fish must make feeding decisions quickly from a very small feeding area. Many things work to your advantage in this sort of setting.

Big Rivers

Starting in about mid-June, the salmonflies begin to appear. They usually work their way from the lowest to the highest elevations (keep in mind the warnings I gave in Chapter 5 about counting on any printed schedule too heavily). The Henry's Fork is one of the earliest in my area, with the hatch starting there about the last week in May. Salmonflies appear on the Blackfoot and the Clark's Fork in northwestern Montana in late May or early June. Because they are geothermally influenced, the Firehole and the Madison in Yellowstone Park will get their light hatch of salmonflies in the middle of June. The Big Hole hatch begins around June 10, and the Madison's first flies appear in late June, maybe the last week of the month. They start on the Yellowstone at the beginning of July. Of course the tributary streams of these big rivers get their hatches more or less as part of the greater upstream movement of the hatch, so that when a hatch is in a certain portion of a big river, the tributaries in that area will probably also have their flies coming off at about the same time.

Notice that many of these streams get their salmonfly hatches in June, which is a period of high water. There may be a great hatch of salmonflies on a given river, but no rise of fish because the water is too high or murky. The Yellowstone, downstream from Yellowstone Park, is a perfect example of the problem of catching this hatch when the water is high; it is usually only good once every four or five years for salmonfly fishing with dry flies because its headwaters are so high and get so much late runoff.

By July 1, most of the western streams are getting pretty clear. Late-clearing streams, like the Sun and the Clark's Fork in Montana, are getting good by then.

Summer is also the time to explore some of the less-known rivers of the West. Some are not known because the fishing is only good at certain periods, or because access is difficult, but they are worth the effort. Wilderness fishing can be had in many parts of the West, with a little help from a trustworthy outfitter. The Middle Fork of the Flathead is a great wilderness float trip, or you could take a pack trip into any of several wilderness areas.

Whatever river you fish, large or small, watch for cottonwood groves along the river. They seem to harbor great numbers of flying ants, and the occasional flight of ants in late summer is a great fishing opportunity. I've often encountered them on the Madison near Varney Bridge, where cottonwoods line the river for a long stretch, and on Slough Creek in Yellowstone Park. Slough Creek is known to the locals for its reliable terrestrial fishing in late summer.

Lakes and Ponds

After ice-out, many lakes, especially those that depend mostly on natural reproduction for their fish populations, go through a slow period during which the fishing isn't that good. It seems to have to do with the lack of vegetation, which is still getting a start at growth. Once the vegetation has gotten into its summertime mode and is helping oxygenate the water and provide cover for newly active insects, fish feeding will increase.

By July and August, the fishing on the bigger lakes usually goes to hell. The best times are late evening and early morning can be good for the "gulpers," but for the most part the peak is past. Of course the fisherman can just follow the lake fishing to higher and higher elevations, staying with those in that active early summer phase.

Spring Creeks

In early summer the spring creeks undergo a transformation more dramatic than do many larger streams. They are small enough that ducks and muskrats can over the course of the winter uproot and remove much of the stream vegetation. People who have often fished western spring creeks in July and August would probably not even recognize those same creeks in April; they're just bare, open meandering trenches.

In June the growth gets a good start, and the fish and insects take advantage of the new cover that is appearing. By late July, the barest, most forlorn looking creek may again be lush, with its flowing channels restricted between thick beds of flowering water plants.

Let me emphasize again that spring creeks are not well enough known for their grasshopper fishing. I suppose most of us who fish them in the summer are especially interested in their challenges for the light-tackle enthusiast, and so we don't notice how many of these creeks are in grasshopper country, or we don't pay enough attention to the occasional explosive rise to a hopper. Fishing hoppers in a spring creek can be challenging, because a carelessly cast fly can just as easily put these spooky fish down as make them rise. But in these small, clear streams, with their unusually large fish, a well placed hopper drifting along a shady undercut bank can give you the most suspenseful moments of the summer.

Chapter 27

Fall

FALL IS A TIME OF MOVEMENT. FISHERMEN THINK FIRST of the movement of brown trout into spawning areas, but all kinds of wildlife are moving. Elk and deer begin their migrations to lower country, and throughout the Rockies fishermen may hear their bugling. Deer begin to appear on the flats along the Madison and the Yellowstone, in numbers that we haven't seen since May.

And something happens to the light. The sun's rays, slanting through increasing angles of atmosphere, give the sky's blue a different, less washed-out quality, and the afternoon is cut short by the early twilight of the long-shadowed mountain ranges. The forest fire season has just passed its peak in August, and the smoke and soot of a dry year give us our most stunning sunsets, as if the aspen aren't giving us color enough for one season.

Here near Yellowstone I especially enjoy the fall in the park. The cold air brings up huge volumes of steam from the thermal features along the Firehole, Yellowstone, and Gibbon rivers, so that fishermen find themselves in a light shifting fog. Just when you think you're alone with the river, a bull elk wanders out of the mist and splashes across the river not 100 feet downstream from you, then just as quickly disappears. At this elevation, and in this setting, you have no trouble believing that at any moment it might snow.

In early fall you still have many good opportunities to use large attractor dry flies. Throughout September and sometimes well into October, you can often pound up fish with a large Royal Trude, Humpy, or Royal Wulff. Don't hesitate to try a #10 or even a #8. We used to routinely use #6 dry flies on the Madison late in the year. There were no risers in sight, and no insects emerging to speak of, but the trout were still looking for food on top.

Though you may always, in any month of the year, find some dry-fly fishing, late fall signals the end of the reliable hatches on most western waters. The dry-fly fishing you find in fall and winter will mostly be to short hatches of mayflies, stoneflies, and occasional midges. Some people call all of these insects "snowflies," and they often do look to be about the size of the snowflakes that may be mixed with them. As we've discussed earlier, "snowflies" is a term that different people apply to different insects; it's a lot like the way some people use the term "*Baetis*" to signify any small grayish-tannish-olive mayfly. The exact terminology isn't as important as knowing that snowflies and the so-called *Baetis* will bring on good rises of trout and whitefish even on the coldest days, especially if there is some bright sun in mid-day, and that a few standard dry flies, such as the Adams, will work wonders on these fish.

As I mentioned in an earlier chapter, in my experience, though I can't explain why it is this way, caddisflies don't appear as part of this fall and winter smorgasbord of hatches.

But most of your fishing, at least the fishing you should go out expecting to find, will be with wet flies. Your best fishing will be with nymphs and streamers, and your success will depend more on your ability to find fish than on your ability to choose a specific fly.

Late fall is a time of some unexpected opportunities. In my area, the Firehole cools off in the fall and provides unusually good late-season dry-fly fishing because of its geothermal sources. There is a period in late September on the Firehole when it appears that the damselfly nymphs seem to concentrate against the banks. One fall I fished a spot on the Fountain Flats, casting a weighted Zug Bug right against those grassy banks. The fishing was very fast, but I didn't realize how good it was until a guy pulled up and got out of his car. He had been watching me from a distance, and he said, "You didn't do too bad there. I fished that pool for two hours before you got here and I've seen you take twelve fish from it."

Times

As the nights get colder the best fishing times move back toward the middle of the day. The feeding periods, that is the times when you might expect rises to floating flies, are correspondingly shortened to a few hours at mid-day.

High Country

The high country becomes less promising in the fall. You can still get in to the subalpine lakes, and may still have some good fishing, but the risk of being snowed in for several days increases as September progresses. Two of my guides went into a small lake called Lousy Springs in the Centennial Range one September and woke up to three feet of snow, which held them there a couple days longer than they'd planned. If they hadn't been familiar with those kinds of conditions they could have been in serious trouble. If you're going to try the high country in September or October, it is more important than ever that you plan your trip with the help and knowledge of the appropriate authorities.

The fish in the high lakes begin to behave like fall fish very early. The spawning runs, or spawning activity, will be earlier and may have dramatic effects on the fishing.

Lakes

Fall is not a prime time on lakes, except in shoreline areas where fall-spawning fish (browns, brooks, lakers) move to spawning areas. Some of these areas may still be too deep for practical fly fishing, but fishermen should know that trout regularly move to both inlets and outlets of lakes to spawn.

Like the streams, trout-food production in lakes declines at the end of summer. There are fewer hatches, and often there is an algae "bloom" that reduces clarity considerably. Unless you are alerted to some specific fishing spot that is known to produce in the fall, you are better off investing your time in streams in fall rather than prospecting for a chance good day on still waters.

Small Streams

The greatest potential for exciting fall fishing in small streams is the result of spawning runs out of bigger waters

downstream. For convenience, I'll cover spawning trout in the section on Big Rivers.

Not all small streams host spawning runs. The little ones may have only a few fish, or only have fish in a few places. The big ones are more promising, but you'll have to check locally, because many streams have had their runs killed off.

Keep in mind as well that a lot of browns spawn right in the main stream. They move to shallower water, or they concentrate off the mouths of smaller streams, and never leave the security of the main stream at all.

Big Rivers

The hatches are pretty much over now, though you may still find the occasional good rise to some small fly. There are still a fair number of fish that will come up to a large attractor dry fly until the snow starts to fall, but even that fishing has started to slow down.

Grasshopper fishing can go well into the fall, even after the hoppers aren't common along the river. I've often seen hoppers work well into late September and even early October. I don't know if that's because the fish are still looking for them, or because hoppers are just good attractor flies at any time. It may be a combination of factors, but don't neglect hoppers. They may be one of the last chances you have in the fall to take fish on a dry fly. I've seen times on the Madison River in the park in late September and early October when larger brown trout would move into shallow water along the banks, where most fishermen would not even be looking for a trout. Those fish are especially vulnerable to a hopper cast from a fisherman standing well back from their bank or standing well below and out from them in the river.

*In late fall, small streams are
often at their lowest level, but the cooler temperatures have energized the trout.*

PAUL SCHULLERY

A broad brown trout taken during the fall on the Madison.

I personally think of the fall as the streamer season. Whether you are fishing for spawning trout or not, streamers work wonders on hungry fall fish.

Spawning Browns

Spawners are very sensitive to light. They are the big exception to the general rule that your best fishing in the fall is likely to be at mid-day. Your best fishing for spawners is likely to be when the direct light is off the water. That may be on a heavily overcast day, or it may just be early in the morning or late in the evening. Evening may be better than morning, because the stream will still have some of the heat of the day. On a bright day, look for sheltered water, maybe at the base of a cliff that keeps the water in shadow. In my guiding, I followed the sun from pool to pool, arriving at each pool about the time the light goes off the water.

In many years of guiding people during the spawning runs, I also noticed a correlation between the catch-rate of spawning brown trout in the fall, and barometric pressure. Our experience showed us that on a day with a fast-falling barometer, brown trout would be much harder to take. We had some theories about why this happened, but it was a priceless piece of information for guides and fishermen, and we earned it the hard way, by watching and keeping track of how the fishing went in relation to all these environmental factors. We got so we watched the barometer in our shop every day.

Remember that much of the time these fish are not feeding. It isn't enough to put a big fly in their general vicinity unless it triggers some defensive or aggressive reaction in the fish; there are periods when they just aren't reacting that way. Many times customers would come into the shop and complain that they were fishing such-and-such a place just as the book told them to, using this fly, casting it that way, and not having any success. I would answer that, "You're about a foot from success."

"What does that mean?"

"Three more split shot."

You are searching for these fish. You are probing their holding lies. You must go to them a lot of the time.

On the other hand, we can get too hung up on fishing for spawners with streamers and big nymphs. There are almost always fish that are feeding in the spawning season, and often you may catch just as many fish with small nymphs and dry flies as with the big patterns. Spawners will take the small flies. I had a customer who fished the Barns Pools on the Madison in Yellowstone Park using beaver and muskrat nymphs in sizes 10-14 all fall. He caught plenty of fish on them, more than many other fishermen. The point is that if you find yourself fishing a spawning run and the big flies aren't working, try giving the trout something that they might just like to eat.

Another relatively little known, or at least little reported, part of the spawner fishing is that it can start surprisingly early. I've taken migratory browns, fish that had obviously moved up from Hebgen Lake, in the Madison in the park as early as late August and early September. The fish moved in long before they went to the spawning beds.

Spring Creeks

Streams of any sort with small flow become more difficult for the fly fisherman in the fall. The water is low, there is little insect activity, and the fish are very spooky.

But on those occasions when you happen upon a good fall hatch on a spring creek, the fishing can be exceptional. It is as if the shortness of the hatch, and the density of food, make the trout reckless. The fishing can be very fast under those circumstances, but you might wait a long time before you find them.

Chapter 28

Winter
(The Season After The Season)

IT'S STILL HARD FOR MANY PEOPLE TO BELIEVE, BUT we have year-round fishing in Montana, especially in the lower ends of the best trout river valleys. You can find great fishing, not just tolerable fishing, any month of the year.

The effects of light and heat become most immediately apparent on fishing in the winter. As mentioned in Chapter 10, a sunny winter day will bring on the snowflies, but there are other effects that you must keep in mind. I've found that in winter it is harder to take fish from the deep pools, which seem to retain their cold temperature and don't get as much sunlight. I assume that fish are not feeding as actively there as are other fish in the shallower riffles, where the sun can more easily trigger insect activity and may even crank up the metabolism of sluggish trout. I look for shallower holding or feeding water in the winter for that reason.

The snowflies are very widespread. This is to say that most big rivers will have some decent winter hatches of the smaller insects, usually #14 and smaller, and some will have

Cold-weather fishing has its rewards.

Cold-weather fly fishermen join duck hunters among those hardy sportsmen for whom a little misery is just part of the game.

really excellent dry-fly fishing now and then. I know that in my neighborhood the Yellowstone, Madison, Big Hole, and Beaverhead all have those hatches.

One of the real blessings of winter fishing in the West is the whitefish. Whitefish are too often looked down upon by fly fishermen when in fact these fish provide some wonderful fast action on streams all over the West in the coldest months. There is no better cure for cabin fever than a couple of hours casting small dry flies and nymphs to a few dozen whitefish feeding daintily along a gravel bar. The action is fast, the fish are exciting sport, and what better way to spend a sunny winter day.

I know that a number of ski resorts are offering winter fly fishing. My son Greg has guided many skier-anglers out of Big Sky here in Montana, and similar trips are available in other areas, such as on the Roaring Fork near Aspen, Colorado. There can be lots of action with steadily rising fish.

Times

You have to fish the warmest time of day. You may get some action at other times of day, but the fish are extremely sensitive to those brief periods of warmth and sunlight (which helps trigger hatches) at mid-day and early afternoon.

The feeding periods will be brief, often just an hour or so. On most winter days out here, you're not really going to be interested in putting in a long day, and an hour or two in mid-day may be just the thing to cure cabin fever until the next sunny day comes along.

High Country

This is once again snowbound and the water is out of reach.

Small Streams

Watch these closely. You may find an occasional freestone stream with some spring sources that keep it open and fishable in the winter. If you find fishing in the small streams in winter it will most likely either be in the lower reaches or in places where spawning trout have lingered in the stream into the winter season.

Big Rivers

These are often the best chance you have in the hard winter. On the coldest days I use large stonefly nymphs. In Chapter 10 I have already reviewed much of the coldwater fishing techniques I use, so I won't repeat them.

I will emphasize, however, that if you get the fly deep enough, and get it to the fish, you will catch trout. I know that there is a common belief, based on various studies, that fish will simply not feed when the water reaches a certain temperature, but even that is not always true. I've taken fish on flies when the water was forty degrees or colder many times. You have to make it easy for the fish, and then the fish will cooperate.

Lakes

The lakes are frozen, though some locals tell stories of trolling from snowmobiles.

Spring Creeks

The spring creeks are tough in winter. The vegetation dies back or is pulled out by waterfowl, the hatches are sporadic and light, and the fish become very spooky because of the lack of cover.

A Trout's Best Friend

"Passing it On," a large bronze sculpture of Bud and
young son Mike, was recently created by Big Timber, Montana, sculptor Dale Wood.

Chapter 29

Why Western Fishing Has Gotten Better

A FEW YEARS AGO, I WAS GUIDING A PAIR OF FLY fishermen from out of state. I had agreed to give a day's guided fishing to anyone who donated $250 to the International Fly Fishing Center, and these two gentlemen had both done so. We were fishing the Yellowstone River a few miles downstream from Yankee Jim Canyon, and we were having a very good day. Both men had caught fish in the eighteen-inch range, and I felt like I'd given them a day they would remember. While we were fishing along one bank, a man and a woman

Back before about 1960, like most Montana fishermen, I kept most of the big trout I caught, and so did my clients. These two browns—four to five pounds each—were taken in the early days of my guiding out of West Yellowstone.

came drifting along the other bank in a rubber raft. The man was spin fishing, and he hooked a very big trout, probably weighing three or four pounds, which he finally beached on a long gravel bar across the river from us. One of my fishermen yelled over at him, "Let it go!"

There was a little more hostility in the air than I would have liked, and the man yelled back, "I gotta eat, y' know!" and mashed this beautiful big brown trout over the head. As long as we keep thinking of our trout streams as our personal pantries, we're not going to do justice to them. Unlike our big game and our game birds, we have a choice when we fish for trout. There is no reasonable alternative for a hunter but to shoot the elk; there is a reasonable alternative for the trout fisherman, who can have all the pleasure of the stalk and the take without killing the game.

I had always promoted conservation in the Trout Shop catalog, but in 1974 I introduced our Catch-and-Release Club. When you joined you got a pin that said you were a member of the club, and then there were additional pins that said you'd released various sizes of trout up to twenty-four inches. You could either buy a set of pins or buy them individually. It was because of the Catch-and-Release Club that our shop got some wonderful attention from Arnold Gingrich. In his book, *The Joys of Trout,* he gave the club some recognition that was helpful in boosting it to national attention. His remarks summed up our philosophy so well that I quote them below.

Catch-And-Release Club

Bud Lilly is a trout's best friend.

Fly-fishing's legion of honor decoration is the lapel recognition button devised by Bud Lilly, which reads "Released 20' Trout" and carries the slogan "Support F.F.F.-T.U." The club's purpose is to get fishermen familiar with the idea of releasing trout. Anybody can join. All that's needed is a dollar, and the simple statement that a trout of a certain size was returned to the water. The statement and the dollar can be sent to Bud Lilly, from November to May, Sourdough Road, Bozeman, Montana 59715, or to Bud Lilly, from May to November, in care of the Trout Shop, West Yellowstone, Montana 59587. Bud's pragmatic philosophy on keeping the membership requirement this simple reflects the belief that all fly fishermen are naturally honest and that any who are not will at least be publicizing the principle.

The principle of trout release, first and best stated by Lee Wulff, has since had many genial variations, one of the nicest of which is the Klamath Country Fly Caster's motto, "Keep your lines tight and your creels empty." But however it's codified it couldn't be better propagandized than by the general adoption and use of the Bud Lilly Catch-and-Release Club lapel buttons. Bud Lilly donates the proceeds from the sale of the release recognition buttons to Trout Unlimited and the Federation of Fly Fishermen

I quote that here not because it lets me show off how much attention the Trout Shop got, but because it reveals something about the attitudes of modern sportsmen, especially those who are willing to travel long distances to find good fishing for wild trout.

When my family first emigrated to what would become the state of Montana, back in the 1860s, there was no such thing as "too big" a kill of fish. There were no restrictions on fishing tackle or on the behavior of fishermen, so long as they didn't murder each other. The fishing was wide open, and the people were few enough that for quite a while the fishing stayed good. But we all know enough about conservation history to realize that it never stays that way. By the time I started fishing, in the early 1930s, we'd already lost a lot of our best fishing, but the state was still so sparsely populated that by any modern standard the fishing was still fabulous all around my home in Manhattan, Montana.

Back when Ma Wiedman and little Buddy Lilly were taking a hundred fish a day from the Gallatin, nobody we knew thought much about the eventual effects of that kind of killing. There weren't that many of us fishing the streams, and we had a fairly simple idea of "waste." If we gave the fish to someone, or ate them ourselves, they weren't wasted. It took a long time for most of us to figure out that there is more than one way to waste a fish. I especially

remember a friend from Deer Lodge coming into my shop in West Yellowstone in the 1950s to tell me about a big fish he'd caught in the Bear Trap. I don't recall exactly how long it was, but I do remember that he told me it was something more than thirty inches, obviously the fish of a lifetime. I was pretty impressed.

"That's a real trophy," I said. "Where is it?"

"Oh, we ate it."

When I bought the Trout Shop I became owner of a big freezer that we used to store and freeze people's fish until they were ready to have them shipped home. Life was simple—you caught a big fish; you killed it. Only an idiot would let it go.

But gradually it dawned on me that we weren't going to be able to go on that way. As there were more and more fishermen, and as we learned about the ecology of a wild-trout stream, we needed more good fishing at the same time that we learned that hatchery fish weren't a good answer. We were going to have to change our ways.

The change took many forms. During that 1960 winter that I spent in Arizona, I sat down and revised the old Martinez fishing map that we'd been handing out for so many years. I was getting uncomfortable with it because of the effects it had on the fishing. Don had put it together back when there were very few fishermen to read it, and he'd been very specific in it—park your car here, walk three hundred feet down the trail, turn left, cast behind the big rock—and now too many people were hitting too few spots too hard.

It was at that point that I decided that maps like ours

The Catch-and-Release Club,
which we promoted with a line of products in the catalog,
was a small-scale effort with big results in encouraging no-kill fishing.

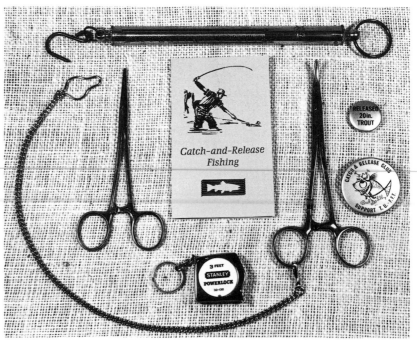

Keeping our fishing good means keeping entire watersheds healthy. If we protect the habitat, the fish and all the other aquatic creatures will take care of themselves.

were creating fishermen who couldn't think for themselves, and that I realized that we needed to show them how. One of the best ways was to give them enough information so that they understood the river, tell them what kinds of flies were good, and send them to a general area with enough skill to find their own trout rather than sending them out to catch a fish that had Don's (or my) name on it.

I also did a lot of soul-searching about the Lunker Club, and though I kept the book for fishermen until the late 1960s, I could see that it was on its way out, too. There again I saw that more fishermen meant more harvest, and the last thing I should be doing was encouraging people to kill fish and bring them in just to get their name in the book.

Of course, I didn't come to realize all these things on my own. Sportsmen went through a lot of changes in the 1960s, and fly fishermen more than most. A few farsighted anglers in Michigan created Trout Unlimited in 1959, and a couple years later Pat Halterman got Dan Bailey, me, and a few other well-known Montana fishermen together to form the

Montana chapter of Trout Unlimited. Pat operated by administrative fiat; she just informed Dan and me that I was to be the president and he was to be the vice-president, and away we went. A few years later the Federation of Fly Fishermen (now the Federation of Fly Fishers) was created, and we began hearing about this organization back East, with people of Ed Zern's caliber as president, named Theodore Gordon Flyfishers. Their motto was "limit your kill, don't kill your limit." A few people, such as Lee Wulff, had been talking about this for a long time, but now it was a true movement, and it became clear that it was fishing's best hope. It also became clear that we weren't going to accomplish any of our goals easily.

Fishing in the West was changing long before we'd ever heard anyone describe it as the New West. But those changes were just part of the attitudes that would become part of life in the New West. We had to ensure the fish a safe place to swim; we had to protect their habitat if we expected them to reproduce and maintain wild-trout populations. We had to regulate the fishing harvest so that those trout populations were not decimated. We had, in short, to overcome a lot of ingrained and traditional ideas about how the West should care for its natural resources. Those of us who lived through that era came to think of it as the Trout Wars.

Governor Mark Racicot presenting Bud Lilly with a plaque for his participation on the Governor's Task Force on Whirling Disease.

Chapter 30

Winning The Trout Wars

THIS TITLE DOES NOT OVERDRAMATIZE WHAT happened. It may not often have been violent, but there were many violent emotions, and there was unlimited hostility. It's something for your soul to get up in front of a group of your neighbors and have them so angry with you that they're booing and hissing like you're a matinee villain. We went through that to drag Montana fishing into the twentieth century.

Yellowstone Park was the pacesetter. Jack Anderson, who became superintendent of the park in about 1967, was an avid fly fisherman and understood the harmful effects of hatchery trout and overharvest. There's a story that when he was superintendent of Grand Teton National Park in Wyoming, he forced the state of Wyoming to stop stocking park streams; he told them that if they sent any of their hatchery people into the park, his rangers would arrest them.

Under Jack's leadership, the National Park Service in Yellowstone set an example with their special regulations. The superintendent has many exclusive powers because the park was created before any of the surrounding states were even states, and Jack used that power well. In the early 1970s, catch-and-release regulations began to appear on park waters, and they spread to several streams. At the same time, the U.S. Fish and Wildlife Service research project in the park monitored the effects of the new regulations in order to see how they were working and if they needed revision. Yellowstone Lake regulations were fine-tuned several times, resulting in a maximum size limit of thirteen inches, which protected the older age classes so important for spawning success. Writers all over the world have praised the fishing in the park, and it really did help us to have that for an example.

But even then the managers in the states around the park would look at the park and say, "Yeah, but those are cutthroat trout. It's different with browns. These approaches won't work with other species." They also pointed out that though Jack Anderson may have had kingly powers to go out and do just what he thought was right, they didn't.

Of course there are lots of kinds of special regulations. The cutthroat is a different fish, but we weren't saying that we wanted all of Montana's trout managed exactly the way the park managed its cutthroats. We were saying that through the use of various kinds of special regulations, Montana's trout could be managed a lot better than they were. And we were right, and have been proven right again and again, and I give the state a lot of credit for coming around, sometimes in the face of strong political resistance, and for gradually increasing the amount of water regulated to improve the sport with no regard for old-fashioned catch-and-kill fishing.

We went from the big-dead-fish philosophy to the idea that we were going to have to share these fish with a lot more people. It wasn't just that the quality of the fishing was going to decline; it was also that the chances of catching that big fish might be less because there was more competition for the fish. The number of big fish is probably greater on many waters now than it was thirty years ago. But there are more people after them.

The variety of special regulations we now have and with which we are experimenting did not come easily. Dick McGuire of the state of Montana has to be credited with acknowledging that dumping hatchery trout in a healthy wild-trout stream was a mistake. It took a lot of work and misery just to get the hatchery trout out of the rivers.

John Peters came to Montana from Michigan in the early 1960s as a project biologist for the state in Bozeman. John deserves a great deal of credit for teaching us that we must start by protecting the habitat. If you don't have a decent place for the trout to swim, there's no point in having them. The second part of the equation, once the habitat was secure, was keeping some trout in the water.

The state put Dick Vincent on the Madison to study the effects of hatchery trout on a wild-trout population. He was one of the resisters, and still may not like the idea of restrictive regulations, but his study did everybody a great service because he proved that you harm the wild trout by putting hatchery trout on top of them.

Cal Dunbar, Charlie Brooks, and I formed a little club called the Southwestern Montana Fly Fishers in the early 1970s, and we used this organization and its letterhead as a vehicle to approach the problem.

We had to have a lot of hearings and bring in people to help. Ennis was really the seat of resistance on the Madison River. There was a group of sportsmen there addicted to hatchery trout. They were devoted to the old philosophy of bringing in the tourist by making sure he caught some fish by whatever means and got to take some home. They believed that that was the only way to have any tourism business. The resistance we faced in those meetings was immense, and I wasn't a very popular man in Ennis. The meetings got pretty hot, and once or twice I think the only thing that kept things peaceable was that Dick McGuire was big and could lick anybody in the place.

There was a lot of talk in Ennis about "our river," and "our valley," and why were people from West Yellowstone coming down and trying to screw up everything in Ennis. It was a terribly provincial attitude, the kind that would have gotten them in trouble in other ways eventually, because trout fishermen just can't afford to have only a local perspective anymore.

We had a meeting in the Silver Dollar Bar in Ennis one Sunday, and we invited all the opposition, sort of bearding them in their den. McGuire, who is about six feet six inches tall and weighs two hundred and twenty pounds, was running the meeting. Dick has not had the credit he deserves for getting the Madison River in the condition it is in today; he fought hard against the hatchery fish, and against the bull-head fishermen, and he did it all while he lived there. He faced those people every day, and it's hard to take on your friends and neighbors no matter how right you are. At this meeting in the bar, things got pretty rowdy, and people were starting to get up and threaten each other. Dick grabbed a salt-shaker in his fist and hammered it on the table a couple times. Everyone looked over, and he declared, "We're going to have to get this meeting back to order." Things were pretty quiet after that.

It wasn't just a matter of convincing fishermen. The state Department of Fish, Wildlife and Parks had the same tendency to drag its feet. Like any political organization, the department has a lot of people to keep happy. They moved very slowly until they saw that the pendulum was swinging the other way, and the evidence against hatchery fish and in favor of special regulations began to build up. There was a period there when the Trout Shop seemed to be singled out for some unusual attention by the game wardens. Of course, they could watch our guides as closely as they wanted because we weren't breaking any laws, but it was an uneasy situation.

Eventually the stream protection bill was passed, primarily through the efforts of John Peters. That protected the habitat through requiring certain instream flows at all times, and by keeping bulldozers and other equipment out of the streambed. A lot of states had laws like that for many years, but in Montana so much was wide open that this kind of change went against the grain. The new law also got rid of the hatchery trout in the Madison and allowed for the establishment of special regulations. This was not a narrowly defined term; it could mean catch-and-release, or a "slot limit" where certain sizes of fish had to be released. Fisheries managers have to be able to experiment with regulations to discover which ones will work best on which water. There are no simple "best rules" for all waters.

The best news, and the real proof that the fights were worthwhile, is that the fishing is getting better. The Madison trout fishing is improving in many parts of the river, and more recently, new regulations on the Yellowstone have shown great promise. I've noticed a big improvement—and it's being documented by the state—in the numbers and sizes of native cutthroat trout on the Yellowstone.

We can do it. We can have fishing like our parents and grandparents did here in Montana. The only difference is that we can't kill fish the way they did. I know that for some people fishing isn't worth it if they can't take some home to eat, and I suppose those people lose out in this situation. But we have to think of the future of the fish populations, and of the recreational industry, and of the young fishermen coming up, most of whom know nothing about the "good old days" when you could kill lots of fish. The new generations of fishermen won't miss that kind of fishing.

It's happening all over the state. Rock Creek, the Big Hole, and other waters are responding to special regulations with better fishing. At the same time, it's become obvious that the new regulations have increased rather than decreased the amount of money out-of-state visitors will spend in areas like Ennis and West Yellowstone (there are excellent fly shops and outfitters in Ennis today, and they promote catch-and-release as enthusiastically as the rest of us). The fishermen who can afford to travel long distances to have good fishing are mostly sportfishermen who aren't especially interested in fish as meat anyway. They just want to know that if they come 2,000 miles to get to the fishing, there will be water good enough to support fish, and fish good enough to be worth catching.

In 1976, a bunch of us—Dick McGuire, Ron Marcoux, Tom Morgan, Charlie Brooks, Dan Bailey, and others—got together and organized the Montana Trout Foundation, a very specifically directed little institution whose purpose is to find ways to encourage the preservation of trout resources, especially but not exclusively in Montana. What we have done is raise enough money so that the interest from it can be used to fund worthy research projects related to wild-trout management. It's a good cause, it's helping, and I recommend it to your attention as much as Trout Unlimited, the Federation of Fly Fishers, and the other organizations.

What is disappointing is how slow people are to see that these new organizations are a sign of big changes. The Snake River in Wyoming could be a great trout fishery, but Wyoming is one of the most reluctant of western states to recognize the possibilities of new regulations. They could restore the area's badly tarnished reputation for sportfishing, generate a big influx in tourist revenue, and do justice to a really outstanding sport fish, the Snake River cutthroat, but though there has been progress there, and though there are a lot of bright, enthusiastic fly fishermen-conservationists in that area, they're still up against too many people locked in to the old ways of hatchery trout and kill-fisheries.

And Montana isn't immune to that same kind of outdated thinking. In 1995, we lost an important battle to a variety of newly elected state representatives who managed to weaken state environmental laws regarding water quality. It's almost as if these people are willfully trying to ruin the state's future, not only in wrecking the great fishing we've worked so hard to protect, but in ruining the wonderful reputation the state has been earning as a good place to visit and spend lots of money. For the moment, the progress we were making all those years in the 1970s and 1980s has been stalled. The next generation of fishermen will, without question, have a hard time forgiving us for this, and I don't blame them.

We now face a whole set of interlocking issues that are very difficult to deal with, and that are going to force us either to change more of our traditional values or accept the losses that those values bring with them.

Like so much else in the New West, fly fishing has gotten tremendously popular. I'm one of the people who made it that way, so I'm as aware as anyone of what it means. It means many things, both good and bad. It means that these great western streams have more friends than they ever have had before, and that never again will the dambuilders and polluters operate with impunity. It means that more people than ever before have found the beauty and peace of a day astream in some of the world's most exciting country. It means that all the other natural residents of the ecosystems through which these streams flow are going to be better off because of healthy watersheds and robust fish populations.

But it also means overcrowding on streams that I remember when they were almost deserted. It means more summer homes being built along the banks. It means that ranches that have been in the same family for generations may get sold off and subdivided, and too many houses aren't any better for a watershed than too many cows. Those big old ranches are one of the best hopes of preserving open country in the West.

The growing popularity of fly fishing means growing competition among far more outfitters than our western waters and their trout can fairly be expected to support. And it means that the quality of the fishing experience is going to be more jeopardized all the time, because there are always plenty of newcomers with no long-term frame of reference of what a good fishing experience can be when the boats are bumper to bumper on the Madison.

These are social issues. We've proven that in some places we can actually manage the trout population well enough that even with extremely heavy fishing pressure there are still lots of trout. But we haven't proven that we have the wisdom to ask ourselves if that's really the kind of fishing experience we want.

We need to face up to this problem. We need to place specific limits on the numbers of boats on the water. This is revolutionary talk; I know that because as a fourth-generation Montanan I know how strongly we feel about being able to do what we want with our natural resources. But these are not just our resources; they are the world's, and they are our children's. We can't afford to sacrifice them just because we have a booming industry rolling here. We have to treat them like any other resource, from timber to minerals. We have to think of them in the long haul, as something we can sustain and use for high-quality recreation for generations.

The late Phil Wright, a colorful outfitter and originator of the Wright's Royal dry fly, suggested we needed a floater's equivalent of tee times, prearranged times when each outfitter or private floater would be launched. I doubt it has to be that rigid, but it has to be a real limiting of use. Otherwise we will soon lose sight of all the wonderful things we fought so hard to restore in these fisheries in the first place. This is an explosive topic, I know, but remember that I made my living from these resources. No one can question that I believe in the rational exploitation of these resources, or accuse me of trying to lock them up like some kind of extremist. I just want to ensure they survive.

And so I propose we consider placing a maximum limit on the number a fishermen on one of the hard-fished rivers like the Madison. We could, for example, try a lottery system of some sort, so that if you want to fish the Madison, you put in like everybody else, and there's a ceiling so that only so many people go by that trout behind that rock, and he gets a break now and then. There are a thousand ways this could be approached, including test closures like the one recently applied to the Madison, and I don't have a preference, except that we reduce the fishing pressure and then be prepared to measure the results. Sectional closures may work, as may closures during spawning, or even some long-term closures that serve as natural nurseries and refuges, as well as giving us a baseline against which to measure the stretches that are being fished. It's a great opportunity to learn, too, because it could be applied as an experiment on some stretches of river, to see how they do compared to others. We can learn from it, and find out just how much fishing is affecting these fish.

My own belief is that, as wonderful as catch-and-release has been, we can still be loving these rivers to death. We all know that catch-and-release works really well in a river like the Yellowstone in the park, but in that fishery the angler catches the fish and lets it go in the same spot. In the Madison, a float fisherman may play a big brown for half a mile or more and then let it go in a different neighborhood. That fish has two choices: it can disrupt the resident fish in the holding water right there, or it can swim home. Either way, it's going to do a lot of work. Catch a few hundred of the fish in the river that way, and you've got a very stirred-up and stressed population.

We still have a lot to learn about how our fishing pressure

Though whirling disease may attack larger hatchery fish, only very small wild fish usually show signs of the disease; these fish show clinical evidence of "blacktail," characteristic of whirling disease.

affects trout populations, and until we know more, we shouldn't be so sure that we can continue to crowd more and more fishermen onto the water without having serious effects on the fish. Perhaps if we start with concern for the fish, we can also figure out a way to limit the effects that over-crowding have on the fishermen and their experience, too.

New Threats

For each generation of anglers, the problems are more complicated. We are always learning more about the resources and we are always getting better at caring for them, but at the same time there are always more of us wanting to fish and there are always new challenges. It is no longer possible to manage a fishery without an eye on the rest of the world because the rest of the world can drop awful problems in our laps.

It seems to be the fate of trout streams that they will always face some new threat. When we solved the over-fishing problems with catch-and-release, we inadvertently helped encourage greater and greater numbers of fishermen, bringing on the social problems associated with over-crowding. The latest, and perhaps most alarming, new

problem facing our western trout waters may be whirling disease.

Whirling disease was first scientifically identified in Europe more than a century ago. The disease is the result of a parasite, *Myxobolus cerebralis,* that damages the cartilege of young fish, leading eventually to nerve damage and a loss of balance; thus the little fish "whirl" or swim in circles. Some 20 states have reported the disease, either in the wild or in hatcheries. It was first detected here in Montana in 1994, and is widely blamed for the spectacular decline in rainbows on the Madison River, from 3,300 fish per mile in 1991 to 300 fish per mile in 1994. But it was already recognized in other parts of the West. For example, it was identified in California in 1965, and in Idaho and Colorado in 1987. Scientists and managers have been scrambling to figure out what is going on ever since, and every now and then the newspapers will report that it's been identified in another drainage somewhere near my home. Late in 1998, it was identified for the first time in Yellowstone Park, in Yellowstone Lake itself.

There are also a lot of ongoing discussions and arguments about how bad things really are, and if other species, such as cutthroats, are as vulnerable as rainbows, and if yet other species, such as browns, will just increase in numbers and fill in the ecological niche vacated by the rainbow trout so that we'll still have good fishing (as if we would willingly lose the rainbow!). The story is changing fast, and for the latest word I encourage you to check the fishing magazines and other publications. The "Trout Line," the newsletter of the Montana Council of Trout Unlimited, and *Rocky Mountain Streamside,* the equivalent publication for Colorado, have both been very conscientious in attempting to sort out the news and the confusion and keep their readers well informed, but many other articles have appeared in publications ranging from *Trout* to *Science.* It's not hard to find reading material about whirling disease.

One of my biggest concerns when we face a new threat like this is controlling the misinformation. Stream ecology is very complex, and though some people seem to think they understand it completely, we're often in the dark. A disease's effects may be tremendously influenced by changing natural conditions, such as high water years, drought, and other factors that really complicate an already incompletely understood situation. I have my own set of theories about why whirling disease does what it does, but none of us dare get too sure of ourselves. Amateur experts can cause almost as much trouble as the original problem.

Everybody has theories about the disease, but for the purposes of this book I'd prefer to concentrate on telling you what you can do to help. First, learn about the Whirling Disease Foundation, and the research that is currently going on to try to solve the problem. The trout need your help with this, and I've included addresses in the appendix (page 157) for how you can learn more and to whom you can send money. We all need to work together on this one.

Second, you can help every time you go fishing. When you finish fishing, make sure you clean all the mud off your gear—waders, boat, trailer axles, anchor, everywhere. Make sure you haven't picked up any aquatic plants, either. The organisms that harbor the disease can easily be transported long distances. Drain your raft or boat of any water. Don't carry any fish, live or dead, from one stream to another. The disease may be in the fish, or it may just be in the water in the bucket. In Montana, and probably in other states, it is illegal to carry live fish or fish parts from one water to another.

But whirling disease now poses other threats besides to the health of the fish. Whatever the experts decide are the real effects of whirling disease, we cannot afford to let it or any other crisis be an excuse for backsliding away from the principles of wild-trout management that have gotten us so far. I mention that because I've heard otherwise-knowledgeable people actually suggest that this whirling disease situation could become so serious that we will want to use hatchery fish to "supplement" or otherwise help prop up the recreational fisheries of Montana.

That simply cannot be considered a sensible option. Whirling disease came to this continent in hatchery fish.

Every known transportation of the disease to a new watershed has been traced to a certain or probable origin in hatchery operations. Hatcheries are exactly the wrong approach. Past experience with hatcheries and hatchery fish taught us beyond any question that the fisheries they create are not worth the costs.

For one thing, they're not worth the costs of maintaining the hatchery programs, which are absurdly expensive. Perhaps more important than those costs are the lost revenue to state agencies and private businesses when trout fishermen refuse to come to our state to fish because they're primarily interested in wild-trout fishing, not some hatchery-supported imitation. Wild-trout fishing has been too successful in places like Montana for fishermen to settle for less.

For another thing, they're not worth the costs to the fishing experience. Anyone who has caught hatchery fish next to wild fish will have trouble considering the two as even belonging to the same species. Esthetically and practically, wild-trout are much better. They survive better, they look better, they fight harder, they represent a greater challenge to the sophisticated fisherman, and, for the person who likes to take one home now and then, they actually taste like something you might want to eat.

Finally, hatchery fisheries are not worth the cost to the trout population. We're way past the days when we thought of rivers as flowing pantries, where we can dump any old fish in there and consider the pantry to be in good shape. As Dick Vincent and others have shown, rather than supplement the wild-trout fishery, hatchery fish directly harm it. It may be that some of our wild-trout stocks are in grave danger right now from whirling disease; that is still being sorted out by the researchers. In the meantime, we owe it to ourselves and to these wild trout we've so carefully guarded all these years to make sure we don't do anything that risks their chances. Dumping a bunch of factory-produced pseudo-trout on top of them would have disastrous consequences. Not only would it stress them through added competition, it would further complicate whatever genetics work our scientists might try to do to sort out the problem.

Whirling disease is symbolic of the changing times in fisheries management. Now that we've learned that we can manage our fisheries for outstanding fishing even with large numbers of fishermen, some of the biggest challenges we face will come from the outside. Whirling disease is an exotic organism, as is the New Zealand snail that is now invading some parts of the Madison drainage in staggering numbers; this invasion is so new that we barely even have any data on it. But again and again, our trout waters are most threatened by organisms we've introduced. We have to become much cleaner fishermen, much more careful about our gear.

We also have to become more ecologically aware fishermen. The western outdoor magazines have carried a number of stories recently about the so-called "bucket biologists" who sneak new species of fish into their favorite lake or stream.

A very young Dave Whitlock with a big Yellowstone cutthroat.

This is such a widespread problem that there are hardly any waters anywhere in the West that are only inhabited by their native species. The most frightening recent case of this is Yellowstone Lake, in Yellowstone Park, where some foolish person, perhaps 15 or 20 years ago, illegally introduced lake trout, which now threaten to wipe out the native cutthroat. Not only does that threaten to destroy the last great cutthroat trout fishery in the lower 48, it will deprive dozens of species of other animals, from bald eagles to grizzly bears, of an important food source as the cutthroat trout population declines (it may already have begun to do so). It will also be an economic disaster to the region's recreational fisheries.

We have to learn to be more careful, and think harder about our actions, and that's good for us anyway. The lesson of whirling disease may be that there will always be some new threat or challenge. It may be social, it may be political, it may be biological; sometimes it will be all three. But though we can keep the West's great fishing great, we can never relax, because the world changes too fast and there is always some new surprise around the corner. The West's fishing is a great gift, and the price we pay for it is vigilance, staying informed, and keeping our eyes open.

The Heritage of Western Trout

One of the unfortunate effects of the recent increase in popularity of fly fishing is that most of the newcomers to the sport have had no chance to understand the traditions and heritage of the sport. Not long ago, the leading writers were people like Arnold Gingrich and Ernie Schwiebert, who celebrated the literature, lore, and values of the sport. I suspect that most new fly fishers have barely heard of Arnold or Ernie, and it's pretty obvious they've not been exposed to all the wonderful, colorful history that helps make fly fishing such an absorbing world.

There is more to understanding our tradition than knowing who Izaak Walton was, or liking old books. When you don't know about these things, you have no way of knowing how to act; you literally don't know who you are. The modern "instant angler" who just walked out of the store with all the new gear, doesn't know how we got here: why we use that gear, what's the right way to use it, how to get along with all the other people who are using it, what our ethics are and how we chose them, what we owe to the resource, and many other things. This isn't about nostalgia, it's about honoring traditions that have made us what we are. You can buy all the fancy gadgets you want and not learn anything about these bigger questions.

In only a few years, we will be celebrating the 200th anniversary of the arrival of Lewis and Clark and their corps of discovery here in the Gallatin Valley. For many of us, Lewis and Clark are important for much more than their historic explorations. They speak to us of what our land was like, and what we have to be grateful for here today. We Gallatin Valley residents found special power in Stephen Ambrose's best-selling book about the Lewis and Clark expedition, *Undaunted Courage,* and Ken Burns' popular PBS documentary on the expedition, because we knew why the story mattered so much. It was an important part of the tradition from which we came.

I take this history personally. When I talk about the pioneers in my family, I am talking about a direct, personal connection between me today and the early settlement and exploration of my home. In their recent book, *Lewis and Clark in the Three Rivers Valleys* (1996), Donald Nell and John Taylor made available the diary extracts from expedition members during their time here, a wonderful portrait of the riches of this little corner of the West. Among many other things, the accounts are full of trout. I think that more than anything else today, it is the rivers and their trout that evoke for us that earlier time, and our need to care about it.

We care about our history because we are still living it. We care about our native trout because they are an essential part of our heritage, because they are part of our legacy and responsibility here, because they're beautiful, and because they're great fun to catch.

But when Lewis and Clark came here they found streams full of westslope cutthroat, grayling, and whitefish. Over the decades, some of those native species were forced out by non-native fish, especially rainbows, browns, and, in a lot of headwater streams, brook trout. Today, the westslope cutthroat, the fish that may best symbolize the great historical rivers of Montana, is gone from most of its former range. Those of us who love browns and rainbows have paid too little attention to what we've lost. We're in danger of letting this fish get away, permanently.

Restoration of native fish is a growing movement, both among the state and federal agencies around the country and among the general public, but it makes some fishermen and some fisheries managers nervous, probably because they're worried that extreme restorationists want to wipe out all the non-native fish and replace them with the original native fish. I don't doubt that there are a few people who feel that way, but that is not what I'm doing when I promote the protection and restoration of our native trout. Nobody cares more about our wild browns and rainbows than I do, and nobody has worked harder to protect them, but I've gradually come to realize that we can keep them without necessarily losing what's left of our native fish.

Because I think our heritage is so important, I've committed a lot of time and energy to working with various groups, especially with American Wildlands, to develop programs to save our remaining stocks of westslope cutthroats. I recently traveled with American Wildlands' leadership to Washington, D.C. to meet with a number of lawmakers and other concerned people, to promote the protection of our native cutthroats. Some of our lawmakers were shockingly uninterested in our natural heritage, but others had already figured out just how priceless this resource was; we were especially encouraged by some of the new leadership of the U.S. Forest Service. The U.S. Fish & Wildlife Service needed a good verbal kick in the pants to get moving on protecting the westslope cutthroat, but I have hopes that we're going to make progress here just as we have in other aspects of wild-trout management over the years. Again and again, anglers have shown that if only they work at it, and communicate the good sense of their wishes, they can make a huge difference in the fishing.

Protection of these native fish means learning more about the surviving strains, and it means giving them stronger legal protection. It also means that we find some waters where they can be protected and given preference, because it long ago became clear that they cannot compete successfully with browns, and are too likely to hybridize with rainbows. In many of our smaller headwaters streams, we have opportunities to ensure the survival of these fish. They pose no threat to the browns and rainbows, and they have a world of things to offer thoughtful anglers who care about traditions and wild trout.

This isn't just a matter of saving some historical oddity. There are other important reasons that justify working on saving these fish. Years ago, Ernie Schwiebert wrote a story in which he compared trout to the canary in the mine, referring to the old mining practice of bringing a caged canary into the working area because if the bird stopped singing or keeled over, the miners knew that the air was getting bad and they'd better run for it. Trout, especially these fragile native trout populations, serve a similar role. Trout provide us with a barometer of the health of our land. If the stream is clean enough, and its hydrology is undamaged enough, to support the original native fish species, then it's a pretty sure bet that the land through which it flows is also in good shape.

For me, the westslope cutthroat, the grayling, and other native western fish are something we can't get along without. We can't afford to lose them and we don't have to.

Chapter 31

Access

FOR MANY YEARS THERE'S BEEN A STORY CIRCULATING in Montana about the rancher who won a million dollars in some lottery, and when someone asked him what he planned to do with the money, he said, "Well, I'm just going to keep on ranching until it's gone." Here in Montana, when you tell people that story, they laugh, but at the same time they nod their heads yes, because they recognize its truth. These are hard times for the traditional industries in Montana. The New West is just as difficult a place to make a living as the Old West. Not only are logging, mining, and agriculture having a rough time economically, they're taking a lot of criticism from people who don't like what they've done to the land. Several generations of good, hard-working people are finding their way of life threatened by pressures and people they don't understand.

A few years ago, I was fishing with a reporter from the *Wall Street Journal.* He was working on a story about fly fishing and how it is changing, and without intending to I walked him into a perfect example of just how much it is changing.

We were fishing the Madison, and I went to a spot where I'd always fished and found it heavily posted. So I went to the ranch house, knowing that a lot of the time if you ask and show yourself to be a responsible person they will let you fish anyway. But with recent battles between sportsmen and landowners over access, especially a few bitter legal cases, things aren't as cordial as they used to be. The guy who came to the door wasn't in the least hospitable.

"Can we go in there and fish?"

"Absolutely not."

"Well, I used to be able to go in there and fish, and I thought maybe . . ." and I gave him a nice polite pitch, thinking maybe I could break him down.

"Nope. With this new access law, and that 'Trouts Unlimited,' we're a lot farther apart than we ever were."

"Well, that makes me feel bad. How long have you been here?"

"I been here thirty years."

"Well, I hope you enjoy it. Thanks." Of course he doesn't even look at the river except to water his cows, but that's his right, even though it hurts me to see all that open water I've fished for years getting closed. But someone has to pay for the fishing, somehow.

We're fortunate in the West that we have not had to totally lose our good fishing before we realized how valuable it is. We've taken some losses, but in many places we've turned the corner now and the fishing is improving. There are still too many Montanans who do not realize the value of good trout fishing. There are still too many degraded waters, too many ranchers losing money with a silted-up spoiled spring creek flowing through their feedlot, a creek that if they just fenced it off for a few years could make them a potfull of money for no investment.

I was visiting a ranch in the Madison Valley recently, talking to the old-timer who owned the place. I noticed a small stream meandering across a brush field. When I asked the owner about it, he told me it was a spring creek. Of course, the discovery of a new spring creek is always exciting, so I asked the rancher about it.

"Jack, are there any fish in that little creek?"

"Oh, yeah, there were a bunch of brook trout in it. We finally got rid of 'em. Had a hell of a time getting them out of there." Brook trout were so unimportant to these people that they actually poisoned them, as if they were rats.

Jack and his family were good people, working a ranch that was losing money badly. He knew nothing about fishing or its potential in the economic future of today's West. He knew ranching, and cattle, and a way of life that is tragically disappearing. We all should mourn its passing, for it produced strong and self-reliant people who made Montana a great state in which to live. But it is passing, and we have a chance to replace it with things that will keep Montana a great place in which to live. Those things include a system of rivers and lakes that are getting the respect they deserve, and are giving back to us the pleasure and fulfillment we need.

Westerners have been spoiled. There are attitudes still common among western fishermen and landowners that have probably outlived their usefulness, and perhaps the most important involve access. Most Americans have a basic sense of their right to public fishing, and I share that conviction, but we are discovering in the West what other nations' sportsmen discovered centuries ago: that a piece of property will eventually rise to its most profitable economic use. That rule holds true with fishing. Though westerners will always be blessed with hundreds of miles of great public fishing waters, a lot of water will only become available to fishermen if they are willing to pay the landowner. What we must keep in mind is that we are not just paying the landowner to fish, we are paying him to manage his land in a way that will permit good fishing to exist. In the past few years anglers have become aware of the terrible damage done to public and private fishing waters by poor management of riparian zones, especially through overuse by livestock. Until someone proves to the landowner (whether it is a federal agency or a rancher) that there is some good reason, especially some economic reason, for him to care about riparian management, that livestock will continue to do harm.

What it comes down to is that a lot of river mileage is never going to become public. The states cannot afford to make it so, and the public fishermen do not have the money to buy it up or rent it. Accepting that reality, and knowing that we need as much good fishing water as we can get, we are left with the choice of finding a way to make it worth the private landowner's trouble to manage for good fishing. Fee-fishing is one way, a very successful way that already provides superb fishing on spring creeks in several western states. A landowner can make a handsome profit simply by doing a little fencing and letting a certain number of fishermen on the property every day.

But even fee-fishing is not all of it. Working with my wife Esther, who is a realtor, I have in recent years made an effort to connect good fishing properties with fishermen-buyers. If the people with the means to buy such properties are alerted to the many potentially great fishing waters that come onto the market in the West, and are willing to make the investment, we can eventually have many new miles of good fishing, some of which will cost the fisherman nothing. It is not that difficult for someone with enough money to own their own spring creek; there are that many creeks around, and they are that easily restored.

You may be wondering, "Why should I care if privately owned water I can never fish is well managed?" The answer is that the more water, private or public, that is well managed, the better the fishing is everywhere else. Many of the private spring creeks have tremendous potential as spawning areas for trout populations in the nearby public rivers, and the exchange of fish between the big rivers and the little streams is important. Besides that, just in principal, isn't it better for all land to be well managed? A well-cared-for spring creek is excellent habitat for ducks and other wildlife, which are valuable to all of us.

There are other approaches being adopted too. I know of a ranch on the Ruby River, in southwestern Montana, where the owners for some years charged a fee to fish on their property. Just recently they built a fishing lodge, a full guest ranch, and they have now excluded all fishermen except for those who stay at the ranch. It's unfortunate that you can no longer fish there for 10 or 15 dollars a day, but it's a reality that good fishing combined with good accommodations is something that many people will pay a pretty stiff fee to have. This one ranch has set the tone for other ranches in the area, so that seven or eight ranches there are now charging to fish on their property. Most are requiring catch-and-release or some other conservation-oriented restrictions, and it appears to me that we could not hope for much more from those private waters. The fishing is improving, there is at least some public access, and the lesson of the economic value of fishing, especially fly fishing, is being learned in places where only a few years ago nobody would listen.

I suspect that it won't be too many years before we are paying more than we used to for access to public waters as well. Here in southwestern Montana we're rich in federal lands, and there is increased talk about access fees for use of the national forests. Just recently, after many years of free fishing, Yellowstone National Park finally had to start charging for fishing, to help cover the costs of administering the program. The message of the 1994 elections was that the public is less willing to foot the bills for the special uses many of us enjoy on public lands. Yellowstone has perhaps the best trout fishing of any area of its size in the lower 48, the kind of fishing people would pay a lot more to have anywhere else.

These are tough times for many ranchers, and they are open to ideas for new sources of income. Most of them allowed little or no access for a long time, so now there is at least some access. Paying for access is better than no access at all.

And these are exciting and challenging issues for fly fishermen. We are in a position now where we can not only improve the fishing on many public waters, as has been happening in many western streams, but we can also add new miles of water to the fishing resource. There are muddy, degraded streams running through feedlots all over my part of Montana that with proper management could rival the most famous spring creeks. There are many miles of collapsing river bank on major rivers that have kept fishermen out of the area for years because the siltation and erosion were so bad. We are in the unique position of actually being able to increase the fishable river mileage, something that most parts of the country haven't been able to do for a century or more. Things are going to get more crowded, and so it's going to be more important that we take care of every mile of fishable stream. The Clark's Fork is being cleaned up. I foresee a day in the future when the Yellowstone River will be a good trout fishery as far downstream as Billings. It's good now as far as Big Timber, which hasn't always been true. Like the spring creeks, Montana's big rivers give us an opportunity few other states have. We can actually increase the number of miles of good fishing rivers, and we are doing it right now.

There will always be a lot of public water in the West, but economics is dictating an increase in fee-fishing on well-managed private waters.

One of the most inspiring and personally enjoyable stories I know about creating a new fishery happened literally in my own backyard. My house is on Sourdough Creek, a historic little stream that runs right through Bozeman before joining the Gallatin. This part of the Gallatin Valley was on important American Indian travel routes, and in the 1800s, starting with Lewis and Clark, many white explorers, trappers, and pioneers wandered up and down this drainage, long before there was a town here. But the development of the town was pretty hard on the creek, and though it might still have had some fish, it wasn't really a place anybody would even think about fishing. Just recently, my neighbors, Bill and Doris Heckerman, acquired a permit from the state to do some restoration work, and they've succeeded in turning Sourdough Creek back into a fine small trout stream (see the pictures of my children Chris and Alisa on page 152 for a look at the restored Sourdough Creek). With careful management and a conservation easement, they've actually added to the mileage of fishable trout waters in Montana. Other property owners up and down the drainage are showing similar new-found respect for this stream, and I know this is going on with other waters as well.

We can get help doing this. The state of Montana recently authorized a Future Fisheries program under the Department of Fish, Wildlife and Parks, who will help landowners restore good trout waters. The American Sport Fishing Association, through its Fish American program, also will provide funds to non-profit organizations to restore streams with some public access. Programs like these can help a lot.

But we will have to be creative about it, and keep our options open. Some streams can best be improved by state and federal agencies. Some may follow the sterling example of Silver Creek, where the Nature Conservancy has done fishermen everywhere a real service by protecting that wonderful stream. Some streams, certainly more than ever before, will only be saved by enlightened private ownership. I support this last category as much as the others; as I've watched my wife Esther's real estate business I've been able to see just how much can be done by private interests in improving and protecting good fishing.

There are many ways to approach the protection of our fishing, but the most important thing for us to keep in mind is that we can do it all, if we try hard enough. We can protect it, and we can make it better. We have great fishing in the West, but we can still make a huge difference in how much good fishing we have tomorrow.

The Total Experience

THIS PHRASE, "THE TOTAL EXPERIENCE," BECAME A way of life as much as it was a business motto for us at the Trout Shop. We believed that one of the most important things we could do for our clients was to improve their fishing by showing them just how much there was to do while they were fishing. We would tantalize them in our advertisements and catalogs with pictures of huge fish, but those same catalogs had pages of items that, back then anyway, seemed out of place to some people when they saw them. We offered wildflower field guides, backpacking equipment, trips with naturalists, and many other things that were intended to broaden their experience.

Some aspects of the total experience are obvious to anyone who has ever fished the West. There is wildlife everywhere, from eagles to ground squirrels to elk. Of course it's especially easy to see wildlife in the West's famous national parks, and it's a great thrill to see wildlife in a park, like Yellowstone or Rocky Mountain, but it's an even greater thrill to see it outside the park. Western game management has come a long way from those days early in the century, when elk, deer, pronghorn, and a variety of other animals were all thought to be destined for extinction, and there is an abundance of opportunities for observing wildlife. We rarely fail to see some large game, either deer or pronghorn, when we fish the Madison in Montana. Along the Yellowstone we often see or hear sandhill cranes, making a strong recovery in our region after nearly being exterminated here by 1920. Black bears wander right into Bozeman and pass within a half a block of my house; moose, deer, and even bear are often seen right along the interstate that connects Bozeman with Livingston. One day that Paul and I were going to go fishing he was late arriving at my house because as he was driving along the Interstate from Livingston he saw a black bear watching the traffic from a road cut. Paul has published several books about bears, and apparently can't resist them; he felt obliged to get out of his car and climb the hill to look for the bear. He couldn't tell me what he planned to do if he found it.

These are things that can be seen without even entering a national park or a national forest, and they are things that enrich your memories of fishing. They are things that are fully worth some time. You may not always see wild animals, but like those big trout we all dream of, they are out there, and they add something precious to western fishing.

But wildlife is only the most obvious part of the total experience. What makes the West so special and so beautiful is what surrounds the wildlife—the land itself. Much of the West is young and raw in geological terms. It is an open geology textbook, just waiting to teach you of its past. As you float through our canyons, millions of years of the earth's biography tower above you to be read by anyone who knows the language of rocks.

In the chapter on guides I suggested that you let your outfitter know if you have any special problems or limitations so that he can plan your trip best. You should also let him know if you have any special interests. Are you a birdwatcher, or a rock collector, or an amateur stream entomologist? Is botany your hobby? He may have a guide with just your special interest. Many guides I know seem to be interested in almost everything, from historic sites along the rivers to the names of every mountain peak they see.

Consider the possibilities. You may stop for lunch along the river, and while the guide is busy making lunch you can go off into the woods looking for wildflowers. I had a guide whose specialty as a university instructor was wildflowers, and he was always booked by a client whose wife loved flowers. All day, while the husband fished, his wife and the guide were chasing around identifying flowers. Another couple, the wife loved to fish and the husband was a rock collector.

One of the great things about western wildflowers is that you can almost always find a good selection of them at any time of the summer. With elevations ranging from 4,000 to 12,000 feet, often within an hour's drive of each other, you can literally drive to another season. If you're a wildflower enthusiast but can only come at a certain season, you have the option of climbing back to an earlier season at a higher elevation.

Or, are you a history buff? If so, would you enjoy a series of floats on rivers that Lewis and Clark floated 180 years ago, passing the very same landmarks they noted in their diaries?

How about spending some time fishing with some of the West's older trout flies? There are popular western patterns that are as old and respected out here as many of the famous eastern patterns. The Trude is older than the Adams or the Hendrickson. The famous Pott series, the "Mites," were developed about the time I was born. Paul and I have had some wonderful fishing with Lady Mites and Sandy Mites. Trout and whitefish take them like they'd just been invented by Gary LaFontaine last week.

Or consider tailoring your trip around the trout, not by size but by species. Would you prefer to catch only brown trout, for example, or would you like the challenge of trying to catch four or more species of trout in a day? Have you ever seen the dorsal fin of a 14-inch Montana grayling? What about comparing the fighting qualities of the Snake River, Yellowstone, and westslope cutthroats, all to be caught within less than 100 miles of each other, all the products of thousands of years of subtle evolutionary divergence. You have many exciting choices out here, and you can make your trip into any of a hundred adventures.

However you might choose to tailor your trip, make a special effort to get to know western fish. The native trout of the Rockies is the cutthroat, of which there are many recognized types. There is an unfortunate tendency among fishing writers to sneer at the cutthroat as a fish that is either "too easy" to catch or "not a good fighter." There certainly are times when cutthroats can be taken easily, just as there are times when they don't fight hard. Studies have shown that they are often much easier to catch than browns or even brook trout. But there are other times, too. I've watched some real "authorities" get skunked by selectively feeding cutthroats, and any time you hook one over 16 inches you're liable to have a real fight on your hands. In places where they've been fished hard, and where good regulations allow them to grow to two or three pounds, the cutthroat has no shortcomings. I know this is not yet widely appreciated among fly fishers, but heavily fished cutthroats can be as finicky and selective, and as spooky, as the savviest brown trout. I've seen it happen too often to doubt it, and I hope you find some just like that; you'll never forget them.

I think I've made the point. You can make all kinds of things out of your trip, and much of the reward will come not from the trout but from the western world in which the trout lives. Don't miss any of this natural glory.

If I could offer the visiting fisherman only one piece of advice it would be this: relax. You're out here to have fun. You wouldn't fish 16 hours a day back home, and you don't have to do it here. You should be after quality, not quantity. If you spend all your time on a dead run, worried that you're not going to cover all the water that day, already planning how early you have to get up tomorrow morning to drive 400 miles to the next spot, you simply aren't getting the best out of your fishing.

A kind of panic sets in when people arrive out here and they've only got a few days. I often have met the client in the morning when he practically had Di-Gel running out of the corner of his mouth. He's wired from the last 50 weeks of working and dreaming about this trip, and now it's here and he is approaching it with the same pace that he approached his job. Everybody fishes at a different pace, I know, but the tendency among visiting fishermen here is to do a lot rather than do a few things right. You're not doing this on contract, and nobody is checking your hours each day. You might unwind enough one day to stretch out on the stream bank for an hour after lunch, and the peace and serenity of that little interlude might end up being one of the most memorable things of the whole trip.

I think that this matter of keeping calm is especially important if you are visiting from another part of the country and you are bringing your family. If they all like to fish, that's great, but often they won't. A family can get pretty torn up in two weeks when they all want to go different directions. Take the time to enjoy what they like too. Spend some time sightseeing, sharing this great country with your family. You'll all remember it, and it will probably make it easier for you to get away when you do insist on some time to fish.

I know you may be thinking that it's easy for me to tell you to take it easy, because I live here and can fish any time I want, but you'd be surprised how little a guide gets to fish sometimes. On those rare occasions that Pat and I were able to get away from the shop for a day or two to ourselves, we would almost always go fishing, but we rarely fished all day. We would usually drive to some small community nearby, get a nice room in a motel, and mix fishing with relaxing, sightseeing, and just enjoying the time together. Pace yourself.

Look for what the area has to offer. Some of my fondest memories of fishing trips are of the lodges and lodge owners, the amazing little restaurants that seem to get by in the most out-of-the-way places, the shops and stores we find, and most of all the people we encounter. I assure you that when I fish I fish hard, but I've learned to enjoy the rest of the day too. Few fishermen (at least the polite ones) will talk much about it, but if you're fishing with a wife, husband, boyfriend or girlfriend, an important item of equipment can be a blanket. Who knows, maybe some sunny afternoon in some secluded stretch of stream the two of you will be fishing away, tuned in to the natural setting, and the mating salmonflies will inspire you. The experience doesn't get much more total than that.

Tuning in is really what it's all about. I love fishing the West because the trout are big and eager and sometimes sulky and reluctant, but I love it just as much for the great open valleys of western rivers, where the foothills are miles away and rise to 10,000-foot peaks that may have snow on them any morning of the year. I don't doubt I've missed many a rise because I was gawking off into the distance, watching a bald eagle soar or a great blue heron rise

Ernie Schwiebert, author of Matching the Hatch, Nymphs, *and other great books, demonstrates perfect form in this Dan Callaghan photograph that suggests the full breadth of the total western fishing experience: catching a fine wild trout in beautiful surroundings.*

from a gravel bar. If you are new to western fishing it may at first seem like there is just too much to do, what with the great scenery, the exciting fishing, and all the rest, and in a way that's true. You can never do it all, but that's just the point. Why try when it's obviously impossible? Instead, work on doing a few things right, each day. I can't guarantee that you'll catch fish, but I can guarantee that you'll go home with the makings of some great memories, and that is probably all any of us can hope for when we go fishing anyway.

Chapter 33

Once a Guide

WHEN PAT AND I RETIRED, WE DECIDED WE WANTED to keep in touch with the many friends we had made at the Trout Shop. So we developed our Western Rivers Club. The purpose of the club was to provide members (who paid fifty dollars to join) with a variety of informational services to help them prepare for fishing trips to our part of the West. We had spent thirty years accumulating knowledge about the fishing, and we still had many contacts that helped us keep up-to-date on fishing conditions. Retirement allowed us the time to explore more of the fishing ourselves, and the club was the best way we knew to put all that to use while continuing to enjoy all the friendships. The club was one way in which we kept active and involved, and there never seemed to be enough time to do everything we wanted to do.

Pat had always had a premonition that she would die young. When she was sixteen she suffered from rheumatic fever and was actually given last rites two or three times. Her mother was always pessimistic about Pat's health after that, and she convinced Pat that she was going to die before her time.

Pat smoked heavily, and during the last few years of her life she was suffering from respiratory problems, including emphysema. Her health had a lot to do with our getting out of the business when we did. In January of 1981 she became very ill with pneumonia, and while she was hospitalized, some X-rays revealed a spot on her lung that eventually was diagnosed as lung cancer. An operation was apparently successful in removing it in February of 1983, but her lungs were in such bad shape that removing the whole lung couldn't be risked. In August of that year they discovered a spot on the other lung, and the doctor told her she didn't have much time. She went through a good deal of suffering as heroically

At the grand opening and dedication of the International Fly Fishing Center in West Yellowstone, in August of 1984. From the left: Yellowstone Park District Ranger Doug Barnard, Grand Teton Park Superintendent Jack Stark, Jan Dunbar, Pete Van Gytenbeek, Bud, Montana Governor Ted Schwinden, FFF Vice President Marty Seldon, and West Yellowstone Mayor Larry Benfit.

as anyone could, though what with radiation treatments and all the other aspects of fighting the disease, it was a very rough time. She passed away on April 14, 1984.

Anyone who has been happily married knows what a shocking loss such a death is, even if you think you're prepared for it. We had thirty-seven wonderful years together. We raised a family anyone would be proud of, and we did it in the beautiful country we all loved so much. She was laid to rest in a small cemetery outside Manhattan, Montana, where a spring creek flows along the edge of the gravesites. The loss of Pat was very painful for all of us. She had been the family's guiding spirit just as she had been the manager of the Trout Shop, and we all agreed that the epitaph on her stone should read simply, "Our Strength."

Early in 1984, shortly before Pat's death, Pete Van Gytenbeek, then president of the Federation of Fly Fishers, called me and asked if I would take on the chairmanship of the International Fly Fishing Center in West Yellowstone. After some false starts and bad luck with fundraising, the FFF had arranged to lease the old Union Pacific dining hall building, known locally as the Convention Center, as the home of the IFFC, but there was a world of work to be done in getting it into shape and developing a program that would make it the functional and important institution it could become. I wasn't too enthusiastic, but Pat encouraged me, pointing out that soon I was going to be alone and I would need a project of this size to keep me occupied and productive.

Esther getting some casting tips from master instructor and writer Mel Kreiger.

For me, the wonderful surprise that came out of all that effort was working with Esther. A veteran of many conservation battles, Esther was a skillful, eloquent advocate for wild trout and fly fishing. Her terrific personality, her great looks,

Chris and Alisa Lilly on Sourdough Creek in Bozeman, summer 1999. (For the story of the restoration of Sourdough Creek, see Chapter 31.)

Working with Esther Simon, executive director of the Federation, I was able to get the IFFC off the ground, and we had a grand dedication ceremony at the Conclave in August of 1984, with Montana Governor Ted Schwinden and several other regional dignitaries attending.

and her obvious personal integrity and commitment made her a natural for the work, and it was my great fortune as a conservationist to get to work with her. It was also my great fortune for more personal reasons, because though it was her energy and enthusiasm that kept me interested in the IFFC,

Bud Lilly's Guide to Fly Fishing the New West

what began as a professional partnership blossomed into a romance that became the true blessing of our lives. Since our marriage in October of 1985, we have been lucky enough to share both home and work (I'll come back to Esther's career as a realtor in a moment), with family always at the center. Anyone who is a parent knows that children give you more than you could ever express, and raising Chris and Alisa has just enriched the romance of our life together.

Long after we finished our work with the IFFC, Esther's encouragement has continued to be important to me. I needed someone to keep me active and in gear, doing things that were important to me but that I might not have done left on my own. I was lucky to be able to retire young, and there are many things I enjoy doing. Being an ardent conservationist who has worked for several important organizations, she encouraged me to get involved with various good causes. In just the past ten years, that has included working, usually on the board of directors, with the Montana Trout Unlimited, American Wildlands, the Greater Yellowstone Coalition, the Montana Ambassadors, the Montana Rivers Action Network,

Bud Lilly's Angler's Retreat, Three Forks, Montana.

Whirling Disease Foundation, the Governor's Whirling Disease Task Force, Trout Unlimited, the Montana Land Reliance, and the Montana Trout Foundation, and her encouragement had a lot to do with me getting around to writing the books that people have been after me to write for so many years. She shares my love of rivers and the West, and though it's quite a challenge being a daddy again, we've built a new life that's very exciting. As we finish up this book, both Chris and Alisa are in high school; all parents know how much excitement that adds to life, and I'm very proud of both of them. They've both shown some aptitude and inter-

est in fishing, but we've tried not to push them into it; they'll eventually decide for themselves if they want to make fly fishing an important part of their lives.

But it seems I always find a way back to helping fishermen. For more than fifty years, my mother, Violet Lilly, ran a small hotel in Three Forks, at the junction of the Madison, Gallatin, and Jefferson rivers—the birthplace of the mighty Missouri. My mother was always fascinated with history, and was a major force for the preservation of local history. As she got older, she occasionally asked me, "What are you going to do with this old place, Buddy?" She was such a pillar of her community and of our lives that I didn't like to even think about what we'd do when she was gone, but it had occurred to me that the hotel might make a nice museum.

Thankfully, my mother lived a long, productive life, passing away in 1994 at the age of 92. All at once her question was serious, and I still thought about a museum. Then one day it occurred to me to turn it into a really special place for fishermen. So Esther and I, with the constant help of my cousin Dave Miller and his wife Norma from Three Forks, overhauled the little hotel, remodelling everything, creating a few single rooms and two suites with kitchens. Esther, Dave, and Norma added a hundred small touches, from trout wallpaper to angling art, that have made it everything a travelling angler might want. The response to all this coziness and angling atmosphere has been wonderful; the people who find their way to the retreat agree with us that the mood is perfect.

We opened for business in the spring of 1995, and with Dave and Norma running the day-to-day operations, it has given me another way to stay involved with fishermen. Now, anglers book their stays well ahead, and I help arrange their trips, advise them on good fishing at the time of their visit, and generally have the same kind of role I had at the shop all those years. What makes me most pleased about this arrangement is that I'm at home in the valley, and know a lot of people who own good fishing water on private land who will tolerate a fairly low level of well-mannered use under my direction.

It's also been a great way to spend time with fishermen. I don't know how many happy conversations we've had on the

PAM LANZA

back porch. Just recently, when broadcaster Tom Brokaw was here, I learned that his family had run a little hotel like my mother's when he was growing up in South Dakota. All the socializing and storytelling just makes the day's fishing more full and memorable.

I don't mind sounding promotional about this hotel because we don't really do all that much promotion; it mostly gets attention through word of mouth. But I have to say that I'm really excited about the fishing opportunities in the Three Forks area. It's within striking distance of the Yellowstone River, Yellowstone Park, and the Big Hole, less than an hour from many of the Gallatin Valley spring

In the summer of 1998, NBC anchorman Tom Brokaw and I donated some time to show the local fishing to people who made a major contribution to the Greater Yellowstone Coalition, an important conservation group in our region. We also found time to take it easy between fishing trips on the deck of the hotel. From left to right: Tom Brokaw, Greater Yellowstone Coalition Director Mike Clark, California angler David Wood, and New Jersey angler Dwight Minton.

creeks, and literally surrounded by the famous trout rivers that gave the town its name: it is here that the Gallatin, Madison, and Jefferson rivers join to form the Missouri. And there are plenty of other waters that only the locals know about. It was because of this concentration of great fishing that I first had the idea for the hotel, and being at the lower end of those drainages, it has much milder winters and thus a much longer comfortable fishing season. If you're interested, check with us at Bud Lilly's Angler's Retreat, P.O. Box 983, Three Forks, MT 59752 (406/285-6690).

One of the most fun things to come out of this project was that I never really lost sight of the idea of a museum. We were able to preserve a few rooms as they were during my mother's long tenure at the hotel, so guests can walk into an authentic little piece of small-town Montana. And we created a comfortable lounge on the second floor full of memorabilia from my own 60 years of trout fishing. And the whole place is an informal gallery of angling art and photography I've accumulated over the years. Here we are in this friendly little western town where the only people wearing cowboy hats are cowboys, out of the recreational mainstream but in the very center of the great fishing, and I get to celebrate all the wonderful local history, a lot of which I personally remember. So far it seems worth all the work.

I have been a businessman, in businesses related to trout

fishing, all my adult life. I have always found it to be a perfectly natural combination of my personal enthusiasm for fishing and my desire to make a decent living, because every one of the conservation organizations I've been involved with has spent most of its time addressing economic issues. When I worked with the Governor's office as a Montana Ambassador setting up "catch-and-release tours" for prospective business investors from out of state, I was trying to educate businessmen and attract the kinds of businesses to Montana that would allow the state's economy to thrive at the same time that the natural resources were protected. It's never easy but it's our only hope.

More recently, in my work with the Montana Rivers Action Network, I'm involved in all the central issues that great trout waters face, from in-stream flows to thermal pollution. People are smart, and if you can show them that clean rivers and good trout fishing are also good sense and good economics, you can make a lot more progress than if you just tell them stories about how much fun fishing is. Everybody likes beauty, but beauty has to pay its way, too.

I'm sure that it is because of my awareness of the central role of economics in the future of trout fishing that I have become so involved with Esther in her real estate business. It is in real estate, as much as in any other direction I've gone, that I think we can offer lessons to conservationists in other parts of the country, because if you're going to save valuable resources like trout, it all comes down to land.

Traditionally, real estate salesmen have been thought of as an even lower form of life than used-car salesmen. When Esther got into real estate, she decided, based on her own career as a professional conservationist with T.U. F.F.F., and other groups, to emphasize special properties with conservation opportunities. There is only so much land out there, and working from within the real estate business has proven to be a great way to get that land into the hands of people who care about nature and wild trout. It's a very intense, competitive business; Bozeman alone has about 300 realtors. But Esther's a great saleswoman, and over time she's developed a broad portfolio of properties with the kind of special values and opportunities that make for good conservation. It's a slow process, with its share of heartbreaks, but if we're going to protect the land our trout streams depend upon we're going to do it a few acres at a time.

On the Alagnak, 1982.

It doesn't end with the sale, of course. Our emphasis with potential buyers is on education. When someone is thinking of buying or developing a riverfront property, for example, is the time to introduce them to the tax advantages of trusts and conservation easements, as well as the practical and neighborly reasons for locating septic tanks safely, not building in the floodplain or right over the water, and finding the most environmentally sensitive and efficient ways to do everything else. The struggle to save the values that we treasure in the West is past the stage where we're going to make huge gains all at once by creating this new national park or that wilderness area. There are still things to be accomplished on that scale, but the future is going to be settled on private property, one lot at a time.

I suppose that my career as a fisherman and a conservationist has evolved along the same lines as trout conservation generally. We all got interested in limiting our kill in the 1950s and 1960s, but pretty soon it became obvious that reducing our harvest of trout was only the beginning; we were going to have get more involved in protecting habitat. Then we realized that a trout's habitat was constantly affected by how we treated the land around the water. Now we look across whole landscapes and try to understand how everything affects everything else, from economics to biology to esthetics. Long ago a wise fisherman said that if a trout can live in it, a man can drink it. Trout are still one of our best barometers of a healthy world; that alone is good enough reason for us to be their best friends.

I finally fulfilled my boyhood dream and went to Alaska in 1982, the summer after I sold the shop. I fished the rivers flowing into Bristol Bay, and a lot of the fishing was so easy that it was possible to lose interest. When you can catch thirty or forty silver salmon weighing eight to fifteen pounds each in one day, you get jaded pretty quickly. They are tremendous fish, great jumpers, and Alaska simply must be preserved so that experiences like that can always be had, but I discovered that I wouldn't want what it has to offer on a daily basis.

We were fishing the Alagnak, and my favorite fishing was for rainbows and grayling. The rainbows were a little larger on the average than those in the Madison, fourteen to twenty inches. It was especially nice because we fished only that one river, which had everything we could have wanted, and spent no time flying around in helicopters and airplanes. I caught silver salmon, king salmon, pike, grayling, and rainbows, and after a week I was ready to come home. The rough, wild country was itself worth the trip, though—the bears were all over the place, we had ptarmigan walking through camp, and so on—and I enjoyed all the things I dreamed of as a child, including some wonderful streamside salmon dinners cooked over open fires. Everyone who loves fly fishing in primitive settings should fish Alaska.

Seeing Alaska with all its fabulous fishing and wild country, was worth it to me for another reason. Forty years ago I had been ready to go up there and be a guide and live what I thought would be a great, romantic life. Now I'm glad I did what I did. I don't think I would have stuck if I'd gone there then, partly because there was comparatively little fly-fishing guiding going on back then and partly because the fishing is not suited to my temperament. We think we'd just love easy fishing for huge fish until we get it, then it pales more quickly than we could have imagined.

Epilogue:

The Best Fish

I HAD A CUSTOMER WHO HAD BEEN A FRIEND FOR many years. Horace had started coming to West Yellowstone in the 1930s, and by the 1950s he was in very poor health. His hearing was shot, he had to carry a little oxygen bottle with him, and he could just barely see. He still wanted to fish, though.

He showed up as usual one summer for some guided trips. We had taken him the year before in a boat, though that hadn't worked out well because it rained on the poor guy all day. The limitations of his health were catching up with him to the point that there was hardly any fishing he could still do.

So Horace asked if I could take him personally. I agreed and said, "Let's go down on the Madison. The salmonflies are on."

"Oh, God, I can't handle that anymore, Bud."

"It's all right," I said. "I know a man who might let us get in and fish Odell Creek above Ennis." So we went down, and my friend, having some sympathy for Horace, let us fish. It was quite a production getting him out to the creek, what with his oxygen bottle and all, but we managed it, though I could tell he was pretty tired by the time we got there.

Luckily the salmonflies were hatching on the main river nearby, and some of them were flying over and laying their eggs in the creek. As I was leading Horace along, I watched the creek and saw a huge boil as a big trout took a fly. Trying to sound calm about it, I said, "I think I got one spotted, Horace." I tied on a Sofa Pillow, and he picked up his oxygen bottle and off we went. I could see a fish sloshing around, and could tell it was very large.

I got him into position. "Horace, he's about in there, just off that bank."

"Huh? What was that?"

"He's over that way!"

"Oh. Okay."

After a little fumbling and a lot of coaching, he did manage to get a cast to within about three feet of the fish, which generously rushed the fly and took it. I yelled, "He's got it!"

"Whatsat?" Horace asked, as the fish hooked himself.

Now Horace, being an experienced fisherman, knew what to do once he had a fish on the line. So it wasn't long before the fish was in, and I got it close enough for him to admire. It was a gorgeous brown trout.

"How big is he?"

"Oh, I'd say he's about twenty-one inches, probably three or four pounds."

"What fly was that I was using?"

"A Sofa Pillow."

"What tippet?"

"4X, Horace." In that little creek, with its clear water, I had to put on a pretty fine tippet even for the large fly.

"Let me see the leader." I handed him the leader, which he started coiling up, so I asked, "What are you going to do?"

"That's it. I'm quitting."

"Quitting? Hell, that's the first fish of the day. There are lots more big fish in here."

"That's right, but that's as fine a fish as I've ever caught, and that's the last one I'll ever catch. Let's go home."

That, whatever else I may tell you about in this book, was my most memorable fish. That man had caught fish for forty years, and he dearly loved the sport, but he had the wisdom to recognize his last trout when it came along. No fishing memory I have will ever equal that one; no trout I catch will ever mean that much to me.

Fly fishing for trout has been an important part of my life for almost 70 years. I have no idea how many trout I've caught, though I do know that back in my early days I killed many more than I should have. There's no point in apologizing for that because at the time, it was just something people did. You caught a fish, you killed it. But those early days did teach me that it isn't the killing that you remember best. It's everything that goes into the day, from the companionship, to the glorious western landscapes, to all the rises struck and missed.

It's amazing how much you remember. Every fish has a certain personality. If you hook a good fish, whether you land him or not, many years from now you will be able to ransack your memory and come up with all sorts of details about what happened right then, and what the rest of the day was like. Whenever I can't be out fishing, I can replay all those fish in my mind and look forward to my next day fishing the great rivers of the West.

Appendix

Organizations dedicated to helping wild trout in the Northern Rockies

American Wildlands
40 East Main
Bozeman, MT 59715

Federation of Fly Fishers
P.O. Box 1595
Bozeman, MT 59771

Greater Yellowstone Coalition
P.O. Box 1874
Bozeman, MT 59715

Montana Council, Trout Unlimited
P.O. Box 7186
Missoula, MT 59807

Montana Land Reliance
324 Fuller Avenue-upstairs
Box 355
Helena, MT 59624

Montana Trout Foundation
c/o Bud Lilly
2007 Sourdough Road
Bozeman, MT 59715

Montana Rivers Action Network
P.O. Box 8298,
Bozeman, MT 59773

Whirling Disease Foundation
P.O. Box 327
Bozeman, MT 59771-0327

Index

A

Abel Reels, 56
Abrams, Rev. Dan, 31
Access, to fishing, 145—147
Adams, 65, 73, 111, 122, 129, 148
Ahrendes, Jim, 36, 39, 48
Aiuppy, Jan, 111
Aiuppy, Larry, 84
Alagnak River, 155
Alaska, 21, 155
Alexandria, 77
Allen, Boots, 23
Alport, Peter, 30
Amato, Frank, 8
Ambrose, Stephen, 144
American Fisheries Society, 112
American Wildlands, 144, 153
Anderson, George, 79
Anderson, Jack, 40–41, 50, 138
Ant, 65
ATH reels, 56
Armstrong Spring Creek, 56, 112
Atkins, Darwin, 47

B

Back, Howard, 23, 48, 77
Backcountry fishing, 119–120
Baetis, 129
Bailey, Dan, 23, 25, 34, 38, 46, 60, 84, 137, 139
Bailey, John, 46
Baker Creek, 16
Bannack (Mont.), 12
Barnard, Doug, 151
Barnes, Pat, 23–24, 27, 75
Barnes, Sig, 24, 73, 75
Barrett, Peter, 40
Bascom, Dave, 26, 82
Baseball, 18–19
Bates, Joe, 36
Bear Trap Canyon, 15

Bear, black, 32–33, 148
Bear, grizzly, 32,62, 143
Beartooth Mountains, 29, 115, 127
Beaver nymph, 131
Beetle, 65, 75
Belgrade (Mont.), 11, 63
Benfit, Larry, 151
Bergman, Ray, 23
Berkley reels, 57
Big Hole River, 67, 128, 154
Big rivers, fishing techniques and seasons, 105–107, 122–123, 124–125, 130–131, 133
Big lakes, fishing techniques and seasons, 117–118, 123, 125, 128, 130, 133
Big Sky, 40
Bighorn River, 54, 64
Billeb, Steve, 22, 29
Billeb, Bonnie, 22, 29
Billings (Mont.), 146
Bird's Stonefly, 88
Bitch Creek Nymph, 65, 76, 125
Black Conehead Marabou Muddler, 66, 78
Blackfoot Reservation, 118
Blackfoot River, 128
Blonde streamers, 84
Bloody Butcher, 16
Blue Dun, 64, 73
Borberg, Charles, 21
Bozeman (Mont.), 20, 21, 26, 35, 42, 54, 110, 111, 122, 148
Brassy, 65, 77
Bright Rivers (Lyons), 36
Bristol steel rods, 14
Brokaw, Tom, 154
Brooks, Charles, 28, 45, 47, 48–49, 74, 76, 138, 139
Brooks, Joe, 84
Brown Drake, 64, 75

Bud Lilly's Angler's Retreat, 11, 19, 154

Bud Lilly's Tackle Catalog and Handbook for Western Trout Fishing, 30
Bunyan Bug, 16, 19
Burns, Ken, 144

C

Call of the Headwaters (Miller), Callaghan, Dan, 50, 150
Carmichael, Bob, 23, 25
Carter, President Jimmy, 42
Catch–and–Release Club, 135–136, 140
Catch–and–release regulations, 101–103
Central Park (Mont.), 16, 20
Clark, Mike, 154
Clark's Fork, 128, 146
Clock, Phil, 28
Clothing, for fly fishing, 60–61
Collins, Christopher Columbus, 19
Collins, Frank, 19
Conservation easements, 155
Conservation of western rivers, 135–147
Continental Divide, 39
Corcoran, Dave, 29, 48
Corcoran, Lynn, 29
Cow Dung, 65, 77

D

Dangers, of outdoor activities, 61–62
Dark Spruce Fly, 66, 78
Darlington Ditch, 112, 123
Dave's Hopper, 88
Decker–Hess, Janet, 112
Deer Lodge (Mont.), 21, 26, 63
Dillin, John, 55

The Dry Fly (LaFontaine), 74
Dunbar, Cal, 121, 127, 138
Dunbar, Jan, 151

E

Eagle's Corner (West Yellowstone), 27
Early spring fishing, 121–123
Earthquake, 1959, 26
Elk Hair Caddis, 65, 75
Emigrant (Mont.), 12
Ennis (Mont.), 15, 139

F

Fairchild, Robert, 118
Fall fishing, 129–131
Farm pond fishing, 117. See also Lake fishing
Federation of Fly Fishermen (Federation of Fly Fishers, FFF), 43, 50, 137, 139. See also International Fly Fishing Center
Fee fishing, 145–147
Fenwick, 28, 57
Field & Stream, 40
Firehole River, 31, 39, 41, 46, 50, 51, 53, 55, 63, 77, 82, 84, 124, 128, 129
Fishing (Bates), 36
Floating western rivers, 94–98, 140
Fly Fisherman, 54
Fly Fishing Always (FFF), 43
Fly Fishing the Blackfeet Country (Fairchild), 118
Fly leaders, 58–59, 83
Fly lines, 57–58
Fly patterns, 63–78
Fly Patterns of Yellowstone (Mathews and Juracek), 75
Fly reels, 56–57
Fly rods, 56, 111–112

Fryingpan River, 53
Fulsher, Keith, 84

G
Gallatin Canyon, 15
Gallatin River, 16, 20, 31, 55, 122, 136, 147, 154
Gallatin Valley, 54, 56, 63, 85, 154
Gapen, Don, 78
Gardiner (Mont.), 24
Gardner River, 46
Gartside, Jack, 47
Gartside Hopper, 65, 75, 88
Gerlach, John, 117
Gibbon River, 46, 73, 129
Gingrich, Arnold, 49, 51, 135, 143
Glacier National Park, 42
Goddard, John, 75
Godfrey, Will, 36
Gold Ribbed Hare's Ear, 65, 77
Goofus Bug, 24, 64, 65, 73, 129
Gordon, Sid, 45–46
Gowdy, Curt, 40–41
Grand Teton National Park, 138
Grant, George, 47, 77
Grasshopper fishing, 80–81, 88, 111, 128, 130. See also Gartside Hopper, Joe's Hopper, Letort Hopper, Dave's Hopper, Parachute Hopper
Greater Yellowstone Coalition, 153, 154
Green, Jimmy, 28
Green Drake, 65, 75
Greenstock, Sir Jeremy, 42
Grizzly Wulff, 75
Gros Ventre River, 79
Guides, 89–93

H
Hague, A.R. (Amos), 12
Hague, W.A., 12
Hair Wing Variant, 65, 74
Halterman, Pat, 137
Hank-O-Hair, 74
Hansen, Norm, 21
Haraden, Bob, 42
Hardy Reels, 56, 57
Harrop, Rene, 47
Hatch-matching, see Imitation
Hatcheries, 142
Hatfield, Dick, 115
Hebgen Lake, 26, 40, 49, 76, 80, 114, 115
Heckerman, Bill, 147
Heckerman, Doris, 147
Henry's Fork, 15, 24, 50, 51, 55, 73, 78 ,80, 100, 121, 124
Henry's Lake, 76, 78, 115
Henryville Caddis, 65, 75
High-country lakes, 115–116, 121, 124, 129, 133
Hodgman waders, 59
Horner, Jack, 25
Horrocks Ibbotson, 14
How to Fish from Top to Bottom

(Gordon), 45–46
Humpy, see Goofus Bug, 24, 126, 129
Huntley, Chet, 40

I
Imitation, theories, 16, 45, 48, 63–64, 73–78, 84, 86, 88, 129
In the Ring of the Rise (Marinaro), 63
International Fly Fishing Center, 43, 135, 151–153
Izard, Jack, 43

J
Jacklin, Bob, 48
Jackson (Wyo.), 23, 31
Jefferson River, 154
Joe's Hopper, 65, 75, 82, 88
John's Elk Hair Hopper, 75, 88
Johnson, Chuck, 22
Johnson, Vint, 23, 45
The Joys of Trout (Gingrich), 135–136
Juracek, John, 75

K
Kast, Don, 90
Kelly, George, 39, 79
Knight, Bobby, 43
Koch, Ed, 28
Kootenai River, 105
Korkers, 59
Kreh, Lefty, 24, 28, 44
Kurrault, Charles, 40

L
Lady Mite, 14, 77
LaFontaine, Gary, 74, 149
Lake fishing techniques and seasons, 117–118, 123, 125, 128, 130, 133. See also Farm pond fishing, High-country lakes
Larger Trout for the Western Fly Fisherman (Brooks), 28, 48
Last Chance (Ida.), 24
Leaders, 58–59, 83
Ledlie, David, 113
Lewis and Clark expedition, 144, 147, 148
Lewis Channel, 41–42
Lewis and Clark in the Three Rivers Valley (Nell and Taylor), 144
Lewistown (Mont.), 36
Letort Hopper, 82, 88
Light Cahill, 65, 73, 111
Light Spruce Fly, 66, 78
Lilly, Alisa, 147, 152–153
Lilly, Annette, 22, 27, 29, 32–37, 51, 58
Lilly, Bonnie, 22, 29, 36
Lilly, Chris, 147, 152–153
Lilly, Esther, 68, 147, 150–153
Lilly, Greg, 23, 25, 27, 32–37, 39, 41–42, 51, 54, 73, 97, 98

Lilly, Karen, 36
Lilly, Mike, 22, 26, 27, 32–37, 48, 51
Lilly, Pat, 20, 21, 23, 30, 34–37, 149–150
Lilly, Violet Collins, 12, 19, 20, 153
Lilly, Walen "Bud" Sr., 12
Lines, 57–58
Livingston (Mont.), 25, 121, 148
Lost River, 124
Lousy Springs, 130
Lunker Club, 25, 44, 137
Lyons, Nick, 8, 36, 51

M
Maclean, Norman, 16
Madam X Rubber Legs, 65, 75
Madison River, 15, 26, 31, 38, 46, 49, 50, 54, 55, 73, 79–80, 84, 87–88, 98, 105, 106, 107, 109, 115, 123, 126, 128, 129, 131, 139, 140, 141, 144, 148, 154, 156
Mammoth Hot Springs, 36, 41, 62
Manhattan (Mont.), 14, 16, 18, 112
Manitoba Nymph, 42
Manners, 98, 99–100
Marathon waders, 33
March brown, 74
Marcoux, Ron, 139
Marinaro, Vincent, 63
Marryat Reels, 56
Martin Reels, 14, 57
Martinez, Don, 21, 23, 25, 73, 74, 76, 136, 137
Martuch, Leon P., 46
Martuch, Leon L., 90
Mathews, Craig, 48, 75, 79
McGuire, Dick, 138–139
Means, Norman, 16
Meisselbach Reels, 14
Merwin, John, 117
Middle Fork, Flathead River, 128
Miller, Dave, 8, 11, 19, 153
Miller, Norma, 11, 153
Minton, Dwight, 154
Missouri River, 54, 80, 105, 121
Mist on the River (Waterman), 46
A Modern Dry Fly Code (Marinaro), 63
Montana Ambassadors, 153, 154
Montana Department of Fish, Wildlife and Parks, 112, 138, 139, 147
Montana Land Reliance, 153
Montana Nymph, 40–41, 65
Montana Rivers Action Network, 153, 154
Montana Trout Foundation, 139, 153
Montana Trout Unlimited, 137, 139, 142, 153
Moose (Wyo.), 25
Morgan, Tom, 139

Mother's Day Hatch, 121, 122
Mountain Creek, 29
Mr. Mite, 14, 148
Muddler Minnow, 46, 66, 77, 78, 122
Muskrat nymph, 131

N
Native fish conservation, 142–144
Nature Conservancy, 147
Nell, Donald, 144
Nelson's Spring Creek, 56, 84, 112
New West, 8, 9, 12, 38, 137, 140, 145–147
New Zealand mud snail, 142

O
Odell Creek, 156
Olive Dun, 65, 73
Olive Stimulator, 65
Olive Zonker, 66, 78
Orvis, 28, 56, 60
Otter Nymph, 65, 77
Outdoor Life, 23

P
Paige, Satchell, 18
Parachute Hopper, 88
Parks, Merton, 24
Parks, Richard, 79
Pat Lilly Art Gallery, 30, 47–48
Pebble Creek, 128
Peerless reels, 56
Peters, John, 138, 139
Pflueger Reels, 57
Pheasant Tail, 65, 77
Pierpont, Robert, 40
Pilgrim's Rest (Mont.), 11
Pondexter Slough, 112, 123
Poltroon, Stanley Milford, see Bascom, Dave
Poppy, the dog, 35, 37
Pott, F.B., 14, 16, 65, 77, 148
Presentation, of flies, 82–88
Prince Nymph, 77
Proper, Datus, 76
Pruett, Jim, 8

Q
Quake Lake, 26

R
Radan, Sam, 46, 88
Racicot, Governor Mark, 137
Ramsbotham, Sir Peter, 41–42
Randolph, John, 54
Rappala, 40
Rather, Dan, 40
Reilly, Hugh, 28
Real estate business, and trout conservation, 147, 154–155
Reels, 56–57
Releasing fish, 101–103
Renegade, 64, 65, 74
Resistol hats, 45
Rhoades, Ray, 46

Richards, Carl, 27, 28, 48, 51
A River Runs Through It (Maclean), 16
Rivers, fishing techniques, see Big rivers, Spring creeks, Small streams
The River's Edge, 29
Rocky Mountain National Park, 148
Rocky Mountain Streamside 142
Rods, 56, 111–112
Roll casting, 83–84
Roundup (Mont.), 21
Royal Coachman, 14, 45
Royal Redball waders, 60
Royal Trude, 65, 74, 129
Royal Wulff, 63, 65, 73, 82, 129
Rubber Legs, 64, 65, 76, 125

S

Salmonfly, 15, 16, 75, 87–88, 128, 156
St. Anthony (Id.), 12
Sam, the dog, 36–37
San Juan River, 77
San Juan Worm, 64
Sandy Mite, 14, 65, 77, 148
Schaplow, Barry, 27, 36, 38, 48
Schullery, Paul, 20, 84, 110, 113, 148
Schullery, Steve, 112
Schwiebert, Ernie, 28, 50–51, 143, 144, 149
Schwinden, Governor Ted, 151
Scientific Anglers, 28, 46, 57
Scully, Jack, 16
Seal–dri waders, 60
Seasons, fishing, 79–81
Seldon, Marty, 151
Selective Trout (Swisher and Richards), 27, 51
Serendipity, 65, 77
Shedd, James, 12, 19
Shenk, Ed, 28, 82
Shrimp, 65, 78
Silkknitter, Ben, 28
Silver Creek, 56, 112, 124, 147
Silver Dollar Bar, 139
Silver Doctor, 77
Small streams, fishing techniques and seasons, 108–109, 121, 124, 127–128, 130, 133

Smith, Chip, 35
Smith, Joseph, 12
Snake River, 54, 139
Snowflies, 129, 132–133
Soda Butte Creek, 128
Sofa Pillow, 64, 65, 75, 87, 88, 156
Sourdough Creek, 147
South Bend Tackle Company, 14
Southwestern Montana Fly Fishers, 138
Spawning fish, 79–80, 130–131
Spring fishing, 124–125
Spring-creek fishing, 54, 110–114, 123, 125, 128, 131, 133, 145–147. See also creeks by name: Armstrong, Nelson and Thompson Spring Creeks, Silver Creek, Poindexter's Slough, Darlington Ditch
Stagecoach Inn, 38
Stark, Jack, 151
Stateler, Rev., 11
Steelfin Reels, 56
Stetson hats, 45
Stillwater fishing, see Farm pond fishing, High-country lakes, Big lakes
Stimulator, 65, 75
Streamer fishing, 84, 122, 124, 125. See also individual patterns by name.
Strong, Irving, 45
Strumm, Ernie, 115
Summer fishing, 126–128
Sun River, 128
Swisher, Doug, 27, 28, 47, 48, 50, 51

T

Taylor, John, 144
Taylor Creek, 128
Temperatures, and trout feeding, 81. See also season chapters and timing
Theodore Gordon Flyfishers, 137
Thompson Spring Creek, 63
Three Forks (Mont.), 11, 15, 16, 19, 154
Thunder Creek streamers, 84
Tibor Reels, 56
Timing, of fishing, 81, 124,

126–127, 129, 133
Tolman, Pres, 49
Townsley, John, 41–42
Trident (Mont.), 16
Troth, Al, 35, 47, 75
Trout (Bergman), 45
Trout (magazine), 142
"Trout Line," 142
The Trout and the Stream (Brooks), 49
Trout Shop, 21–38, 51, 135–137, 148
Trout Unlimited, see Montana Trout Unlimited
A Trout's Best Friend (Lilly and Schullery), 8
Trude, 148
Trueblood, Ted, 40, 44, 46
Turck's Tarantula Rubber Legs, 65, 75
Two-fly rigs, 86

U

Undaunted Courage (Ambrose), 144
U.S. Fish and Wildlife Service, 138, 144
U.S. Forest Service, 144

V

Van Gytenbeek, Pete, 151, 152
Van Nice, C.A., 54
Varley, John, 109
Varney Bridge, 46, 128
Vincent, Dick, 138, 142
Virginia City (Mont.), 12

W

Waders, 33, 59–60, 120
Wading socks, 60
Wading staffs, 46, 60
Wall of Fame, Dan Bailey's, 25
Wall Street Journal, 145
Walton, Izaak, 143
Warden, Mr., 26
Waterman, Charles, 46
The Waters of Yellowstone with Rod and Fly (Back), 23, 48, 77
Weighting flies, 84–85
Weighting leaders, 85
West Yellowstone (Mont.), 21–25, 27, 40, 42, 54, 63, 76, 84,

151–153. See also Trout Shop.
Western Rivers Club, 151
Wet flies, casting, 85–86
What the Trout Said (Proper), 76
Whirling disease, 141–142
Whirling Disease Foundation, 142, 153
Whirling Disease Task Force, 153
White Conehead Marabou Muddler, 66, 78
White Zonker, 66, 78, 97, 121
Whitlock, Dave, 28, 47, 48, 76, 78, 143
Wiedman, "Ma", 15, 136
Wilkinson, Charles, 8
Wind casting, 83
Winter fishing, 132–133
Wood, David, 154
Wood River, 124
Woolly Bugger, 65, 77–78, 97, 121, 125
Woolly Worm, 23, 64, 65, 75, 76
Wretched Mess News, 26
Wright, Leonard, 75
Wright, Phil, 140
Wright McGill hooks, 19
Wright's Royal, 140
Wulff, Joan, 50
Wulff, Lee, 50, 82, 137
Wyoming Outfitters, 30

Y

Yankee Jim Canyon, 123, 135
Yellowstone Lake, 29, 117, 141
Yellowstone National Park, 29, 40–41, 49, 55, 84, 88, 102, 115, 124, 128, 131, 138, 140, 146, 148, 154
Yellowstone River, 31, 54, 80, 88, 106, 107, 121, 129, 135, 139, 148, 154
Yellowstone Valley, 12, 112, 121, 123, 146
Yates, George, 11
Yates, Mary Wells "Granny", 11
Young, Brigham, 12
Young, Paul, 46, 56
Yuk Bug, 97

Z

Zern, Ed, 44, 46–47, 137
Zug Bug, 65, 77, 129

About the Authors

BUD LILLY, A FOURTH-GENERATION MONTANAN, IS perhaps the best known of modern western fishing guides, and has been fly fishing for nearly 70 years. From 1950 to 1982 he and his family operated the world-famous Trout Shop in West Yellowstone, from which he advised generations of anglers on the fishing possibilities of the West. Profiled in countless articles and books, he has appeared on CNN's "Portrait of America" Series and ABC's "20/20," and was recently the subject of the film "Three Men, Three Rivers," a tribute to him, Dan Bailey, and George Grant, produced by the Montana Department of Fish, Wildlife and Parks.

Bud's work as a conservationist has brought him many awards and honors. He was a founder of the Montana Trout Foundation, was founding president of Montana Trout Unlimited, and was the first chairman of the International Fly Fishing Center. He has served as a director, trustee, or lead advisor of numerous organizations, including the Whirling Disease Foundation, the American Museum of Fly Fishing, the Federation of Fly Fishers, American Wildlands, the Montana River Action Network, the Montana Land Reliance, and the Montana Ambassadors. His latest fishing enterprise is Bud Lilly's Angler's Retreat, housed in a historic hotel in Three Forks, Montana. Bud and his wife Esther, also a lifelong professional conservationist and angler, live with their children Alisa and Christopher in Bozeman, Montana.

PAUL SCHULLERY BEGAN FLY FISHING IN 1972 WHEN he became a seasonal ranger-naturalist in Yellowstone Park. From 1977 to 1982 he was executive director of The American Museum of Fly Fishing, in Manchester, Vermont, and has written or cowritten several books about fish and fishing, including *American Fly Fishing: A History* (1987), *Shupton's Fancy: A Tale of the Fly-Fishing Obsession* (1995), and *Royal Coachman: The Lore and Legends of Fly Fishing* (1999).

A historian by training, most of Paul's writing has been about nature and conservation. Ten of his 29 books are about Yellowstone Park, including *The Bears of Yellowstone* (1992), *Mountain Time* (1984), *Searching for Yellowstone: Ecology and Wonder in the Last Wilderness* (1997), and *Yellowstone Fishes: Ecology, History, and Angling in the Park* (1998), which he co-authored with John D. Varley. In 1997, Montana State University presented Paul with an honorary doctorate of letters in recognition of his work as a historian and nature writer. In 1999, the University of Colorado Center of the American West gave Paul the Wallace Stegner Award in recognition of his work as a writer who has made a "sustained contribution to the cultural identity of the West." He and his wife Marsha Karle live and work in Yellowstone Park.